LOUISIANA STATE UNIVERSITY STUDIES

Humanities Series

WALDO F. MCNEIR, Editor

———

Number Eleven

Studies in Comparative Literature

1962

LOUISIANA STATE UNIVERSITY STUDIES

MAX GOODRICH, General Editor

The Louisiana State University Studies was established to publish the results of research by faculty members, staff, and graduate students of the University. Manuscripts of exceptional merit from sources other than aforementioned are considered for publication provided they deal with subjects of particular interest to Louisiana.

The Studies originally appeared as a unified series consisting of forty-two numbers, published between the years 1931 and 1941. In 1951 the Studies was reactivated, and is now being issued in the following series: Social Sciences, Humanities, Biological Sciences, Physical Sciences, and Coastal Studies. Other series may be established as the need arises.

The Studies in each series will be numbered only serially, without volume designation.

Requests for exchanges should be addressed to the Gift and Exchange Division, Louisiana State University Library, Baton Rouge. All other communications should be addressed to the Louisiana State University Press, Baton Rouge.

STUDIES
IN COMPARATIVE
LITERATURE

Edited by

WALDO F. McNEIR

+

LOUISIANA STATE UNIVERSITY PRESS
BATON ROUGE
MCMLXII

Preface

THE FIFTEEN ESSAYS in this collection are a joint undertaking by seven faculty members in the Department of Foreign Languages and seven in the Department of English at Louisiana State University, plus a contribution by a visiting European scholar.

Since comparative literature has broad dimensions in both space and time, these studies are wide-ranging. One of them deals with aesthetic theory and two deal with folklore, subject areas that scarcely admit either geographical or historical limits. The others are somewhat more circumscribed. They concern a variety of relationships in a variety of periods between the literatures of ancient Israel and England, England and Spain, France and America, Provençal and France, France and England, Italy and France, America and Germany. They are presented as illustrations of the variety of methods and approaches characteristic of modern investigations of cultural cross-currents. If they illuminate in some sense the kinship or contrast between the national literatures and writers of different provenance brought under scrutiny, their purpose will be served.

Professor Horst Oppel, director of the Englisches Seminar in Phillips-Universität in Marburg, is the visiting European scholar included. He lectured at Louisiana State University on October 1, 1958, and at that time visited with us for several days. But we already knew him, for relations between his university and Louisiana State University have been close. And several contributors to this volume, as well as the editor, have a lasting sense of obligation to his broad humanism, his penetrating scholarship, and his energetic promotion of German-American understanding. "Dieses Buch ist ihm gewidmet."

WALDO F. McNEIR
University of Oregon

v

Contents

vii

Ananda K. Coomaraswamy:
The Perennial Philosophy of Art

by
Fabian Gudas

ANANDA K. COOMARASWAMY was born in Ceylon in 1877, the son of a distinguished Singhalese father and British mother. Two years later his father died, and his mother, who had brought her child to England the previous year, never returned to Ceylon. Thus Coomaraswamy was reared in England, and his education culminated in his receiving a Doctor of Science degree from the University of London. Gradually his interests shifted from botany and geology to Oriental culture; and for the last thirty years of his life he was a member of the staff of the Boston Museum of Fine Arts in charge of its Oriental collection.

Despite these Western associations, Coomaraswamy never identified himself with the Western way of life. During his extraordinarily prolific writing career, which lasted almost half a century,[1] one of his chief aims was to interpret to the West the culture of the Orient, particularly the art and philosophy of India. Another aim was to reverse the judgment of Kipling that East is East and West is West and never the twain shall meet. In his earlier essays he was constantly pointing out correspondences between Oriental and Western thought: Nietzsche's Superman is similar to the Chinese and Indian Superior Man; Shakespeare's plays reflect the canons of Indian dramatic theory; Indian aesthetics anticipates the views of Goethe, Croce, and Clive Bell.[2] As Coomaraswamy's knowledge of Sanskrit, Chinese, Greek, Islamic, and medieval philosophy deepened, he began

1

to see more fundamental correspondences in the doctrines of the great thinkers of the East and West. From the early thirties to his death in 1947, he was a vigorous advocate of what he called the "traditional" or "perennial" philosophy, a metaphysics once universally accepted but now in great danger of being wholly forgotten as impatient modern man rushes to construct his utopias. Coomaraswamy set himself adamantly against the dominant intellectual currents of modern times (except science), and pleaded for a transvaluation of the West's most cherished values.

Many of his later publications were intended to document his claim that the great thinkers of the East and West taught the same doctrines. By a laborious comparison of philosophical texts, he tried to show that these teachers not only shared a common metaphysics but also made the same applications of metaphysical principles to the solution of problems in ethics, politics, and the arts. Coomaraswamy also extended his comparative studies to the practices and dogmas of the world's great religions and to the arts, myths, and other folklore of all races. Here, too, among seeming diversity he found a remarkable similarity in essence. He raised the question, "How is it that so many and different kinds of men have thought alike?"[3] The answer seemed to him to be obvious: universal consent can be explained only by the hypothesis of an original revelation which receives a continuous verification in the lives of those who choose to live by it.

The present essay confines itself to an analysis of the theory of art as taught by the perennial philosophy, with special emphasis on what it has to say on myth and symbol, on folklore, and on the aims and methodology of comparative literature. These are subjects to which Coomaraswamy devoted a great deal of attention in the last fifteen years of his life. The development of his views on the theory of art is beyond the scope of this essay, although it is a very interesting subject. For example, in his earlier writings on art, he seemed content to work within the categories established by contemporary aesthetics; later, after he had formulated the perennial philosophy of art, he recommended the abandonment of aesthetics as an autonomous discipline, and he called "disinterested aesthetic contemplation" a contradiction in terms and pure nonsense.[4]

I

Modern Western man regards himself as the heir of all the ages, the happy culmination of a long line of cultural evolution. He prides himself on his clearheadedness, the expansion of his encyclopedias, and his freedom from the confusions and errors of the early stages of human thought. He believes that he is living a life vastly better than that of any of his ancestors and that his standard of living is destined to rise further to inconceivable heights. He looks upon the other peoples of the world as his intellectual and cultural inferiors; he smiles condescendingly at their narrow foreheads, primitive mentality, superstitious beliefs, exotic ways, and quaint works of art; but he magnanimously accepts the white man's burden to bring light and civilization to the backward and static nations of the world.

Coomaraswamy asks this man to pause in his song of praise of himself and to ponder the realities of his present situation. He also asks him to look at himself from a fresh historical perspective. All the peoples of the past had accepted some version of what Lovejoy has called the "other-worldly" philosophy—the belief in a world order which has a spiritual reality as its ground —and had organized their cultural institutions in accordance with the implications of this philosophy.[5] In fact, the majority of the peoples of the world today (Coomaraswamy was writing before the Communists came to power in China) still guide their lives by this great tradition. Thus modern Western man is almost unique in that he has tried to found a culture on a "this-worldly" philosophy.[6]

Beginning with the Renaissance, Western man committed himself increasingly to nominalism and empiricism. His philosophers argued that the belief in "spirit" is a relic of ancient animism, that metaphysics is just a sophisticated game played with words, that ultimate truth is impossible to attain, that therefore agnosticism is the religion of all sensible men. Western man, at first reluctantly and later with evident satisfaction, accepted the recommendation to give up the "quest for certainty" and to make observation and experience the only tests for valid knowledge. He turned to the temporal and sensible world to see what he could make of it: he developed science into the power that it is today; he constructed political systems which give each citizen the freedom to do and believe and enjoy what he likes as long as he does not infringe on the similar rights of others; his ethical insight provided him with a single, all-embracing categorical imperative—the obligation to make his decisions in accordance with his conception of what makes for the greatest happiness of the greatest number; he invested his treasure in an expensive educational system and hired teachers to instruct his children in reading, writing, arithmetic, and personality development; he built factories to provide the abundant life for everyone. Above all, Western man believed in progress. His philosophers told him that dislike of change and the preference for the immutable—attitudes characteristic of older societies without a sense of history—were, after all, only prejudices; his biologists gave him a theory of evolution which he interpreted as a continuous progressive development; his poets assured him that through the ages one increasing purpose runs; and his prophets described brave new worlds which made the utopias of the past seem like the dreams of children.

But this experiment of cultivating an earthly Garden of Eden with no God and no snake is now a demonstrated failure; the devastating effects on life, liberty, and the pursuit of happiness of two world wars and a world-wide depression within thirty years and the possible ugly consequences of the harnessing of atomic energy have shaken the faith of even the most convinced believer in inevitable progress. And Coomaraswamy joins the increasing number of writers (and he quotes many of them) who are analyzing "the modern predicament" (or even "the human situation") and tinging the modern consciousness with the note of anxiety and the sense of crisis.

In the harshest terms Coomaraswamy condemns the Western way of life as the cause of all our present discontents: it is "barbarous," "sinister," "diseased," "rotten to the core," "chaotic," "despairing." What Western man understands by "civili-

zation" is a "vicious and destructive force," and the continued acceptance of his definition of "progress" is "suicidal and mur-
derous"; the modern Western world is like "a headless corpse
of which the last motions are convulsive and insignificant."[7] Its
psychologists, who are increasingly influential in government
and industry, are teaching a behaviorism of conditioned reflexes.
Its ethics has become a science of "approvals," of likes and
dislikes, and its politics a balancing of competing likes and dislikes. Democracy, where it survives, is a state of internal war
with occasional periods of peace when a balance of power among
competing pressure groups has been established. Assembly line
industrialism and the division of labor have dehumanized the
workman by depriving him of intellectual responsibility for the
product he is helping to make; and manufacture for profit has
resulted in the production and overproduction of shoddy goods.
The destruction of the caste system has made impossible a functional social organism. Thus modern Western man lives in a
world of "impoverished reality"; he has "forgotten who he is";
he has "lost his way." And the worst is that colonialism has
spread the "virus of civilization" so widely that there is scarcely
an ancient culture left in the world which is not disintegrating
under its influence. However, even in India, where two centuries
of British education have left indelible traces, "an Indian peasant's face has neither the vacancy of the greedy children, grin-
ning apes and whores that are the ideal of the American ad-
vertiser, nor the expression of anxiety that marks the American
'common man' in real life."[8]

Western man's abandonment of the otherworldly philosophy
caused profound changes in the practice of artists and the theory
of art. The appearance, about two hundred years ago, of a new
autonomous branch of learning to which the name "aesthetics"
was given, was dramatic evidence of the crystallization of the
new point of view. The subject matter for this new discipline
was created by classifying all artifacts into two groups: those
made to serve a functional purpose and those made to be "ends
in themselves,"*i.e.,* to produce the terminal value of "aesthetic
pleasure." Thus a distinction, unknown in the past, was established between the "useful" arts and the "useless" or "fine" arts,

and the latter became the special province of aesthetics. Whereas older theories dealing with poetry, painting, music, sculpture, and the dance had assimilated these arts to religion, ethics, rhetoric, politics, or some other discipline, aesthetics insisted on treating art as art and not another thing; by this it meant that it was committed to study only those objects or only those aspects of objects which are specialized to produce aesthetic experience. Thus the relations of art to the other disciplines were considered to be largely external and, in any case, irrelevant, and the artist was proclaimed "emancipated" from all loyalties except to his art. "Disinterested aesthetic contemplation" and "art for art's sake" became the new slogans.

Actually, says Coomaraswamy, aesthetics has done little more than codify what poets and painters and other artists had been up to ever since the Renaissance. With the gradual abandonment of metaphysics, the artist found he had nothing to say about a (fictitious) supersensual reality; his only alternatives, then, were to describe external nature, especially the beauty of its sunsets, flowers, and women, or to describe what goes on within himself, especially his interesting emotional states. Thus a type of art was produced which was almost without precedent in the history of the world,[9] and the new branch of philosophy, aesthetics, came into being to justify and encourage this art.

Such is Coomaraswamy's summary of the aesthetic theory and artistic practice of modern Western man. He condemns both almost without reservation.[10] Aestheticians have redefined the honorific term "art," which had an established meaning in traditional theory, and have tried to persuade others to call and honor as art only those objects which arouse aesthetic pleasure in the receptor. Aesthetics has thus achieved its autonomy, but at great cost. In recommending that the expression and excitation of feeling for pleasure's sake be the end of art, it has cut art off from man's active and contemplative life. Painting becomes the art of seeing and poetry merely emotive language. The meaning and use of art are ignored or declared irrelevant. Thus art has become a "spectacle" and an "aphrodisiac"; the artist is an "exhibitionist"; the appreciators of art are "sybarites" and "idolators"; and the professors of aesthetics and historians of art are "leaders of the blind." In spite of its pride in its autonomy, aesthetics is really a branch of psychology, animal psychology at that, for feelings are something that man has in common with the lower orders. The novelty and intensity of the emotion aroused become the standards of judgment; and since emotional reactions are notoriously variable from person to person, a relativity of taste is defended.

Another consequence of this new conception of art is that the plain man has lost interest in art; he considers it a luxury product or mere ornament or, if he is wealthy enough, a status symbol. Thus today poetry, music, and the visual arts are cultivated by small cliques of artists and connoisseurs who claim to understand these arts and thus feel themselves superior to the bourgeois and proletarian philistines. But the connoisseurs are really only "sentimentalists," "dilettantes," and "playboys." The artist complains of his neglect, but rather than prostitute his genius he continues to express what he really feels, that is, his idiosyncrasies and especially his rare and novel emotional states. In this quest for novelty and individuality, he has gradually become unintelligible. Naturally he is flattered by the reverence which is paid to his personal genius; and since it is commonly accepted that genius is to madness near allied, he affects an unstable temperament which is reflected in a certain costume and coiffure and in personal vices for which he, like some minor deity, expects to be (and is) forgiven. His genius makes understandable his neglect and isolation, and his privileges warm his cold Ivory Tower. Thus the modern artist is not a responsible member of society but a "parasite," and his hard-won emancipation is nothing but "his final release from any obligation whatever to the God within him, and his opportunity to imitate himself or any other common clay at its worst; . . . all wilful self-expression is auto-erotic, narcissistic and Satanic, and the more its essentially paranoiac quality developes, suicidal."[11] Such artists were rightly banished by Plato from the ideal state.

Finally, aesthetics has made impossible the full understanding and appreciation of the literature, painting, and music of the past. The modern theorist, assuming that aesthetics sets up principles which govern all art, praises or condemns traditional

works of art for the wrong reasons. He commits the unfortunate
fallacy of assuming that these works were created by men interested in aesthetic surfaces, naturalism, and expressionism;
and so he often makes himself ridiculous by saying that a traditional artist was trying and failing to do something which this
artist was, in fact, deliberately avoiding. The truth is that it is
impossible to understand or judge a work of art (or anything
else) without first knowing its formal and final causes. Traditionally, the highest function of art was conceived as the illumi-
nation of a thesis. If the artist used natural forms, he used them
as symbols through which he conveyed an ideology. Thus no
one can appreciate traditional art unless he identifies himself
with it. For an atheist to be an authority on medieval art is
impossible; to teach the Bible, or even the *Divine Comedy,* as
"literature" or to have a Mass performed by a secular choir is
sentimental dilettantism or fetishism.[12] The present academic
study of the art of the past is concerned mainly with its accidents
rather than with its essence, which is its meaning. The symbols
of traditional art have been "secularized," "emptied of content,"
and turned into mere "art forms." The principal worries of the
art historian are when, where, and by whom a work was done.
Much time is devoted to the study of influences, the characteristics of the styles (the element of personal expression in a work)
of different schools or artists, and the technical processes of the
various arts. All such studies have little value.[13]

II

After enumerating the symptoms of his patient and convincing
him that he is ill with a mortal disease, Coomaraswamy proposes
a cure: Western man must abandon his "provincial" and historically "anomalous" philosophical position and return to first
principles as taught by the perennial philosophy which has been
the "normal" or "traditional" or "orthodox" metaphysics of
peoples everywhere. He insists that he is not presenting a systematic philosophy of his own.[14] He is simply making a comparative study of the doctrines of the great teachers of mankind

to show that these doctrines, when freed from localisms which had been necessary for different cultural conditions, are the same.

The greatest teachers of mankind (e.g., Krishna, Buddha, Moses, Christ) have similarly claimed only to fulfill the old law, to renew an insight into the nature of things which had lost its immediacy, to return society to first principles, or to adapt these principles to changed cultural conditions. They have created "scriptures" which describe the perennial philosophy clearly, directly, and concisely. This philosophy has also been taught by the keenest minds of all ages, and Coomaraswamy draws into his comparative net (in addition to the great Hindu and Buddhist thinkers) Plato, Aristotle, St. Paul, Plotinus, Philo, Hermes, Dionysius, St. Augustine, Boethius, Dante, Meister Eckhart,[15] St. Bonaventura, St. Thomas, William Blake,[16] and others; he also quotes Chinese and Islamic philosophers.[17] When examined closely, the doctrines, symbols, and even the very words of these great teachers are identical.[18] Thus Coomaraswamy regards his own work as showing the possibility and necessity for a new *Summa,* a "Summa of the Philosophia Perennis," which would be "impartially based on all orthodox sources whatever."[19]

But Coomaraswamy extends his comparative method even further. The reports of anthropologists on the institutions, mentality, myths, art, and way of life of contemporary primitives (those least affected by Western penetration and education) convinced him that the folklore of these peoples is the same throughout the world and agrees remarkably with the basic teachings of the perennial philosophy. These parallels are so numerous and so close that no hypothesis of "independent origin" or "borrowing" can conceivably be correct. The only hypothesis which explains the facts is that the perennial philosophy was a primordial revelation to the progenitors of the human race.[20] Thus the perennial philosophy is a heritage of all of mankind and, after the fall, was carried to all parts of the world by the migrating races of man. It was preserved for millennia by oral tradition and later set down in literary texts. It is reflected in scripture, myth, popular folk tale, religion, rite, and philosophical teaching. Periodically, it has been revitalized, extended, and explicated by the "masters." If this be the true view of the matter, then man's historical development can no longer be regarded as progress but must be viewed as a degradation from an original state of pure spiritual insight to the complete loss of this insight by modern Western man.[21]

The perennial philosophy teaches that the ultimate reality is a Supreme Identity of which the universe is the manifestation.[22] Of the Supreme Identity not much can be said except negatively; conceptual language, which has been developed to enable man to deal with the world of appearance, is inapplicable to the supersensible ultimate reality. However, this much is axiomatic: the Supreme Identity, which exists in the "Eternal Now," must be conceived as "omniscience independent of any source of knowledge external to itself, and a beatitude independent of any external source of pleasure."[23]

The manifestations of the Supreme Identity exist in time and space. They are on different "levels of reference" (gods, angels, the social organism, individual men, animals, vegetables, matter).[24] There are "correspondences" between each of the levels and the others (a parallelism of microcosm and macrocosm).[25] And lastly, the manifestations are to be thought of as sets of "contraries" or "polarities": for example, male and female, light and darkness, heaven and earth, subject and object, archetype and particular. The extreme positions within each of these polarities "are never absolute values but only the logical extremities of a divided form."[26] The polarities are necessary characteristics of any "conditioned" world: "A 'world' without pairs of opposites . . . would be an 'unconditioned' world, a world without accidents, change or becoming, logically inconceivable and of which experience would be impossible."[27]

The more important of these polarities become the key terms of the perennial philosophy. Because of the doctrine of correspondences, the terms naming the polarities can be used analogically or with systematic ambiguity; thus "male" refers not only to sex, but becomes the "male principle" in the universe functioning together with the "female principle" in the creation of new wholes, their "children," who reflect the divine biunity of the Supreme Identity in which there is a coincidence of all opposites. Thus the same principles govern all disciplines—theology,

ethics, politics, psychology, art, or science—and all these disciplines are only "logically" and not "really" distinct from each
other. The best state for anything is always a unity of opposites,
but a unity in which one principle is subordinated to its superior: God is male and properly dominant over His creation,
which is female to Him; the priest is male and dominant over
the king, who is male and dominant over his realm; an ordinary man is female to the king and priest, whose authority
he must respect, but he is male to his wife; she, on the other
hand, is male over his estate; in all men and women the empirical self is female to the Spiritual Self; and in art (that is,
in all making) the intelligible idea or form is male and dominant over the feminine visible materials.[28]

The perennial philosophy teaches that each man has two
selves: a Spiritual Self (the Brahma, the God within), which
is one and the same in all men and identical with the Supreme
Identity, and an empirical self, which is a manifestation of the
Spiritual Self. Thus the pronoun "I" is ambiguous in that it
can refer to either self. A man must not make the mistake of
identifying his essential being with his body and soul, which
together make up the psycho-physical mechanism of the empirical self. Since this "personality" exists in time, it is always,
like the rest of the phenomenal world, in a state of flux; it is
a process, a causal continuity, brought into existence at birth
and destroyed at death. Traditional doctrine here agrees with
modern psychology in regarding "individuality" as "nothing
but a transitory association of sensuous data, mere name and
phenomenon, and 'the very mother of illusions.' "[29]

To recognize the existence of these two selves is the beginning
of wisdom.[30] To perceive that all human activity must be directed to establishing the proper relationship between them is
to take the first step on the way to salvation. The ultimate
beatitude for man is to achieve metaphysical realization (Awakening, Deliverance, Liberation, Deification, Enlightenment),
that is, to experience the Spiritual Self directly and become a
Comprehensor.[31] Though relatively few are granted this blessed-
ness, their testimony is of the utmost importance for mankind:
it is through them that the perennial philosophy receives its

most authoritative restatement in each generation; and their having reached the common goal provides what amounts to an experimental proof for the truth of the perennial philosophy (such personal verification—knowledge by direct acquaintance— is the only one possible for metaphysical claims).[32]

The way of contemplation, which leads to metaphysical realization, is an arduous one and open only to the spiritually qualified. Most men for most or all of their lives remain committed to the active life, the "way of works." Yet even on this level there are analogues of the divine happiness of realization, which can be experienced by any person who strives to become "perfect of his kind" (his "kind" is determined by his inherited capacities). The great danger for anyone is to give free rein to his empirical self, the accidents of his being, and to cultivate his individuality with its private opinions and preferences; the untransformed psycho-physical mechanism of the empirical self, driven chaotically by passion and desire, controlled by pleasure and pain, is the fundamental cause of all human suffering.

III

The perennial philosophy derives its definition of art from metaphysical principles. The basic polarity constituting human nature—the empirical self and the Spiritual Self—is reflected in the distinction between man's active and contemplative lives. These two "lives" are not distinct or autonomous aspects of human living, at least of human living as it ought to be. Contemplation, until its goal is reached, is itself an act or operation; and, after its completion, it ordinarily expresses itself in action. Action without contemplation is a mere cause-and-effect sequence; action after contemplation becomes a manifestation of universal principles. Thus the course of life of the "good" or "whole" man will be a unity in which both of these aspects are present and in the proper relation to each other.

The active life may be divided (very roughly) into doing and making. Making, or art, is subordinated to doing, since making (from the standpoint of the consumer) is for the purpose of more efficient doing (or contemplating). Coomaraswamy then completes his definition of art by adding a value term: "art" (as distinguished from "work of art") is "the right way of making things," or "the making well, or properly arranging, of anything whatever that needs to be made or arranged, whether a statuette, or automobile, or garden."[33] Coomaraswamy recognizes that there are degrees of "well making" and that therefore his definition is vague; the best one can say is that the closer a thing is to being perfect of its kind the more it has a right to the name "work of art."

Ordinarily Coomaraswamy uses the word "art" to refer to a class of human activities and "work of art" to the products of these activities, but he does not allow us to forget that human art has analogues on other levels of reference. For example, God (mythologically) has frequently been called the Supreme Maker or Artist and his creation a work of art. In fact, in traditional cultures human art is "a rite, consciously imitative of the formative work of the Father by whom the earthly, feminine material was given form in the beginning."[34] Thus the perennial philosophy gives the name "work of art" (in its broadest extension) to any unity (however temporary) which has been created by the conflation of opposing forces in the proper hierarchical relation to each other.

Useful classifications of works of art may be made in various ways: in terms of their efficient cause (God, man); their material cause (wood, marble, words, etc.); their formal cause (the particular intellectual prototype imitated in the object); and their final cause (the satisfaction of some need or needs of the consumer, who may be the artist himself). All these possible classifications, though practically useful, must not be allowed to suggest that the differences among well-made objects are more important than their similarities; all the arts are the same in essence and are governed by the same first principles. Furthermore, these classifications do not establish discrete genres. For example, the needs of the consumer or patron, reflecting the polarity of human nature, are divided into the needs of the empirical self and those of the Spiritual Self. This division seems to justify a classification of the arts into the useful (or functional or practical) arts and the spiritual arts. However convenient such a classification may be for talking about the arts in terms of their proximate intentions, it must be remembered that in the traditional view the best state is always a union of opposites. Thus all art objects should serve both practical and spiritual needs, at least to some degree: "the fresco invites us to consider its thesis, the house to warmth and shelter, at the same time that the fresco is a piece of furniture, and the house by its proportions and design appeals to the intellect as well as to the shivering flesh."[35] Elsewhere Coomaraswamy explains in greater detail how the house appeals to the intellect: it symbolizes the architecture of the universe in that it has "a ground below, a space between, a vault above, in which there is an opening corresponding to the solar gateway by which one 'escapes altogether' out of time and space into an unconfined and timeless empyrean. Functional and symbolic values coincide; if there rises a column of smoke to the luffer above, this is not merely a convenience, but also a representation of the axis of the universe that pillars-apart heaven and earth, essence and nature, and is itself although without dimensions or consistency the adamantine principle and exemplary form of temporal and spatial extension and of all things situated in time or space."[36] There is also a metaphysics of embroidery and weaving, and the shape and function of even the humble safety pin have symbolic values.[37]

While it is true that because of the doctrine of correspondences "functional and symbolic values coincide," it is not necessarily true that my house or your safety pin, regardless of how efficient either is for practical purposes, will automatically carry a spiritual message. Probably Coomaraswamy would say that to endow an ordinary safety pin with symbolic values would be to sentimentalize.[38] In any case it is desirable that these values be "expressed" by the object. An artist produces a practically useful object by skillfully incorporating his idea of its correct form into the appropriate matter. The object can then become the matter for the expression of a metaphysical truth. This is done by "adorning" or "ornamenting" the object: "it is generally by means of what we now call its decoration that a thing is ritually transformed and made to function spiritually as well as physically." [39] The term "ornamentation" must not be used with the modern meaning of adventitious or non-functional or useless embellishment, serving an aesthetic or merely decorative purpose. Ornament, traditionally, is the "completion" or "fulfillment" of an object; it endows a person or object with his necessary "accidents" so that he or it can function properly. It is like the judge's robes or the king's crown, the "equipment" by which a man becomes a symbolic figure and assumes a certain function. In traditional societies, even cosmetics, hairdressing, and jewelry have their specific significance. God's attributes are his adornment, and the creation of the world an act of adornment. Naturally, overornamentation or "mere" decoration is always bad. But an object "devoid of all symbolic ornament . . . is not 'simply and truly *useful*,' but only physically serviceable, as is the trough to the pig."[40]

According to the traditional view, all men are artists. Each man inherits (or brings with him to the world of becoming) a specialized knowledge and skill that guarantees his success in some one branch of the arts. The discovery of his way of life is of supreme importance, for only by following his "vocation" can he attain self-realization and happiness. In traditional societies the social order, with its hierarchy of castes, assists a man in making this discovery; and then, through education and initiatory procedures, helps him to develop his inherited capacity to its fullest extent. Within his own realm each man is considered a "priest"; his work is a "ritual"; and his reward is realization of the Spiritual Self.

The traditional artist, regardless of what he makes, works not to earn a living but to fulfill himself (his salary merely enables him to go on working). Since his art is a part of his nature, he is bored by leisure and prefers to practice his art than to do anything else. He is not the "hired hand" of modern industrial societies, but has hereditary standing in a culture which does not regard any necessary work as being below human dignity. He considers himself nothing more than a skilled craftsman, a servant of his patron or of society as a whole. And in striking contrast to our modern geniuses in love with their personalities, he is content to remain anonymous; he knows that the essence of his art derives not from himself (his empirical self) but from the God within him who is the same in all beings.

Also in contrast to the modern artist, the traditional artist does not prize originality, novelty, or individuality, either in subject or workmanship. His spiritual message is not expected to be an independent vision of the nature of things. His job is simply to reproduce a form, a portion of the Eternal Truth which does not change; there is no private property in ideas except those conceived by the empirical self.[41] To be truly original means to derive the form from its intellectual source. Almost inevitably all artists reflect something of themselves in their work (by some idiosyncrasy in the handling of their materials or by some shade of interpretation), but the traditional artist considers even such self-expression to be an imperfection in his work. [42] The artistic works of the East and those of the Middle Ages, produced in accordance with these prescriptions, may seem monotonous to Western man especially when he compares them with the work of modern "creative" genius; but Coomaraswamy reminds us that Plato praised the art of Egypt whose forms, he thought, had not changed for 10,000 years.

The process of making, the same for all the arts, consists of two steps. The first is the artist's intellectual apprehension of the form[43] to be imitated, and the second is the "servile" employment of his skill in embodying this form into the chosen material. The first step is the more important and difficult one. The artist's intellectual apprehension of the form is the direct realization of it, analogous to the Comprehensor's realization of the Supreme Identity. The artist becomes "one" with it; as knower, he is no longer distinguished from the known. In India this discipline of spiritual perception has been rigorously formulated and is analogous to the discipline of the yoga.[44] Unless the artist submits to this discipline and achieves a realization of his form, his work, however skillful, will necessarily be at a third remove from reality and fall under the censure of Plato. The realization which occurs through the contemplative process is a recollection, a true inspiration or supernatural influence. In contrast, when the modern artist talks of being "inspired" by a chance observation, he is perverting the meaning of the word; he can only mean that he is "excited" by the chance observation.

The consumer of traditional art expects the simultaneous satisfaction of both his physical and spiritual needs; art nourishes the whole man. An important part of his total experience with the artistic object is his response to its beauty. Beauty is defined as the qualities in an object which when seen or, better, "apprehended" will cause a spectator to be attracted to it as to something desirable or excellent of its kind. Although beauty is as important in traditional theory as it is in modern aesthetics, it is a concept that must be analyzed with great care.

In the first place, beauty exists on various levels of reference. It may be "occasional" or "relative" or due to the aesthetic surfaces of the object (Coomaraswamy calls such beauty "loveliness" and the response to it "aesthetic pleasure"). But this beauty will be a snare if the aesthetic surfaces are ends in themselves or, worse, are used to hide functional inadequacy. The enjoyment of such beauty is legitimate only if it is a reflection of ideal beauty, which is one of the names of God. Any object which is perfect in its kind will reflect ideal beauty even in its aesthetic surfaces. Therefore the general condition for the beauty of a human artifact is the same as that for its being a well-made object: the beauty of an object is "proportionate to its accuracy . . . or truth," where "accuracy" and "truth" mean "the proportion of essential to actual form, paradigm to image."[45]

In the second place, it must not be assumed that the artist works to create beauty; if he tries to do so he will surely fail or, at best, produce mere decoration. Rather, he strives to make an object which will have a physical and spiritual use, and he trusts traditional theory which says that anything which is well and truly made will inevitably reflect ideal beauty. For him, beauty is a necessary consequent, an "inevitable accident," and not a final cause.

In the third place, beauty has a variety of functions for the consumer. Its immediate function is "to attract us to the theme or use of the object before us"; thus beauty is a "means to an end," a "symptom and an invitation."[46] True beauty is a sign to the consumer that he has before him a genuine work of art, a well-made object that will effectively serve his needs.[47] Of course, the consumer must be a qualified judge, one who will not be misled by the attractiveness of aesthetic surfaces; it is the automotive engineer rather than the housewife who has a right to make the judgment, "This is a beautiful automobile." But beauty has a higher function than that of sign or symptom. The experience of true beauty can itself be (at least a part) of the spiritual use of the object. This experience is an intellectual ecstasy (or rasa, as the Indian rhetoricians call it), an analogue of the Divine Beatitude and the only experience truly worthy of being sought after as an end in itself.[48] It is a purely contemplative experience, joy in the knowledge of the things of God, and occurs when the spectator penetrates to the meaning behind the externals of aesthetic surfaces. This is what modern aestheticians should mean by their "awkward" and "self-contradictory" expression "disinterested aesthetic contemplation."[49]

The evaluation of a purported work of art consists of two steps: (1) the determination of the adequacy of the object for achieving the end or ends for which it was made (the "good" of the work; (2) the judgment of the value of its final cause (the "good" of the consumer).

The first step, the province of artistic criticism, in effect results in a decision as to whether or not the object deserves the name "work of art." It is a judgment normally made by the artist himself, who, if he has an artistic conscience, will not offer an object to the consumer unless he is satisfied it is a well-made object, that is, unless the finished object corresponds to its archetype in his mind. The next best critic is an authority, another master in the craft. However, under certain conditions (e.g., when dealing with the art objects of the past or those produced by modern mass manufacture), the consumer-critic may be forced to appraise the artifact himself. One way of doing so is to make the empirical test of actual use; the degree of an object's effectiveness is a rough measure of the correspondence of the object to its prototype. But the empirical test is only a second best; the judgment which it justifies is in the realm of opinion and is not true knowledge (scientific laws themselves are only statistical probabilities).[50] And furthermore, for various reasons, the empirical test may not be possible or even appropriate (e.g., in the evaluation of the religious art of a culture foreign to that of the consumer). In such cases the best that the critic can do is first to determine as accurately as he can (admittedly a difficult procedure) the formal and final causes of the work—the intention of the artist—and then to inspect the work to see how adequately it fulfills this intention.[51]

The second evaluative step, the appraisal of the final cause of the object, is a moral judgment. It involves answering the question, "Does this object, though a genuine work of art, satisfy the *true* needs of the consumer?" This evaluation is necessary because the artist as artist has no moral responsibilities (his concern is only with the good of the object he is making) and therefore artistic skill may be used to make objects to satisfy any need, real or apparent, of the consumer. Of course, in traditional societies both the artist and consumer are whole men; hence the latter does not demand, and the former does not produce, anything which does not conduce to the satisfaction of the consumer's real needs. In cultures not controlled by the perennial philosophy, the artist's skill may be perverted to the making of bombs, poisons, pornography, and other objects with noxious effects. If these objects effectively fulfill their purpose, they cannot be refused the name "work of art," but they can be morally censured. Thus a skillful murderer or modern dictator is to be praised as an artist but judged unfit as a man;[52] objects produced by modern industrial methods may be "good as utilities, but bad as *mere* utilities";[53] and the modern "fine" artist may be a skillful exhibitionist or a skillful arouser of pleasurable feelings, but his works are to be condemned as corrupting influences.[54] A Platonic censorship of the work of artists is therefore necessary, a censorship guided not by opinion but by permanently true first principles: "To justify the exercise of a censorship, we must *know* what is right or wrong, and why; we must have read Eternal Law before we can impose a human code."[55] The only qualified censor and judge of the merits of works of art is the metaphysician. He will place a work of art higher or lower in the scale of value depending on how effective it is in bringing wayfaring man closer to his goal. Thus *"mere* utilities," although true works of art, will fall low in the scale, whereas spiritual works of art, initiating man into life's deepest mysteries and providing him with an analogue of the beatitude of God, are of the highest value.

In an important sense the metaphysician is unable to make "absolute" evaluations of works of art. Since men are born on different levels of reference, what is true, good, useful, or beautiful at one level will not necessarily be so at another (except analogically). A work of art fitted to the needs of a wayfarer who is near his goal (the Comprehensor can dispense with all works of art) will be vastly different from a work of art efficacious for a wayfarer at the beginning of the journey. Thus Coomaraswamy says that "beauty and validity are relative. There is nothing made that can be either beautiful or apt in all contexts."[56] Beauty, validity, and aptness are relative to their total context, an important part of which is the degree of spiritual development in the consumer. This principle has wide applications. A religion, for example, regardless of how anthropomorphic it is, must not be judged absolutely. It is true and good if its formulae analogically reflect first principles and are adapted to the level of spiritual need of its adherents.

IV

The special characteristics of the spiritual arts require a fuller discussion. Most of the arts which moderns class together as the "fine arts" originally had an intimate connection with practical objects or activities of which they were the ornaments or ritualizing elements. Some of these arts may have had a "pure" or "specialized" spiritual function from their first invention; for example, the earliest poets were prophets and the earliest poetry was scripture. However, even those arts which are the most highly specialized for performing a spiritual function (for serving as guides to contemplation) necessarily retain a close connection with the needs of the empirical self; the pleasure which a spectator gets from the loveliness of aesthetic surfaces (the *delectatio* recommended by traditional rhetoric) not only is legitimate but also is essential as a means for attracting him to the theme of the work of art (the aesthetic surfaces are also the indispensable means for conveying the theme).

At the present time all the "fine arts" (except perhaps architecture and the decorative arts) have been completely dissociated from practical objects and activities; furthermore, they have been secularized, and their original spiritual function has been replaced by aesthetic considerations. The purpose of the perennial philosophy of art is to re-establish the unity of all of man's activities and to return these arts to their original function as parts of the art of contemplation which is the greatest of all arts—the art of knowing God.

Traditionally, the spiritual arts have been classed together, along with sermons and orations, as species of rhetoric.[57] Their common purpose is "effective communication" or "the effective expression of theses."[58] These theses are metaphysical principles, statements about God or one of His aspects. Spiritual art, then, is an appeal to the intellect through the senses; the thesis is the form which controls and transforms the tangible matter that gives it expression.

The end of the spiritual arts, the translation of the consumer to a level of reference higher than his habitual one, can be achieved only through an intellectual activity on his part. What the consumer sees in the work of art or what he gets out of it will depend, to a large extent, on what he brings to it and how actively he participates in it. This necessary co-operation of the consumer in the artistic act means that the work of art is not the cause of the final experience but only its occasion.[59] It also means that the highest levels of the experience are accessible only to those who are spiritually qualified.[60] Thus the work of art is only a "reminder" of what the Spiritual Self already knows; it is an "aid" or "support" for contemplation; it is a "point of departure" or a "signpost" which invites the spectator "to the performance of an act directed toward that form for the sake of which the picture exists at all."[61] The climax of the act occurs when the participant directly realizes the artist's thesis; then no real distinction is possible between artist, work,

and spectator. Coomaraswamy describes the onset of this climax
as a "shock."[62] The participant feels as if he were struck by a
whip or a thunderbolt. Though emotion is involved, no arousal
of ordinary feelings can explain this body-blow. It occurs as a
consequence of intellectual realization occasioned by a work of
spiritual art which is a "perfect and therefore convincing statement of truth."[63] It is followed by the peace and beatitude of God.

One of the most characteristic features of works of spiritual
art is their pervasive symbolism. Since the form or thesis of a
work of art is always a metaphysical content and since this content is something which cannot be observed by the senses, the
artist, like the authors of the scriptures, is forced to use physical
objects or qualities as symbols for that content. (In literature
the words are signs for objects or qualities which then become
the symbols.)

Symbols are of various kinds, but Coomaraswamy is particularly interested only in what he calls the "adequate symbol."
A symbol is adequate if it can represent "a reality on a certain
level of reference by a corresponding reality on another."[64]
This representation obviously cannot be a visual likeness, but
the doctrine of correspondences makes it possible for the symbol
to be like the content analogically. Thus the Christian cross is
one of the great analogues of mythological literature; it symbolizes "the crucifixion of unitary being on the dimensions of time
and space; the nail that fastens beam and upright is within you,
and there lies the ultimate significance of the image and of
life."[65]

Another way of defining "adequate symbol" is to say that it is
a symbol which (formally, not materially) "participates" in or
is "one" with its content. This doctrine of participation seems
strange only to modern Westerners with their "paleface pre-
conceptions."[66] Coomaraswamy is pleased to accept the testimony
of Lucien Lévy-Bruhl who says that one characteristic of the
"prelogical" mentality of primitives is their inability to distinguish between subject and object, name and referent, representation and thing represented; they regard the relation between the elements of each of these pairs as one of "mystic

participation."[67] This doctrine is as old as the perennial philosophy itself (Lévy-Bruhl was ignorant of this fact), but it is valid only where there is a true correspondence of realities on different levels of reference. An example of participation still widely familiar even to modern Western man is the Eucharist which, during the Mass, without losing its physical properties, is transformed into the body of Christ. The different levels of reference of physical and spiritual nourishment are thus brought together; and the formal participation of the first in the second is complete, for it is obvious that the body of Christ is indivisible.

Traditional symbols, like the cross and the Eucharist, are always adequate because they are "not conventionally but *naturally* correct."[68] They are not a product of human invention (images to which more or less arbitrary conceptual meanings have been assigned) but are "revealed" and therefore "inevitable" and inseparable from the meanings which they convey.[69] They are visible images which display their corresponding invisible forms that exist on a higher level of reference. Thus, as Coomaraswamy is fond of saying, traditional symbols are not figures of speech but figures of thought, the only adequate language for talking about metaphysical reality. Further, these traditional symbols are truly a "universal language" and not the private property of any individual artist, historical period, or nation.[70] There are, of course, "dialectical" differences (Coomaraswamy's favorite example is the interchangeability of the Eastern lotus and the Western rose)[71] but Indian and medieval art (and, in fact, any other traditional art) differ "neither in principle nor in essential content, but only in local colour and specific phrasing."[72]

Thus the finding of an adequate symbolism is no problem for the traditional artist. His traditional symbols, handed down from antiquity, are a rich vocabulary, precise as mathematics, and far better as a means of expression than any he could have invented for himself. It is the modern consumer who has difficulties. His own artists do indeed use symbolism, but they have resorted to private symbolism which effectively defeats the purpose of communication.[73] And when he turns to traditional art, he finds that the meaning of the ancient symbols has disappeared and is no longer familiar even to art historians.

The most urgent problem of practical criticism is to restore the lost significance of these symbols, whose power, though dormant, can spring back to life even after long neglect.[74] But the study of symbolism is no job for the amateur. Only the metaphysician can avoid the hazard of subjective interpretation or determine correctly whether a quality or object represented in a work of art is in fact a symbol. Blue may be a symbol of infinity, but if the amateur reads infinity into the eyes of a realistically painted girl he is sentimentalizing.[75] The hazard of subjective interpretation will occur if an amateur, like Carl Jung, comes to the ancient symbols with a point of view developed in modern times.[76]

As a guide to correct interpretation, Coomaraswamy suggests that the student (besides becoming a metaphysician) study the authoritative texts (especially the Indian) in which explicit statements are found about the meanings of symbols; make a comparative study of the symbols found in the works of art of all races; and secure the testimony of those (mainly primitives) who still use the traditional symbols with understanding.

Myth is but a system of symbols presented in narrative form. The rationalistic inquiry as to whether or not a particular myth is historically true or what portion of it is true is wasted labor: "The vulgarity of humanism appears nakedly and unashamed in all euhemerism."[77] To try to determine what the historical Christ really did and said is to be blind to the whole significance of myth, whose authentication is not historical but ideal. The miracles and other wonders usually reported in a myth, which the rationalizer particularly wishes to excise, are the most important elements contributing to its symbolic significance.

Myths are the "relics of an ancient *wisdom*"[78] which is as valid now as it ever was. Their ultimate source is a primordial revelation. As the races of man migrated over the face of the earth, the original Ur-myth took on local color (particularly when it was revivified by some historical figure like Buddha or Christ), but its essence was carefully and precisely transmitted.[79] Myths must be approached not with the superior at-

lern sophisticated scholar, but with a childlike
e deepest mysteries are concealed in them:
st must be, not so much a psychologist as a
..ietaphysician."[80] Even the "immoral" stories
ₒ₋ₐs must be accepted. In ritual, things may be done
which on a human ethical level of reference are "improper."
But the content of both myth and ritual is intellectual and
therefore amoral.[81] Myths are not ethical treatises or influences
but, like the rest of the spiritual arts, supports for contemplation; they are re-enactments of the cosmic relationships revealed
by the perennial philosophy.

Myths must be interpreted with great care. The hazards to
be avoided and the procedures to be followed are the same as
for the interpretation of symbols. Again Coomaraswamy em-
phasizes the usefulness of the comparative method and the value
to the Western student of Indian exegetical literature.

A vast mass of Coomaraswamy's publications are applications
of the comparative method to the interpretation of symbols
and myths. These publications do not form a systematic treatise
on universal symbolism; rather they are iconographical studies
of particular works of art, illustrations of the value of the comparative method, or explorations of the meaning of such great
analogues as the puppet show, the loathly lady, the dome, the
sun, the lotus, the tar baby, the thread, the beheading, the
world tree, archery, the sunkiss, the chariot, the clashing rocks,
the world wheel, and the Golden City. These analogues are to
be interpreted as parts of one great Monomyth, the essential
points of which, in the Christian version, are as follows: the
theme of Christian art is "the cosmic drama of the procession
of the will to life, in terms of the conflict between the powers
of light and darkness, good and evil. Man in his universal aspect
having eaten of the Tree, entered into time, and being thus
disintegrated and individualized, stood in need of redemption,
which was conceived as a reintegration in the likeness of one
who though he had taken on mortality as the Son of Man had
never been diminished of his wholeness as the Son of God apart
from time, who said of himself 'Before Abraham I am.' "[82]

Myths are the highest form of literary art, identical with

scripture. The great writers of the past, the epic poets and 1.
the dramatists, used these myths as the themes for their wor.
Then literature descended to romance and finally to the realistic
novel. At each level of this descent there was some obscuring of
the original materials until they disappeared altogether in the
modern novel. It was also a descent from the universal to the
general to the particular—from the mythical imitation of first
principles, to the imitation of ideal types, and finally to the
photographic imitation of individual character. The seculariza-
tion of literature of all kinds is now complete among intellectu-
als in Western cultures.

The folk, where they survive in any country, are more fortu-
nate. Folklore is the "form in which metaphysical doctrines are
received by the people and transmitted by them."[83] This popu-
larized metaphysics is, of course, an exoteric doctrine adapted
to the level of spiritual understanding of the folk; only a metaphysician can explain the full symbolic significance of such
stories as those about Snow White and Santa Claus.[84] But these
stories are of value even when not fully understood; on a lower
level of reference they propound the same doctrines that are
taught to the initiates into the Greater Mysteries; they are,
therefore, analogically true and suitably guide the folk (whether
the folk realize it or not) in the direction of spiritual progress.

V

Coomaraswamy's writings are a plea for a return to metaphysics, to the functioning of the intellect as "the habit of first
principles," to symbolic thinking as the normal operation of
the human mind, and to viewing all of human activities as having analogical relations to higher levels of reference and as
leading to the same end. Metaphysics is not a rigid body of
doctrine or even a systematic one. Although the first principles
are indeed immutably true, metaphysics allows for infinite development; also it is adaptable to new conditions, to different
human needs, and to different stages of spiritual development.
Thus the acceptance of the perennial philosophy does not mean

uniformity in all social arrangements for all times and places.[85]
Nor would such acceptance interfere with our interest in the
empirical world or the understanding of it through science. As
a matter of fact Coomaraswamy sees in science the one bright
spot in contemporary culture: "The only surviving artists in the
Scholastic, Gothic sense, are scientists, surgeons, and engineers,
the only ateliers, laboratories."[86] And, more important, the
hypotheses of contemporary theoretical science have striking
analogies to the first principles of the perennial philosophy;
the invisible "energies" which science postulates are, after all,
one of the names of God,[87] and so "where modern science uses
names and algebraic formulae in establishing its hierarchy of
forces, the East has attempted to express its understanding of
life by means of precise visual symbols."[88] Thus it is possible
"that the mathematical development of modern science . . . and
the penetration of Asiatic thought and art into the Western
environment . . . may represent the possibility of a renewed
rapprochement" between the East and the West.[89]

A summary of the perennial philosophy of art should, perhaps, be presented in the analogical mode which Coomaraswamy
so strongly recommends.[90] Art is the wedding of the masculine
intellect (the God within, the lawful husband, the concept) and
the feminine power (the empirical self, the bride, the Voice)
whose child is a winged word. If the Voice, tempted by her
appetites, forgets the Divine Maker and allows herself to be
played upon by a seducer, she gives birth to a bastard, a heresy,
the deadly music of secular art, which flatters herself and the
deities of this earth. She becomes a lost woman and, as she
wanders in uncharted ways under the sun, sings only of what she
sees or feels. A true work of art is a Divine Incarnation and
requires for its production the death and transfiguration of the
sensitive powers; it is a union of the sacred and profane, the
eternal and secular. But these are the universal conditions for
any good state, and so life itself becomes the most important
of the arts. The art of living is only an extension of the process
of symbolic transformation which is the essence of the spiritual
arts. Of course only the Comprehensor is completely free, each
of his actions being a spontaneous manifestation of spiritual

reality. But every person can travel the *via analogia*. He can enjoy an analogue of the Comprehensor's freedom and happiness if he transforms the empirical events of his time-bound existence into symbols of eternal metaphysical principles; that is, if he regards "every operation and experience of life without exception . . . as a reflection of the single uneventful act of the divine being, desire and dormition being taken then no longer for what they are empirically, but as reflections and as indices of a more real Love and Death."[91]

Hebrew Parallelism in Doughty's
Travels in Arabia Deserta
by
Annette M. McCormick

CHARLES MONTAGUE DOUGHTY'S *Travels in Arabia Deserta,*
published in 1888, is a unique book not only for its material,
a full record of the life of nomad Arabia, rarely seen by Europeans, but also for its style. It is a very complex kind of writing,
composed of archaisms and innovations; it is at once a patch-
work of fifteenth, sixteenth, and seventeenth century English
words and phrases and Latin construction. A completely new
material is woven by an artist who took as much delight in this
execution as did his contemporary, William Morris, in the de-
signing and weaving of beautiful tapestries. It has generally been
recognized, by the few critics who have been attracted to this
craggy book, that the Bible plays a part in the formation of its
style, but heretofore that assumption has rested on rather cur-
sory observation. The real extent of the biblical influence on
the style of *Travels in Arabia Deserta* is much larger than it
has been thought to be: indeed, the difficulties of Doughty's
sentence structure are largely resolved when his debt is fully
understood.

Like many others of his time, Doughty was attracted to the
English Bible, whose deep, full tones vibrated through the
writing of the nineteenth century. From his childhood he must
have been familiar with it, for his father was a clergyman and
his mother was the daughter of a prebendary of Rochester and
rector of Dennington, Suffolk. Such a household in the fifties
and sixties would not permit a child's growing up in ignorance

29

of the Bible. Nor did his acquaintance with it cease during his
university days. In the list of books that he read in the Bodleian, from the autumn of 1868 to the early winter of 1870, in
what seems to have been a strong desire to saturate himself in
more virile periods of the English language than that in which
he was living, appears the English Bible of 1578. This is the
so-called Breeches Bible, an edition of the Geneva Bible of
1560, translated by William Whittingham, Anthony Gilby,
Thomas Sampson, and perhaps others. The Geneva Bible, as
Doughty must have known, was one of the great translations.
It was the work of religious exiles who had far more than the
ordinary translators' interests at heart; they were intent on
presenting the "living word of God and the one guide for the
upright man in the conduct of his everyday life."[1] Doughty
appears also to have been familiar with the Coverdale translation (1535) as well as the Authorized Version of 1611, although
neither of these appears on the Bodleian reading list. In all of
these Bibles he found, of course, that which he was seeking:
words fallen out of use which he could reintroduce to augment
and enrich the language of Victorian England. And, as we
might expect, biblical rhythms came into his prose.

There are two ways in which Doughty's familiarity with the
Bible exhibits itself in *Travels in Arabia Deserta*. One is not
unexpected—the same thing is to be seen in E. H. Palmer's *The
Desert of the Exodus* and in most accounts of those who explored
the Near East: description and explanation of persons and
places in terms of their biblical equivalents. Any explorer with
an historical sense would be expected to do a certain amount
of such comparing. Doughty felt very keenly that the Semitic
peoples had changed little in their customs since the days of
Isaiah. What better way of showing this than by comparing
what he saw with what had been recorded in the Old Testament?
The other manifestation of biblical familiarity is far more en-
grossing. This consists of the employment of parallelism, the
principle of ancient Hebrew poetry, in English prose sentences.
What appears to the reader of Doughty a complex and distorted
style, if read with the understanding of this principle becomes
lucid. The debt to Chaucer and Spenser which Doughty ac-

knowledges ought indeed to have been paid to Old Testament poets, for their contribution to *Travels in Arabia Deserta* far outweighs those of the English poets.

An application of the structural principles of Hebrew poetry to the prose of the English travel book may seem an odd enterprise. But the oddness must lie with the creative artist rather than with the critic. To have chosen deliberately a writing technique so remote from the prose of his own day argues one of two things: an excess or a deficiency of artistic sense. The casual reader of *Arabia Deserta* (if indeed there be such a person), finding the prose difficult or perplexing in a degree that he has not encountered elsewhere, will have no reservation about condemning the obscurity of the book. But he who sees in the sentences the biblical pattern and the Semitic development of the ideas will marvel at the real purity of Doughty's art. For it is true, as what is to follow will, I hope, show, that the sentence and paragraph structure are perfect in their conformity to the Semitic subject matter.

The structure of ancient Hebrew poetry was first satisfactorily explained by Bishop Robert Lowth, more than a century after the appearance of the Authorized Version. His findings, which, with some additions by more recent scholars, stand as the best explanation of Hebrew prosody, can be used to test the extent of Doughty's biblical debt. With any writing of biblical flavor, there is the question of how much one must attribute directly to the Bible, how much to intermediate stages in themselves largely biblical in tone. With Doughty the answer is not difficult to come by. Although he did read theological writing and although he was familiar with *Pilgrim's Progress*, and borrowed occasionally from both, his great source must have been the Bible itself. For the Semitic cast of his sentences is quite different from that of the other writings, which are constructed on what has been called an Aryan pattern. A study of the system of parallelism, explained by Lowth, of the Semitic linking of sentences into blocks of thought, together with an examination of the imagery and vocabulary of *Travels in Arabia Deserta* will reveal the book as lavishly biblical.

Lowth's great discovery is the governing principle of Hebrew poetry, parallelism. "The poetical conformation of the sentences, which has been so often alluded to as characteristic of the Hebrew poetry, consists chiefly in a certain quality, resemblance, or parallelism between the members of each period; so that in two lines (or members of the same period), things for the most part shall answer to things, and words to words, as if fitted to each other by a kind of rule or measure. This parallelism has much variety and many gradations; it is sometimes more accurate and manifest, sometimes more vague and obscure."[2]

This rhythm of symmetry which is parallelism resides in the poetry of other Semitic tongues as well as Hebrew: it is found in Abyssinian, Sumerian, Babylonian-Assyrian, Egyptian, and Arabic, both classical (including Turkish and Persian) and neo-Arabic.[3] But Doughty did not come upon it through the Arabic, I feel certain. His knowledge of Arabic was slender. He had great difficulty acquiring the basic essentials with which to go into the desert in 1876; the records of the twenty-one months in the desert contain no passages from Arabic writing; there is no Arabic poetry written down in the little notebooks he kept during his wanderings; and there is no evidence that on Doughty's return to England he read Arabic literature. Nor have I found evidence that he read ancient Hebrew. He came to parallelism through English translations of the Bible. The loss of poetic quality in the process of translation is, as John Livingston Lowes observed in "The Noblest Monument of English Prose," minimal for a poetry resting upon such principles as those observed in Hebrew, which, as he says, is "supremely translatable." Parallelism is "the rhyme of thought"[4] rather than that of words. It moved as poetry into the King James translation, and from there Doughty wrought it into one of the most curious and powerful of English prose styles.

As a constituent of English prose, parallelism is infrequent. To find it so heavily used in this Victorian travel book may be at first surprising. But the choice of language is with Doughty a slow and exceedingly conscious process: *Travels in Arabia Deserta* was ten years in the writing, and its author sought to revivify a language which had become blunted. He reclaimed, from sixteenth and seventeenth century works and from Anglo-

Saxon, words which had long been archaic or obsolete, and he recast the structure of sentences for the sake of impressive rhythms.

Parallelism is the perfect medium for this prose, for it is in complete accord with the setting in which the author had immersed himself for almost two years.[5] The consciousness that in the Arabian desert he was living with biblical customs and amidst Semitic desert peoples who might have been contemporaries of the ancient Hebrew prophets never left him. He found the ruins of Medáin Salîh as they might have stood before the birth of Christ: "The Semitic East is a land of sepulchres; Syria, a limestone country, is full of tombs, hewn, it may be said, under every hillside. Now they are stables for herdsmen, and open dens of wild creatures. 'Kings and counsellors of the earth built them desolate places'; but Isaiah mocked in his time those 'habitations of the dead.' "[6] Amongst the nomads he was constantly witnessing practices recorded in the Bible: a Beduin treated for megrims covered the blood which had been let from him with a little heap of dust, and Doughty remarked, "So it is read in Ezekiel"; the women's nose-rings were the same as those worn by Rebekah and those women who moved Isaiah to anger; the men's arm bracelets were like those of Saul; the nomad tents were "black as the tents of Kedar"; the binding oaths of the Arabs were like those of David and Ahab; and, indeed, the habit of confirming every word by an oath had its Old Testament origin; the herds of sheep and camels, the rocks and dry water courses, the harsh conditions of life in the desert were those of the ancient Hebrews. Impressed as he was by the continuance of Old Testament manners and modes of living, he found quite naturally that the language of parallelism was the best form for the recounting of Arabian life. It was succinct, even sparse, but emotionally charged, and it suggested antiquity.

The three kinds of parallelism Lowth observes are synonymous, antithetic, and synthetic or constructive. Instead of depending for its effects upon meter and rhyme, as does English poetry, ancient Hebrew poetry rests upon patterns of sentences with parallel disposition of clauses and phrases of approximately the same length. The "members" referred to by Lowth, either phrases or clauses, occur in groups of anywhere from one to six, groups of two, three, or four being most common. We may find, for example, a verse in which there are two clauses, the second repeating the thought of the first in different, though similar, language, as

> The mountains skipped like rams,
> And the hills like lambs. (Ps. 119:4) [7]

This is a distich of synonymous parallelism. Or we may find a distich in which the second member expresses a thought not the exact equivalent of the first but similar to it, such as

> Sun, stand thou still upon Gibeon;
> And thou, Moon, upon the valley of Aijalon.

This, too, is a variety of synonymous parallelism in a distich. Instead of repeating the thought of the first member, the second member may present a contrasting thought; it is then antithetic parallelism, as

> A wise son maketh a glad father:
> But a foolish son is the heaviness of his mother.

When neither a repetition nor a contrast is presented but when there is a parallelism in the form of construction, there is synthetic or constructive parallelism. "A comparison, a reason, a consequence, a motive, often constitutes one of the lines in a synthetic parallelism."[8] Hence the following are all instances of the same type of distich:

> Yet I have set my king
> Upon Zion, my holy hill.

> Better is a dinner of herbs where love is,
> Than a stalled ox and hatred therewith.

> Answer not a fool according to his folly,
> Lest thou also be like unto him.

> As a bird that wandereth from her nest,
> So is a man that wandereth from his place.

To these three kinds, S. R. Driver adds climactic parallelism, in which the completion of the thought is delayed by the insertion of a parenthetic element and the consequent repetition of part of the first member. Another term for this construction is ascending rhythm. This kind of parallelism occurs almost uniquely in the most elevated poetry; hence its rarity.

> Give unto the Lord, O ye sons of the mighty,
> Give unto the Lord glory and strength.

> The voice of the Lord shaketh the wilderness;
> The Lord shaketh the wilderness of Kadesh.

In the more complex patterns, of more than two members, and as many as six, the same principles of similarity and contrast are observed. In a tristich, for example, all three members may be parallel, as

> But let all those that put their trust in thee rejoice;
> Let them ever shout for joy, because thou defendest them:
> Let them also that love thy name be joyful in thee.

The first two may parallel and the third complete the thought:

> The kings of the earth set themselves,
> And the rulers take counsel together,
> Against the Lord, and against his anointed.

The first may be introductory and the second and third parallel:

> Arise, O Lord; save me, O my God:
> For thou hast smitten all mine enemies upon the cheek bone;
> Thou hast broken the teeth of the ungodly.

Or the first and third may be parallel and the second parenthetical:

> Hear me when I call, O God of my righteousness:
> Thou hast enlarged me when I was in distress;
> Have mercy upon me and hear my prayer.

Tetrastichs and the rarer pentastichs and hexastichs have similar arrangements. These last are of relatively little importance: like octameter lines in English verse they are most frequently compounds of simpler forms. As Driver observes, "The finest and most perfect specimens of Hebrew poetry are, as a rule, those in which the parallelism is most complete (synonymous distichs and tetrastichs), varied by an occasional tristich."[9]

The principle of parallelism in ancient Hebrew poetry is an astoundingly large element in Doughty's sentence structure. There is hardly a page where it cannot be observed.

Distichs of synonymous parallelism of the two types illustrated above are frequent. For that type in which the second member enforces the thought of the first by repeating, we might illustrate with some sentences which have, if the principle of parallelism be not recognized, a strangely attractive simplicity:

> They comforted themselves by the way with tobacco,/ and there was none, said they, better in the whole world than this sweet leaf of their own country (I,5).[10]

> There was a great stillness in all their camp;/ these were the last hours of repose (I,6).

> His usher found me slumbering in my makhzan;/ worn and broken in this long year of famine and fatigues, I was fallen into a great languor (II,11).

> Great are their flocks in this dîra, all of sheep, and their camels are a multitude trooping over the plain (II,62).

> How pleasant then seemed to me the sunny drought of the wilderness,/ how blessed the security of the worsted booths in the wandering villages! (II,75-6).

These are frequent in *Travels in Arabia Deserta* and unmistakably biblical in tone.

The second type of synonymous distich, that in which the second member expresses a thought not identical with but parallel and similar to that of the first, Doughty did not use so frequently as the first. But it is to be found occasionally, as in:

The morrow was one of preparation,/ the day after we should depart (I,6).

Enough it seemed to them that the stranger was the hakim,/ they would not cavil with a guest or question of his religion (II,8).

In the antithetically parallel distichs there is a varying degree of length in the members. They may be long and uneven, as in

The new dawn appearing we removed not yet./ The day risen the tents were dismantled, the camels led in ready to their companies, and halted beside their loads (I,6).

Or they may be short and of approximate evenness, as in

Under the kella is a new cistern to be filled by the freshet,/ for the well of stinking water within the tower is ruinous (I,27).

Mohammed is childless, and ajjr, a man barren in himself;/ the loyal Hamûd el-Abeyd has many children (II,18).

Synthetic or constructive parallelism has no place in Doughty's prose, as far as I have been able to discover. This is hardly surprising. For in his prose style the manner in which clauses and sentences are brought together is Semitic rather than English. In the one relationships are expressed through the juxta-position of ideas, without connectives (or with very slight con-nectives, and those usually co-ordinating); in the other, they are expressed through connectives which subordinate or heighten certain parts. One may be called a constructive or artificial style, the other a cumulative style.[11]

The latter may be seen at a high degree of perfection in the prose style of Milton. Phrase is locked to phrase, clause to clause, so that as the sentence is built each part is joined inseparably to the whole; and the entire thought, which cannot be grasped until the end of the sentence or paragraph, is one usually of great complexity. The Semitic style, on the other hand, conveys its ideas through the placement of statements beside each other, without benefit of subordination. Ernest Renan has summarized this difference thus:

> Dans la structure de la phrase, comme dans toute leur constitution intellectuelle, il y a chez les Sémites une complication de moins que chez les Ariens. Il leur manque un des degrés de combinaison que nous jugeons nécessaires pour l'expression complète de la pensée. Joindre les mots dans une proposition est leur dernier effort; ils ne songent point à faire subir la même opération aux propositions elles-mêmes. C'est, pour prendre l'expression d'Aristote, le *style infini,* procédant par atomes accumulés, en opposition avec la rondeur achevée de la periode grecque et latine.[12]

This peculiarity of the Semitic languages may have been borne in upon Doughty as he heard the Arabs talk: certainly the same lack of subordination and of transition is observable in their conversations recorded in his book. But he himself, in the parts of the book that do not reproduce Arabian speech but convey his own observations, used it widely, page after page.

The phenomenon is most easily understood in single sentences, where phrases and clauses, simply by being placed together, have a relationship, implicit in this Semitic or constructive style rather than explicit as in the Aryan or cumulative manner. J. H. Gardiner, in his chapter on Hebrew narrative,[13] maintains that in Hebrew sentences the verb could be omitted, and gives as an example Prov. 26:3, "A whip for the horse, a bridle for the ass, and a rod for the fool's back." Doughty makes use of this technique not infrequently. "His strength failed him here, the fever returned upon him: I gave him rhubarb in minute doses and quinine." Normal English would insert "and" between the first two clauses; to Doughty the relationship is apparent without it. And normal English would subordinate the first two clauses, probably with either "when" or "since"; to

Doughty the temporal or causal subordination is implicit in the way in which the clauses are placed. This device is probably responsible for a good part of the irritation some readers experience in *Arabia Deserta*. Because normal English prose makes suitable subordination, giving proper emphasis to the main ideas, sentences which do not render this service to the reader seem fragmentary and rude. Unless we recognize the Semitic principle in Doughty's style, when we read such a passage as "Samn is the health of man in the deadly khála; the best samn has the odour of the blossoming vine.—The negroes gladly anoint their black skins with butter" (II,209), we may think it merely a collection of rough notes.

Doughty's paragraphs conform to this principle of implied relationship in a way that is hardly believable until one has really examined them for it. A short paragraph, that recording part of his experience at Hâyil, will do:

> Few or none of the pilgrim strangers while lying at Hâyil had entered the town,—it might be their fear or the Arabians. Only certain Bagdad derwishes came in, to eat of the public hospitality; and I saw besides but a company of merry adventurers, who would be bidden to a supper in Arabia, for the novelty. In that day's press even the galleries of the Mothîf were thronged; there I supped in the dusk, and when I rose, my sandals, the gift, of Hamûd, were taken. From four till half-past six o'clock rations had been served for "two to three thousand" persons; the Emir's cheer was but boiled temmn and a little samn (II,53).

All four sentences in the paragraph embody parallels of one kind or another, synonymous or antithetic. It is true that there are certain transitional devices: *and, besides, who, that, these;* there is even one *when*. But even these do not serve to draw the passage over the line into Aryan style. Each sentence is a unit connected to the sentence on both sides only by its placement. The austerity of the Emir in contrast to his great wealth is implied in the biblical fashion.

The paragraph in which the Kahtân and their sheykh Hayzàn are described starts in a more normal English style, "The Kahtân who talked with me in the Méshab were pleased when I confirmed the noble antiquity of their blood, in the ears of the tribesmen of Nejd, who until that hour had never heard anything in the matter" (II,38). But with the second sentence Doughty begins to slip into Semitic style; there is no transitional device linking it to the first sentence. With the third sentence, a tetrastich, begins parallelism. There follow a tristich, a tetrastich, a distich, and a tristich, all lacking transition and subordination:

> These Kahtân came not into the great public coffee-hall of the Kasr, whether because of the (profane) bibbing there of tobacco smoke, or that they were at enmity with most of the tribesmen: they drank the morning and mid-afternoon and evening cup apart, in their own makhzan; but they received the coffee-berries from the Emir's kitchen. After supper I sought them out: their young sheykh Hayzàn immediately bid me sit down on the saddleskin beside him, and with a good grace he handed to me the first cup of kahwa. This was a beautiful young man, of manly face and stature; there was nothing in him that you would have changed, he was a flower of all whom I have seen among the Arabians: his life had never suffered want in the khala. In his countenance, with a little ferocity of young years, appeared a pleasant fortitude: the milk-beard was not yet sprung upon Hayzàn's hardy fresh face. His comeliness was endowed with the longest and greatest braided side-locks, which are seen among them; and big he was, of valiant limbs:—but all this had no lasting!

Temporal, causal, concessive clauses—all are lacking in this paragraph, yet the relationship of the ideas is perfectly clear; we cannot miss the tragedy of Hayzàn.

Synthetic or constructive parallelism for the most part is, then, a deviation from the normal Semitic habit of mind. Doughty's prose consciously or unconsciously rejects it.

Rare though it is in the Bible, climactic parallelism appears in *Arabia Deserta,* and in a proportion which is, I think, in the same ratio to the other forms of parallelism as in the Bible. "Bitter is the heart, and the sword is sharp, of him who rules over the wandering tribes of the Khála" (I,561). "How good!

seemed to me, how peaceable! this little plot of the nomad earth under the dripping curtains of a worsted booth, in comparison with Hâyil town" (II,67). It is this kind of parallelism with its readily seen emotional height which has led some readers of *Arabia Deserta* to feel, without knowing exactly why, that Doughty's style is biblical in part.

When we find the more complicated patterns of parallelism in the prose of *Arabia Deserta,* the dependency on the Old Testament becomes far more obvious: tristichs, tetrastichs, pentastichs, and even hexastichs crowded into the pages are incontrovertible evidence that the Bible was Doughty's model.

Among the numbers of tristichs there are some of all kinds. We shall find those in which all three members are parallel, iterating the same idea, as in

> The Peraean Beduw are more easy in their religion than the Wahabish tribesmen of Arabia;/ they make little account of pattering the daily formal prayers,/ nor do they rightly know them (I,17).

> When this land came to be weakened, it would be soon partly forsaken, as lying open upon the Beduin marches:/ the few people would draw together in the stronger villages,/ the outlying hamlets would be left without inhabitant (I, 22-3).

> The first houses I found to be but waste walls and roofless,/ and the plantations about them forsaken;/ the languishing palmstems showed but a dying crown of rusty leaves (II,7).

And there are those in which the first two members are parallel and the third completes the thought, as in

> Malcontent, as has been often seen, they would assault the Haj march or set upon some corner of the camp by night, hoping to drive off a booty of camels:/ in warfare they beset the strait places, where the firing down of a hundred beggarly matchlocks upon the thick multitude must cost many lives;/ so an Egyptian army of Ibrahim Pasha was defeated in the south country by *Harb* Beduins (I,10).

> Months before, when I came riding hither in an eventide
> from Kerak, Beduin booths were pitched in the waste without
> the walls;/ the sun was setting and the camels wandered in
> of themselves over the desert, the housewives at the tents
> milked their small cattle./ By the ruins of a city of stone
> they received me, in the eternity of the poor nomad tents,
> with a kind hospitality (I,20).

In this instance the third member has been cut off as a separate
sentence. Notice in the next instance how the use of the colon
becomes defensible when the operation of parallelism is apparent.

> The Aarab have no religious elders in their miserable encamp-
> ments,/ nor have any of them learned letters:/ who then
> should teach the Beduw their religion? (I,17).

The third type of tristich, that in which the second and third
members are parallel and the first is introductory, can be seen in

> It is their caravan prudence, that in the beginning of a long
> way, the first shall be a short journey;/ the beasts feel their
> burdens,/ the passengers have fallen in that to their riding in
> the field (I,7).

The fourth type of tristich, that with the parenthetical second
member, is used by Doughty thus:

> Already we saw the flies of the oasis:/ Kheybar was yet cov-
> ered from sight by the great descending limb of the Harra;/
> we felt the air every moment warmer and, for us, faint and
> breathless (II,74).

The numbers of tetrastichs in *Arabia Deserta* are indeed surprising. As in the distiches and tristichs there is variation in
the length and composition of the members; sometimes the
divisions come between parallel phrases, sometimes between
parallel clauses; and the disposition of the parallel parts is also
varied. The most common type, that in which the first two
members and the last two are parallel, can be seen in Gen. 49:7,

"Cursed be their anger, for it was fierce;/ and their wrath, for it was cruel:/ I will divide them in Jacob,/ and scatter them in Israel"; and Deut. 32:21, "They have moved me to jealousy with that which is not God;/ they have provoked me to anger with their vanities:/ and I will move them to jealousy with those which are not a people;/ I will provoke them to anger with a foolish nation." Doughty uses this type again and again:

> Tell me (said he), since thou are here again in the peace and assurance of Ullah,/ and whilst we walk, as in the former years, toward the new blossoming orchards, full of the sweet spring as the garden of God,/ what moved thee,/ or how couldst thou take such journeys into the fanatic Arabia? (I,1).

> There go commonly three or four camels abreast/ and seldom five;/ the length of the slow-footed multitude of men and cattle is near two miles,/ and the width some hundred yards in the open plains (I,7).

> But the day was rainy,/ the pilgrims' bedding, commonly a cotton quilt, in such a march is wetted through;/ yet the present evils cannot last/ and each moment we are nearer to the sun of tomorrow (I,20).

> The soil is now good loam,/ no more that sharp granite grit of Hâyil;/ the dates are good,/ they are the best of the country (II,7).

Other types of tetrastichs Doughty uses less commonly. That in which the first and third members and the second and fourth are parallel, as in Ps. 55:21, "The words of his mouth were smoother than butter,/ but war was in his heart:/ his words were softer than oil,/ yet were they drawn swords/" can be seen in these examples:

> The Moslem town-sheykh deals tolerantly with them,/ they are part of "many",/ but the Christians complain of vexations;/ they are all rude men together (I,24).

> If any marketing nomads dismounted at her door,/ she re-

ceived them bountifully;/ if any in the village were in want,
and she heard of it,/ she would send somewhat (II,89).

The type in which the first three members are parallel and
the fourth is independent, as in Ps. 1:3, "And he shall be like a
tree planted by the rivers of water,/ that bringeth forth his
fruit in his season;/ his leaf also shall not wither;/ and whatsoever he doeth shall prosper/," occurs in *Arabia Deserta* in sentences such as "The hearts of the Arabians waxed cold at that
sight,/—the black death, when they thought themselves secure,
was there in the midst of them!/ also the bullets of the Dowla
fell to them from very far off;/ nevertheless they passed on to
the assault" (II,35). The tetrastich of introverted parallelism,
in which the first and last and the two middle members are
parallel, as in Prov. 23:15-6, "My son, if thine heart be wise,/
my heart shall rejoice, even mine./ Yea, my reins shall rejoice,/
when thy lips speak right things/," appears occasionally, in sentences such as "What mean these lofty walls;/ is not the site
too small for a city?/ neither is the soil very fit hereabout for
husbandry;/ less town than fortress it might be a *praesidium,*
in these parts, upon the trade road" (I,30). The tetrastich in
which the first member is independent and the remaining three
are parallel, as in Prov. 24:12, "If thou sayest, Behold, we knew
it not;/ doth not he that pondereth the heart consider it?/
and he that keepeth thy soul, doth not he know it?/ and
shall not he render to every man according to his works?"
is to be seen in, "Now we descended into a large bottom ground
in the lava-field, *el-Húrda,* full of green corn:—/ that corn I saw
ripen before my departure from Kheybar!/ Here Ghroceyb
dreaded to meet with the ghrazzu,—/ the robbers might be
grazing their mares in the green corn of the settlement" (II,74).
In short, the only type of tetrastich which is not found in *Arabia
Deserta* is that in which the four members are in no determinate
relationship (as in Ps. 40:17). It is possible that they too are
there, though rarely; but because they do not appear frequently
we may conclude that Doughty employed the tetrastich for effects of repetition or contrast, which this type does not afford.

Even the rare pentastich, which can be seen in Cant. 3:4, "It was but a little that I passed from them,/ but I found him whom my soul loveth:/ I held him, and would not let him go,/ until I had brought him into my mother's house,/ and into the chamber of her that conceived me/," occurs in *Arabia Deserta:*

> We should think them sprawling riders;/ for a boast or warlike exercise, in the presence of our armed company, they let us view how fairly they could ride a career and turn;/ striking back heels and seated low, with pressed thighs, they parted at a handgalop, made a tourney or two easily upon the plain;/ and now wheeling wide, they betook themselves down in the desert, every man bearing and handling his spear as at point to strike a foeman;/ so fetching a compass and we marching, they a little out of breath came gallantly again (I,30) .

There are at least two instances of the hexastich, which has varying patterns of parallelism (as in Num. 29:17, I Sam. 2:8, Cant. 4:9, and Hab. 3:17):

> Little was my practice of medicine,/ yet this name procured me entrance amongst them, and the surest friends./ A man of medicine is not found in Nejd;/ but commonly they see some Ajamy hakîm, once a year, at Hâyil amongst the Persian pilgrims./ I was called to visit suffering persons;/ yet because they would not leave with me the smallest pledge of their good faith, I remained with hardly any daily patients (II,4) .

> The Emir sat now in Hamûd's place,/ and Hamûd where Sleyman daily sat./ The light scimitar, with golden hilt, that Mohammed carries loose in his hand, was leaned up to the wall beside him;/ the blade is said to be of some extremely fine temper./ He sat as an Arabian in his loose cotton tunic, mantle and kerchief, with naked shanks and feet,/ his sandals, which he had put off at the carpet, were set out before him (II,11) .

There is more than one sentence in each of these passages, but because the subject matter in each has a unity, it does not seem an unwarranted application of the term hexastich. It is, after all, the juxtaposition of thoughts, not the employment of punctuation nor containment in a sentence unit, which constitutes parallelism.

There can be, I think, little doubt that the inspiration the Bible gave to Doughty was very great. The employment of parallelism in sentence structure may seem at first a highly artificial technique for an English writer, but as the book progresses and we see the same structure constantly in the recorded conversation, we come to accept it as natural to the subject matter and to the man who became so much a part of that world he was describing. The notebooks reveal that the Bible was not remote from Doughty's mind; but we do not really need that evidence to tell us. The comfort of Psalm 90 is obvious when he writes, in the midst of suffering in the summer famine, that the "languor of hunger, the desert disease, was in all the tents," and again when he writes: "Hither lies no way from the city of the world, a thousand years pass as one daylight; we are in the world and not in the world, where Nature brought forth man, an enigma to himself, and an evil spirit sowed in him the seeds of dissolution/" (I,473). When, in the often quoted second sentence of the preface to the first edition of *Travels in Arabia Deserta,* he warns the reader, "The book is not milk for babes," he speaks in the metaphor of St. Paul, "And I, brethren, could not speak unto you as unto spiritual, but as unto carnal, even as unto babes in Christ. I have fed you with milk, and not with meat: for hitherto ye were not able to bear it, neither yet now are ye able/" (I Cor. 3:1-2). Beyond the shadow of a doubt a very great part of *Arabia Deserta* was fed from the fat pastures of the Bible.

Louise Labé and the Comtessa de Dia

by
Elliott D. Healy

ALTHOUGH SOME THREE and a half centuries, as well as differences in civilization and language, separate Louise Labé and
the Provençal poetess, the Comtessa de Dia, their spiritual kinship as women who owe their poetic achievements to the sufferings of love is inescapable. This relationship has not gone
unnoticed. For example, Charles Camproux, a recent historian
of troubadour literature, says of the poetic compositions of the
comtessa: "Ils expriment, avec une passion que la Belle Cordière
ne dépassera pas au XVIᵉ siècle, les sentiments éternels de désir,
de joie, de mélancolie et de jalousie qui ont toujours fait la
réalité de l'amour depuis Sapho jusqu'aux héroïnes de Racine
et aux amoureuses modernes."[1] Such a statement perhaps does
more honor than the facts warrant to the Provençal poetess, or
trobairitz, as the feminine singers of the *langue d'oc* were called;
yet the Comtessa de Dia, shadowy figure though she may be,
is a not unworthy predecessor of the Lyonese poetess, as an examination of their *romans d'amour* will abundantly demonstrate.

Although Louise Labé is considerably closer to us in time and
civilization than the lady of Dia, we know disappointingly little
about her. Much that has been written about her life is highly
romanticized and often based upon nothing more solid than
ingenious conjecture. There is, however, general agreement on
a number of facts. Louise Labé was the daughter of a well-to-do
ropemaker of Lyons named Pierre Charly, but known as Labé.
She was the wife of another and equally prosperous manufacturer
of ropes named Ennemond Perrin. Hence the nickname of "la

47

Belle Cordière." She was born in Lyons close to the year 1520 and died at her property of Parcieu-en-Dombes, outside that city, in 1566. Her one book, containing a little-read prose comedy, three elegies, and the twenty-four unforgettable sonnets on which her fame rests, was published in 1555 by the Lyonese printer Jean de Tournes. Louise possessed, for a woman of her time, an extraordinarily broad education, for in addition to competence in various feminine arts, she was widely read in Latin, Spanish, and Italian as well as in French, possessed gifts as a musician, was skilled as a rider and knowledgeable in arms, and was in brief a young woman whose education Rabelais himself might have planned. She may or may not have been a *cortegiana onesta* as some have claimed,[2] but she was highly esteemed by many poets and scholars of her day and was a well-known figure in the literary circles of Lyons in the bustling years of the forties and fifties of her century. We do not need the legends which have grown up about her name in order to see her across the centuries as a vigorous, fascinating personality, nor do we need to accept the conjecture that the man to whom she addressed some of the most ardent love poetry in all French literature was the poet Olivier de Magny in order to feel the full impact of her *roman d'amour* as revealed in her poetic legacy to posterity.

As little as we know about Louise Labé, far less has come down to us concerning the Countess of Dia. By a strange quirk of literary and historical research, less is known of her today than was accepted as fact a generation ago. For then we would have called her Beatritz de Dia, and we would have assumed without question that her lover was the well-known nobleman and troubadour Raimbaut d'Aurenga, exponent of *trobar clus,* and author of some forty extant poems. Furthermore we might not have questioned her composition of the woman's argument in a *tenso* which has traditionally been assigned to her and to Raimbaut. These interesting assumptions come to us largely from her Provençal *vida,* which reads as follows: "La Comtessa de Dia si fo moiller d'en Guillem de Peiteus, bella donna e bona. Et enamoret se d'en Raimbaut d'Aurenga, e fez de lui mantas bonas cansos."[3] The traditional attitude of provençalists has been to regard statements found in the *vidas,* usually written long after the death of their subjects, with great caution. There has been, however, a tendency to lend some credence to assertions which do not appear illogical and which could not have been derived by the biographers from the troubadour's own compositions. Since nothing in the four *cansos d'amor* ascribed to the Comtessa de Dia by the manuscript rubrics touches upon the information given in the *vida,* it is not surprising that she was long assumed to be the wife of a Guillem de Peiteus and to have loved Raimbaut d'Aurenga. Because the most likely Guillem de Peiteus was known to have married a lady named Beatrice, the *trobairitz* came to be called Beatritz de Dia, and she is still often referred to under this name. We now consider it unlikely that she was married to a Guillem de Peiteus and equally unlikely that she was in love with, or even a close contemporary of, the well-known troubadour Raimbaut III d'Aurenga. Thus even the period in which she lived is not definitely determined. Jeanroy suggests, and Walter T. Pattison, in his excellent edition of Raimbaut, urges quite plausibly that the Raimbaut d'Aurenga mentioned as the countess' lover in the Provençal *vida* may well have been the nephew of the great troubadour or Raimbaut IV, who was also a poet of sorts.[4] This Raimbaut d'Aurenga must have been born about 1185, and he died in Montpellier in 1218.[5] Consequently, our *trobairitz* may be presumed to have flourished during the last quarter of the twelfth century and the first decades of the thirteenth, or possibly some twenty-five years earlier if her Raimbaut should ever be proved to have been the first of the two in question.

Thus the Comtessa de Dia is at best a nebulous figure, and the few apparent facts which can be assembled about her are partly matters of deduction. Jeanroy goes so far as to question the sincerity of her poetic utterances: "Je me figure que nos 'trobairitz,' esclaves de la tradition, incapables d'un effort d'analyse, se sont bornées à exploiter des thèmes connus, à user d'un formulaire courant. . . ."[6] His thought is that the *trobairitz,* several of whom sang in a forthrightly passionate manner, are simply utilizing in reverse the usual courtship procedures of the troubadours. It would be extremely difficult, however, to find any troubadour, no matter how frank, expressing himself quite so openly on the subject of amorous yearning as did the Comtessa de Dia.

In any event, her poetry, although limited in quantity, speaks for itself, and it does not really matter who she was, when she lived, or who her lover was, when she, like Louise Labé, has left us a story of her love which is still capable of reaching out and speaking to us in strikingly poignant fashion. Although, as a product of her time and culture, she demonstrates much that is typical of the troubadour approach to poetry, there is in her revelation of deep-felt emotion such strength and sincerity that we are constrained to see in her the beginnings of a more enduring lyric tradition and to find her not unworthy of her Lyonese sister, or of any of the later feminine poets which the Gallic strain has produced.

The uncertainties and lack of circumstantial knowledge about the relationship of Louise Labé and the Comtessa de Dia with the two men whom they addressed in their sonnets and *cansos d'amor* are not here a matter of primary concern. It is reasonable to assume that they were men of flesh and blood, for it would seem contrary to human experience that either could have written such powerful and personal verses to an imaginary lover, and thus in each case the *roman d'amour* may be considered a *roman vécu*. Of greater concern is the essence of their poetic dedication and the manner in which each, speaking for herself in particular and for womankind in general, sought to achieve a full expression of the deepest emotions of her heart.

We obtain a clearer insight into the full range of Louise Labé's reaction to the role of love in her life than is the case with the Comtessa de Dia, for the greater extent and scope of her poetry, aided by our wider knowledge of the surroundings in which she lived, tell us more than the four *cansos d'amor* and the one doubtful *tenso*[7] of the latter. Yet the inequalities in breadth and variety between the literary productions of the two are in large measure offset by the high degree of emotional impact which both possess. This is not to say that the Comtessa de Dia measures up in all respects to the poetic stature of Louise Labé, for the Lyonese poetess in a number of ways surpasses the lady of Dia. Nevertheless, they have much in common, sharing a place among the most vigorous of all the singers of the sorrows and sufferings of love.

One of the most consistent traits of both women is the whole-hearted singleness of purpose that motivates them. Their fidelity to a single theme, despite the variations which add to its rich-ness and color, is remarkable in its purity of intensity and in the clear contours of its expression, so that we are rarely con-scious of any monotony or repetitiousness. The sentiments vary little, but the expression is ever fresh. Speaking of Louise Labé, Bernard Jourdan, a recent editor of her elegies and sonnets, says: "Son œuvre n'est en effet presque jamais parée de grâces inutiles, mais nous étreint au plus profond de nous-mêmes par ce que nous découvrons de vérité passagère et de vérité éternelle dans la plus belle lamentation, le plus beau cantique amoureux de notre langue."[8] While M. Jourdan appears to have a penchant for superlatives, it is perhaps demonstrable that he is right, even when he proclaims further, "Cette jeune femme, qui naît cent ans après Villon, cent ans avant Racine, est sans doute la plus grande poétesse de notre langue."[9] We will find no such enthusiastic praise applied to the Comtessa de Dia, but it must be remembered that it is not yet the habit of provençalists to evaluate the work of the troubadours from the point of view of the literary critic. The traditional methodologies of the historical linguist and the literary historian too often narrow the horizon of the student of troubadour literature to the detriment of a fuller under-standing of the genuine accomplishments of these earliest singers of the neo-Latin languages. Joseph Anglade, perhaps more fully alert than most scholars of his generation to the poetic excellence of troubadour verse, does have this to say of her poetry: "On y sent une émotion sincère, à peine contenue; c'est un douloureux roman, où la passion s'exprime avec une simplicité et une ab-sence de recherche qui donnent à cette œuvre si brève un charme de plus."[10] Charles Camproux adds this apt observation, "C'est d'amour tout simple et brûlant que sont pétris les poèmes de celle-ci. . . ."[11] And Anglade has noted elsewhere, speaking of the *trobairitz* in general, "Il semble que les poétesses provençales n'aient écrit que sous le souffle de l'inspiration."[12] In other words, the few feminine poets of the *langue d'oc* who have come down to us, unlike many of their masculine counterparts, wrote from the heart when composing their *cansos d'amor*.

Both women follow much the same pattern in developing their *roman d'amour*. Both dwell at some length on their sorrows and sufferings, crying out at the injustice of the neglect which they must endure. As Jourdan graphically puts it, speaking of Louise Labé, "C'est . . . un halètement de bête blessée qui lèche encore la main qui l'a frappée."[13] Both protest their own fidelity, and both berate their lovers for their absence and lack of constancy, although in this respect Louise Labé is more urbane and the countess more forthright. Both heap praise upon their absent lovers and extoll their virtues, at the same time expressing sadness at the lovers' lack of perceptivity. There is, beyond doubt, a measure of self-pity in their eloquent lamentations, and finally there is some of the most honest, outspoken, and unabashed expression of physical longing that one is apt to find in any sophisticated literature.

To a greater degree than Louise Labé, the Comtessa de Dia seems to feel that she is too beautiful and high born a lady to be treated with indifference by her lover, that if he were not sadly lacking in discernment he would surely return to his lover's allegiance. She states in effect that she is all that any man has a right to desire, but that he treats her as if she possessed none of the qualities which he ought to appreciate:

> Vas lui no·m val merces ni cortesia,
> Ni ma beltatz, ni mos pretz, ni mos sens,
> C'atressi·m sui enganad'e trahia
> Cum degr'esser, s'ieu fos desavinens.[14]
>
> II, 4-7.

We find little attempt on the part of Louise Labé to urge her good qualities upon her lover. She prefers, rather, to pour out her own love in tumultuous phrases which seem at times to pursue each other in their effort towards utterance, and thus reach straightway the one to whom she calls. Consider the headlong impetuosity of such lines as these:

Je vis, je meurs: je me brule et me noye.
J'ay chaut estreme en endurant froidure:
La vie m'est et trop molle et trop dure.
J'ay grans ennuis entremeslez de joye.[15]

VIII, 1-4.

When she speaks of beauty it is with the recognition that love itself is a creator of beauty. Might this not reflect a realization that her own beauty, often attested by her admirers, was not so much a physical attribute as an inner loveliness, a radiance which shone forth from her animation, and particularly from an animation born of happiness? In the fifteenth sonnet she exclaims:

Fay mon soleil devers moy retourner,
Et tu verras s'il ne me rend plus belle.

XV, 13-14.

Later admirers of Louise Labé, thinking of her in literal fashion as "la Belle Cordière" and aware of various contemporary tributes to her beauty, sometimes find the one surviving portrait of her, done by P. Woeiriot at Lyons in 1555 when Louise was approximately thirty-five years of age, disconcertingly thin-lipped and grim. It seems likely, therefore, that her face in repose may have been reproduced faithfully enough by the painter and that her beauty was a result of animation, play of features, and spirited responsiveness. Only once in the sonnets does she make direct reference to her own beauty, and this is, interestingly enough, within much the same context as the reference already cited from the Comtessa de Dia, namely, that in view of her beauty she cannot understand her lover's coldness and lack of interest:

Las! que me sert, que si parfaitement
Louas jadis et ma tresse doree,
Et de mes yeus la beauté comparee
Tira les trets causes de ton tourment?

XXIII, 1-5.

As for our *trobairitz* we have only her own statements, plus the otherwise unsupported evidence of her *vida* to attest to her beauty, but her complacent confidence that any discriminating man would find her beautiful is doubtless worthy of acceptance.

Little appears in the verses of either poetess which might serve to produce a definite impression of the personalities of the unknown lovers. In fact, surprisingly little is said which may be construed as direct praise of either man. This may be explained by the complete absorption of each lady in her own unhappiness, her own anguish of soul. "Elle ne connaît que sa prope misère," says Jourdan of Louise Labé,[16] and the same observation applies equally well to the Comtessa de Dia. Yet both, at intervals, so far forget their own sufferings as to permit us a brief glimpse of their lovers. The countess, writing in the normal fashion of troubadour poetry, uses all too often the familiar clichés which leave us at best a vague and formless impression:

> Q'ieu n'ai chausit un pro e gen
> Per cui pretz meillur' e genssa,
> Larc et adreig e conoissen.
> On es sens e conoissenssa.[17]
>
> > I, 25-28.

Pro, gen, pretz, conoissenssa, all represent qualities which are so much a part of the troubadour stock in trade that sometimes it is difficult to know precisely how they should be rendered in terms of present day concepts. The countess tells us, however, in clearer and more meaningful terms, that her lover is *gais,* therefore of a joyful and outgoing temperament, wherefore she in turn, responsive to him, is gracious and gay: "Car mos amics es lo plus gais/ Per q'ieu sui coindet e gaia."[18] On only one other occasion does she speak directly and in detail of her lover's qualities, but here the tone is different. She no longer sings his praises with joy and pride, but, in a darker mood not untinged with jealousy, wonders that any woman could resist his attractiveness. One has the impression that perhaps the rift which was to separate the two lovers is just beginning, that there is as yet no definite separation, and that it is with a gentle melancholy rather than with discouragement or despair that she sees once again in her memory her lover's pleasing qualities:

> Proesa grans q'el vostre cors s'aizina
> E lo rics pretz q'avetz m'en atayna,
> C'una non sai loindana ni vezina
> Si vol amar vas vos non si'aclina.[19]
>
> II, 22-25.

With an assurance, however, born perhaps of that faith in her own beauty and lineage already noted, she continues at once to point out that he with his natural discernment ought to realize that he should return to her:

> Mas vos, amics, etz ben tant conoisens
> Que ben devetz conoisser la plus fina,
> E membre vos de nostres convinens.[20]
>
> II, 26-28.

Louise Labé, though unrestrained in most of her lyric effusions, is likewise relatively conservative in describing her lover's prowess and virtues, almost as if, loving as she did from the deepest recesses of her passionate nature, she felt no need of explaining why. It would be sufficient to her to recognize the simple fact of her adulation without wondering to herself or explaining to others why it should be so. Thus we find only a few fleeting comments, rather stylized and lacking in originality, offered in praise of her lover. These lines from the tenth sonnet are representative:

> Quand j'aperçoy ton blond chef couronné
> D'un laurier verd, faire un Lut si bien pleindre,
> Que tu pourrois à te suivre contreindre
> Arbres et rocs: quand je te vois orné,
>
> Et de vertus dix mille environné,
> Au chef d'honneur plus haut que nul ateindre:
> Et des plus hauts les louenges esteindre:
> Lors dit mon coeur en soi passionné:

> Tant de vertus qui te font estre aymé,
> Qui de chacun te font estre estimé,
> Ne te pourroient aussi bien faire aymer?
>
> X, 1-11.

Once again we learn little about the man toward whom her thoughts are ever directed. That he was blond, possessed of a thousand virtues, able to draw away to himself the praise destined for the loftiest of men—these statements evoke no image, constituting rather the prelude to a reproach, in which she says in effect, "Possessed of so many virtues, virtues which cause you to be beloved of all, could you not, in your turn, bring yourself to love?"

When they seek to pour forth the deepest yearnings and sorrows of the heart, both women not only reveal the depth of the emotion that obsesses them but also demonstrate a gift for the fullest expression of the heart's turbulence. It is then that they attain the eloquence that enables them to reach out beyond themselves, projecting the essence of their feeling across the years so that we, looking back, feel the impact of their loneliness, sense of loss, pain of separation, and yearning passion. With both women the desire to record the pent-up emotions with which they live, for the sake of their own *soulagement d'âme*, expresses itself in the poignant phrases of sorrow and devotion, but in both there is also more than a touch of asperity, of lament mingled with accusation, of loneliness shot through with an echo of pride which has been hurt.

The Comtessa de Dia, for example, in her best known *canso*, begins with an expression of forlorn bitterness:

> A chantar m'er de so qu'ieu no volria,
> Tant me rancur de lui cui sui amia
> Car eu l'am mais que nuilla ren que sia . . .[21]
>
> I, 1-3.

She then goes on to remind her lover somewhat sharply, in verses already cited, that he does not treat her as her beauty, noble lineage, and intelligence demand. In the doubtful *tenso* the lady accuses her lover of being carelessly unaware of her pining and heartache and even incapable of sharing her pain, for she tells him with some asperity:

> Amics, en gran cossirier
> Suy per vos, et en gran pena,
> E del mal q'ieu soffier
> No cre que vos sentatz guaire . . .[22]
>   III, 1-4.

Much the same thought is repeated in a later strophe of the same *tenso,* in which the lover is accused of not being able to suffer a quarter of the grief which she must endure. Elsewhere, she speaks bitterly of having been betrayed, attributing this to the fact that she had not given her love, a puzzling statement unless we accept it as meaning that she had not granted it in the full physical sense:

> Ara vei q'ieu sui trahida
> Car eu non li donei m'amor,
> Don ai estat en gran error
> En lieig e qand sui vestida.[23]
>   IV, 5-8.

Such verses as these emphasize the countess' preoccupation with her lover's indifference to her sorrow, his unwillingness to share her grief, and her sense of betrayal. They seem to reveal, in effect, that in her surpassing confidence in her beauty and desirability, she cannot accept, either humbly or despairingly, the thought that the one she loves may in cold reality be indifferent to her.

Louise Labé also occasionally speaks out with her accustomed vigor in chastisement of her lover. In the eleventh sonnet she exclaims with a mixture of asperity and anguish:

> O cœur felon, ô rude cruauté
> Tant tu me tiens de façons rigoureuses
> Tant j'ay coulé de larmes langoureuses
> Sentant l'ardeur de mon cœur tourmenté . . .
>   XI, 5-8.

And again in the second sonnet, picturesquely and directly:

> De toy me plein, que tant de feus portant,
> En tant d'endrois d'iceus mon cœur tatant,
> N'en est sur toy volé quelque étincelle.
>
> II, 12-14.

But, unlike the countess, she seems somewhat ashamed of such an outburst, even though the thread of reproof is on the whole a slender one, and she asks forgiveness for uttering such sentiments of scarcely concealed bitterness:

> Pardonne moy, Ami, à cette fois,
> Estant outrée et de despit et d'ire:
> Mais je m'assure quelque part que tu sois,
> Qu'autant que moy tu soufres de martire.
>
> XXIII, 11-14.

It is not surprising that Louise Labé often surpasses her predecessor in vigor and diversity of language. As flexible an instrument for the expression of emotion as was the language of the troubadours, the poetic idiom in which the Lyonese poetess worked was an even more highly developed medium for the subtle analysis of feeling. Again, the impeccable sonnets of the latter seem better equipped to produce the delicate, sometimes whimsical, often impetuous, and always appealing verses which it was her gift to write, than were the more formalized *cansos d'amor* of the Comtessa de Dia, limited as they were by the conventions of troubadour phraseology.

Nevertheless, the Comtessa de Dia conveys a deep impression of the quality and the pathos of her feeling, coupled as it often is with assurances of her own loyalty and suggestive of her effort to be worthy so that no shadow of blame may attach to her for whatever had happened to mar the tranquil course of her love. In words tinged with distress and sadness she tells us:

> D'aisso·m conort car anc non fi faillenssa,
> Amics, vas vos per nuilla captenenssa,
> Ans vos am mais non fetz Seguis Valenssa,

E platz mi mout qez eu d'amar vos venssa,
Lo mieus amics, car etz lo plus valens. . . .[24]

> II, 8-12.

She is not, moreover, devoid of feelings of jealousy, and we may
be justified in assuming that she knows full well that she has
reason to be jealous when she exclaims:

Non es ges dreitz c'autr'amors vos mi tuoilla
Per nuilla ren qe·us diga ni·us acuoilla;
E membre vos cals fo·l comensamens
De nostr'amor, ia Dompnidieus non vuoilla
Q'en ma colpa sia·l departimens![25]

> II, 17-21.

We have encountered this note before, and indeed it recurs
throughout the countess' poems; a nostalgic harking back to
an idyllic moment of happiness with the firm assurance that
the separation which has obviously taken place was not of her
making. She has been ever faithful, wishing always that she
could count, in equal fashion, upon her lover's faithfulness:

E pois eu li sui veraia
Bei·s taing q'el me sia verais,
C'anc de lui amar no m'estrais
Ni ai cor que m'en estraia.[26]

> I, 5-8.

Confident in the knowledge of her own integrity, she may well
expect similar loyalty from him.

It would be difficult, on the other hand, to surpass the poignant
nostalgia and sheer lyric power of the most moving sonnets of
Louise Labé, verses which Jourdan refers to as "la cendre chaude
en notre main, de·ce cœur et de ce langage qui se brûlent l'un
l'autre."[27] This she often achieves with commendable economy
of phrase, as in these lines from the eleventh sonnet:

Tout aussi tot que je commence à prendre
Dans le mol lit le repos desiré,

> Mon triste esprit hors de moy retiré
> S'en va vers toy incontinent se rendre.
>
> IX, 1-4.

And in more mystic vein:

> On voit mourir toute chose animee,
> Lors que du corps l'ame sutile part:
> Je suis le corps, toy la meilleure part:
> Où es tu donq, ô ame bien aymee?
>
> VII, 1-4.

This same sonnet ends on a note of longing and entreaty, in which the poetess, with a touch of the neo-Platonism which was esteemed in the Lyons of her day, comments on the union of soul and body which her lover's absence makes impossible, and then pleads gently that he, if he should return to her, might do so with gentleness:

> Non de rigueur: mais de grace amiable,
> Qui doucement me rende ta beauté,
> Jadis cruelle, à present favorable.
>
> VII, 12-14.

But love to Louise Labé is seldom without cruelty. The occasional contentment which she achieves is of briefest duration, for no matter where it leads her, and no matter how dear the thought of the absent one may be to her, happiness is quickly superseded by the more nearly constant companion of sorrow:

> Ainsi Amour inconstamment me meine:
> Et quand je pense avoir plus de douleur,
> Sans y penser je me treuve hors de peine.
>
> Puis quand je croy ma joye estre certaine,
> Et estre au haut de mon desiré heur,
> Il me remet en mon premier malheur.
>
> VIII, 9-14.

Both women are perhaps equally effective in painting a clear and graphic picture of their *misère d'amour,* of the wounds they have suffered, and of the sorrow they bear. On the other hand, only rarely do we glimpse, even in the Comtessa de Dia,[28] heiress though she is to the troubadour tradition of the *ioi d'amor,* the delight which lovers are wont to share. She is, in fact, somewhat more personal and specific in speaking of love's sorrow than is Louise Labé and typically adopts a questioning attitude, asking herself again and again why her lover should be arrogant or indifferent toward her. In her case, we have the impression that her reluctant lover is nearby, that he may well be the immediate recipient of her *cansos,* whereas Louise Labé, perhaps because she addresses herself to someone who is actually far away, perhaps because of greater sophistication, leaves us with the feeling that her outpourings of emotion are largely for her own solace and that her lover, genuine though he must be, is not really expected to return. Thus the countess, using the frequent troubadour device of referring to a poem as a messenger to the one to whom it is addressed, exclaims:

> Valer mi deu mos pretz e mos paratges
> E ma beutatz e plus mos fis coratges,
> Per q'ieu vos mand lai on es vostr'estatges
> Esta chansson que me sia messatges . . .[29]
>
> II, 29-32.

It is not possible to know to what extent such songs were actually sent to their intended recipients, but there is no reason to doubt that they often served as real missives. In the *tornada* or *envoi* of the same poem she makes another reference to this special function of her verses, pointing out succinctly and forcefully that pride can indeed be the cause of downfall or loss: "Mas aitan plus vos diga lo messatges/ Q'en trop d'orguoill an gran dan maintas gens."[30]

The countess expresses once more her constant questioning and apparent bewilderment in the following verses:

> Meravill me cum vostre cors m'orguoilla,
> Amics, vas me, per q'ai razon qe·m duoilla.

. . . .
> E voill saber, lo mieus bels amics gens,
> Per que vos m'etz tant fers ni tant salvatges,
> Non sai si s'es orguoills o mals talens.[31]
>   II, 15-16 and 33-35.

Her distress is further increased by a sense of jealousy resulting from his kindness to others, so that she is constrained to cry out, elsewhere in the same poem, "Mi faitz orguoill en digz et en parvenssa/ E si etz francs vas totas autras gens."[32]

By comparison with this, Louise Labé's love lament, inevitably longer and more detailed than that of the countess, is indeed a more nobly expressed one, avoiding for the most part the element of petty complaint. She is able to express in comparatively simple phrases her deep sense of melancholy and grief without indulging in undue bitterness or recrimination. Such simple verses as these have both dignity and pathos:

> Et quand je suis quasi toute cassee
> Et que me suis mise en mon lit lassee
> Crier me faut mon mal toute la nuit.
>   V, 12-14.

At times she is inclined to invoke death while confessing that she has no real wish to die:

> Je ne souhaitte encore point mourir.
> Mais quand mes yeus je sentiray tarir,
> Ma voix cassee, et ma main impuissante,
>
> Et mon esprit en ce mortel séjour
> Ne pouvant plus montrer signe d'amante:
> Priray la Mort noircir mon plus cler jour.
>   XIV, 9-14.

At other times her words become unrestrained, and we are led to feel that in her heart she is seeking to give expression to a double measure of despair and passion. She experiences love as a mixture of divine fire and of the deepest cruelty of pain, and from her comes this cry of anguish:

> Depuis qu'Amour cruel empoisonna
> Premierement de son feu ma poitrine,
> Tousjours brulay de sa fureur divine,
> Qui un seul jour mon cœur n'abandonna.
>
> IV, 1-4.

So swept away by the headlong rush of her emotions does she become that in utter abandonment of hope that her longing and yearning will come to fruition she even wishes that she may have, for lack of the reality, at least the semblance of love's happiness. Her cry is piteous in its naïveté:

> Et si jamais ma povre ame amoureuse
> Ne doit avoir de bien en verité
> Faites au moins qu'elle en ait en mensonge.
>
> IX, 12-14.

Something of the same desperate yearning appears in those poems which are frankly sensual and which have given Louise Labé her reputation as a composer of burningly passionate verse. These same poems have almost certainly given weight to the belief held by many who have written about her that she was, to use Jean Larnac's phrase again, a *cortegiana onesta*.[33] These lines of outspoken desire and physical longing carry the impact of conviction. Only a woman dreaming of other such occasions in the past would be likely to call out with bodily hunger implicit in every vivid word:

> Oh, si j'estois en ce beau sein ravie
> De celui là pour lequel vois mourant:
> Si avec lui vivre le demeurant
> De mes cours jours ne m'empeschoit envie. . . .[34]
>
> XIII, 1-4.

or again with even greater passion:

> Si m'accollant me disoit: chere Amie
> Contentons nous l'un l'autre, s'asseurant
> Que ja tempeste, Euripe, ne courant
> Ne nous pourra desjoindre en notre vie. . . .
> XIII, 5-8.

Such union with her lover has for her so great a promise of happiness that if she could only possess him in the fashion which in her impetuous way she postulates, building up in her mind a fantasy vividly real in its intensity, she would look upon death coming to her at such a moment as offering the culmination of earthly happiness:

> Si de mes bras le tenant acollé,
> Comme du Lierre est l'arbre encercelé
> La mort venoit, de mon aise envieuse:
> Lors que souef plus il me baiseroit,
> Et mon espirit sur mes levres fuiroit,
> Bien je mourrois, plus que vivante, heureuse.
> XIII, 9-14.

Occasionally, however, her revelation of her passion is less intense, happier, and more carefree, when thoughts of despair and death do not intrude, and she sings with the ingenuous joyousness of a woman who looks forward with the ardor and freshness of youth to the exuberant enjoyment of her lover's embraces. Thus in her eighteenth sonnet she exhibits a kind of *esprit gamin,* playing with provocative words as if each is a gleaming jewel to be tossed into the air only to be recaptured and used again:

> Baise m'encor, rebaise moy et baise:
> Donne m'en un de tes plus savoureus,
> Donne m'en un de tes plus amoureus:
> Je t'en rendray quatre plus chaus que braise.
>
> Las, te pleins tu? ça que ce mal j'apaise,
> En t'en donnant dix autres doucereus.
> XVIII, 1-6.

This can be no studied effort to achieve full expression of physical yearning. It is rather the impetuous, spontaneous utterance of a woman swept along by the tempestuousness of her delight in anticipation of her lover's physical presence. She is almost guilty of poetic negligence in the forward rush of her feeling, projecting herself toward the concrete expression of her love, as if somewhere her brightly shining words must strike a responsive chord, and lifting herself toward a lover's goal with an *élan* which carries conviction and truth, as she concludes:

> Ainsi meslans nos baisers tant heureus
> Jouissons nous l'un de l'autre a notre aise.
>
> Lors double vie à chacun en suivra.
> Chacun en soy et son ami vivra.
> XVIII, 7-10.

Where was the absent lover that he did not feel and respond to so much outward reaching and bright yearning? In the immediately succeeding verses she appears to answer this question, suggesting that she is perhaps trying to create an illusion of happiness and well being, a substitute for the reality of happiness— *en mensonge.* As she puts it, rather sadly:

> Permets m'Amour penser quelque folie:
> Tousjours suis mal, vivant discrettement,
> Et ne me puis donner contentement,
> Si hors de moy ne fay quelque saillie.
> XVIII, 11-14.

Physical longing with the Comtessa de Dia is no less intense, and she is somewhat more frank, if not so artistic, in presenting this phase of her feeling for her lover. In her brief utterances on the subject, one feels more sensuality and less poetry than in those of Louise Labé, but nonetheless she reveals herself to be a completely womanly woman, who does not hesitate to admit that she is no laggard in any aspect of love. Nor does she hesitate to confess that she would gladly have her lover fulfill the role of husband, on condition that he would have given his promise to do her will.[35] She makes it clear, however, that in order to love openly, she must know that she is dealing with a man of honor:

> E dompna q'en bon pretz s'enten
> Deu ben pausar s'entendenssa
> En un pro cavallier valen,
> Pois ill conois sa valenssa,
> Que l'aus amar a presenssa. . . .[36]
>
> I, 17-21.

And in verses which must belong to days of happiness, she speaks of her gladness in desiring one who fulfills this essential condition, at the same time expressing her gratitude to the one who first brought her lover to her:

> Mout me plai car sai que val mais
> Sel q'ieu plus desir que m'aia,
> E cel que primiers lo m'atrais
> Dieu prec que gran ioi l'atraia. . . .[37]
>
> I, 9-12.

We can, of course, only guess at the chronology of the countess' poems, but it must be rather later and perhaps after having endured much loneliness that she tells us directly and with engaging frankness:

> Ben volria mon cavallier
> Tener un ser en mos bratz nut,
> Q'el s'en tengra per ereubut
> Sol q'a lui fezes cosseilier. . . .[38]
>
> IV, 9-12.

In the following strophe she asks somewhat plaintively when she may expect to enjoy the *solatz d'amor* with him, indicating that for this he must be completely hers, that he must surrender completely:

Bels amics, avinens e bos,
Cora·us tenrai e mon poder?
E que iagues ab vos un ser
E qu·us des un bais amoros!
Sapchatz gran talan n'auria
Qe·us tengues en luoc del marit,
Ab so que m'aguessetz plevit
De far tot so qu'eu volria.[39]

IV, 17-24.

No more than Louise Labé does the countess believe in trifling with love. Not only does she admit her desire to herself, but she is quite ready to tell her lover about it, stating frankly that she will have him only if he is as willing as she to be a complete lover.

In these forthright statements by both ladies we have, in a sense, the capstone of their amorous declaration, the assurance that they were in deep earnest, permitting us to attribute to them both a high degree of honesty and sincerity in the apparently conventional as well as in the deeply poignant expressions of their anguish. Only a little sympathetic perceptiveness is required to see that we are in close touch with a real and profound emotion.

Thus we round out the *romans d'amour* of these two women of another age, both of whom possessed the poetic power to record their stories in such fashion that they have continued to live, maintaining their freshness and vigor despite the passing centuries. Their full personal histories will probably never be known, but the story of their hearts' desire stands fully revealed.

Few would deny that "la Belle Cordière" was a more gifted poetess than her Provençal predecessor, that her sonnets attain a high level of lyric expression, and that she uses the *genre* with fluency and power, making it flexible enough for her varying purpose. If the Comtessa de Dia lacks the reach and scope of Louise Labé and does not have so soaring an imagination or so facile a gift of phrase, she occupies nonetheless an honored place in the history of the poetry of love. Her deficiencies stem in large measure from the literary conventions within which she worked, and we should not forget that she ranks as the first of the *trobairitz* in importance and most probably in time, and that she is in all probability the first lyric poetess to compose in a neo-Latin vernacular upon the soil of France. The differences we note between the two women are in part those which we may expect to find between the medieval world, still in the process of perfecting its arts, and the Renaissance, bursting with the energy and love of life which constitute its greatest charm. Thus we may, without undue concern for the differences and inequalities which appear in their work, appreciate them both as women who had the independence and literary skill to express the inmost impulses of their burdened hearts, and thus to prove, as Alfred de Vigny was to put it centuries later, that "La vie est double dans les flammes."

Some Folk-Motifs in *Don Quixote*

by
John J. Guilbeau

IN HIS ANALYSIS of *Don Quixote* Paul Hazard devotes considerable space to a study of Cervantes and the literary currents of his time. He points out that Cervantes was not only well versed in the literature then in vogue, formal as well as popular, but that with his gift for assimilation and with an exuberance not unlike that of other famous writers of his period, he incorporated into his novel all current genres and forms: the romance of chivalry, the typically Spanish picaresque novel and the *romancero,* and more general European types, such as classical literature, mythology, and legendary history, the Italian *novella,* the pastoral novel, the "burla" (the type of hoax played on Don Quixote and Sancho throughout the novel), the proverb, the popular tale.[1] On this point R. Schevill states that Cervantes was influenced as much by popular fiction and current tradition as he was by the formal types of literature in poetry and romance which had preceded him.[2]

The occurrence of all these forms in *Don Quixote,* the place they occupy in the structure of the novel, and the sources the author may have used have been the subject of numerous notes, commentaries, and longer studies.[3] Of these various forms, the popular traditional elements—folk tales, popular anecdotes and riddles, popular beliefs, and the like—have frequently been difficult to identify precisely. The annotators of the standard Spanish editions and of the English language translations have commented on various items of this kind, but in some cases have either not appreciated the popular nature of them or have failed

69

to relate them to the general stream of traditional fiction to which they belong. This is, of course, not surprising when we consider the difficulty of working with literature of this type; for, as Stith Thompson has pointed out, "The material with which the student of traditional narrative deals is so enormous in its bulk, so varied in its form, so widely distributed geographically and historically that an actual first hand acquaintance with it all is beyond one man's power."[4]

With the publication, in fairly recent times, of the *Motif-Index of Folk-Literature*,[5] the task of the researcher in this type of material has been greatly facilitated. This work permits the easy identification and classification of a large number of themes or motifs underlying traditional genres and gives for each a sufficient number of bibliographical references to start the researcher off in a study of their occurrences in the great body of traditional fiction. It is a useful tool not only for pure folklore classification, but for the study of popular elements in literary works as well. In this paper I shall investigate some of the main popular elements in *Don Quixote* along the lines made possible by the *Motif-Index* to see what light such a study may throw on Cervantes' sources and his use of popular material.

Of the items classified for this study, a fairly large number fall into the category of popular forms which are simply alluded to or used as figures of speech. For instance, in the story of Grisóstomo and Marcela the body of the former has been brought to the foot of the mountain to be buried. At this point Marcela, for whom Grisóstomo had died, appears on the summit of the rock. As soon as Grisóstomo's friend sees her, he exclaims indignantly, "¿Vienes a ver, por ventura, ¡oh fiero basilisco destas montañas! si con tu presencia vierten sangre las heridas deste miserable a quien tu crueldad quitó la vida?" (I, 14) .[6] Here the references are to two well-known motifs: the basilisk whose fatal glance renders powerless or kills (B12.2) , and the belief that a corpse will bleed in the presence of its murderer (D1318.5.2). Again, when Don Quixote and Sancho are about to take leave of the Duke and Duchess, the maid runs out and in an amazing ballad accuses Don Quixote of having stolen three kerchiefs and garters. A scene, embarrassing to Don Quixote, follows, at the end of which the maid admits having the garters and begs pardon, saying, ". . . he caído en el descuido del que yendo sobre el asno, le buscaba" (II, 57). This is clearly an allusion to the folk tale about the man who had bought seven donkeys and was returning home mounted on one of them. Halfway home he stopped to count them, and forgetting to count the one on which he was mounted, found that he was one donkey short. A man came along, told him to get off his donkey, and then count them. Upon so doing the owner found that his donkeys were all there. The newcomer added that there were now eight donkeys going home instead of seven (J2022).[7]

It is sufficient here to note that occurrences of these motifs in traditional fiction are mentioned in the standard annotated editions of the novel, particularly Rodríguez Marín's and R. Schevill and A. Bonilla's. In eny event such motifs belong to the general stream of traditional material and are not limited to a period or a country.

There are in *Don Quixote*, on the other hand, a number of short narratives constructed on popular motifs and presented as anecdotes or riddles, related outright as folk tales, or woven into episodes acted out by the characters. Let us proceed to an examination of these.

Of the popular narratives I have classified, perhaps one of the most interesting is the anecdote told by Sancho about the wine tasters. One evening Sancho and the Squire of the Grove are seated under a tree discussing their masters and relating the story of their lives. At one point in the conversation the Squire of the Grove offers his wineskin to Sancho. The latter takes a long draught from it and exclaims that it must be a good Ciudad Real vintage. Thereupon, the squire compliments Sancho on his ability as a connoisseur. Sancho boastfully admits his special talent and adds that there is nothing unusual about this, since related to him on his father's side were two of the best wine tasters La Mancha had known in many a year. He illustrates this with the following story. The two wine tasters were given a sample of wine from a certain vat and asked to judge whether it was good or bad. One of the men tasted it with the tip of his tongue while the other merely brought it up to his nose. The first man said that the wine tasted of iron, the second that it smelled of leather. The owner said that the vat was clean and there could be nothing in the wine to give it a flavor of iron or leather. Nonetheless, the wine tasters stuck to their point. Time went by, the wine was sold, and when they came to clean out the vat, they found in it a small key hanging on a leather strap (II, 13).

While the Spanish and American annotators of Cervantes have been aware of the popular nature of this tale, none, so far as I know, has pointed out the currency of its underlying motif in traditional fiction. Rodríguez Marín, in his edition of the novel, remarks that it probably was a simple tale used to praise the ability of wine tasters.[8] R. Schevill and A. Bonilla, in their edition of the plays of Cervantes, state that it is probably a popular anecdote that antedates him.[9] More significantly, M. A. Buchanan has pointed out that this little story is not unknown in America where it is told of two southern judges, with a leather-headed tack found in the cask.[10] Schevill and Bonilla, in their critical edition of the novel, refer to Buchanan's note and imply that the story may have been brought over by the Spaniards.[11] Putnam merely states that it is a popular tale, judging from Buchanan's note, and it may have been translated by the Spaniards from some other language.[12]

It seems clear, however, that this anecdote is merely a version of the tales woven around the motif of "Clever deductions by eating, smelling, drinking, etc." (J1661.2), which is widespread both geographically and historically. N. M. Penzer has pointed out its occurrence in an old Sanskrit collection, the *Vetālapañcha-viṃśati*, in the story "The Three Fastidious Men."[13] A rich sacrificing Brahman had three sons who were distinguished for preternatural acuteness. One day, when they had been sent out to get a turtle, none of them wanted to touch the animal, each giving as an excuse the fact that he was extremely fastidious: one about eating, another about women, and the third about beds. In order to settle the argument they appeared before the king and explained their problem. At meal time the three brothers sat with the king at his table. The one who was fastidious about food did not eat but puckered his face with disgust. To the question of the king he answered that he perceived in the cooked rice the evil odor of a corpse. An investigation revealed that the food had been made from rice grown in a field near the burning-ghat of a certain village. The second brother later felt quite faint in the presence of a beautiful girl, for he detected an odor of goat about her. It turned out that she had been reared on goat's milk as a child. The third brother got a bruise from a hair which was found under several mattresses on which he slept.

According to Penzer, this motif concerning the ability to discover the fundamental origin of a thing by eating, smelling, or drinking it, and which he calls the "Quintessence motif," found its way all over the East and migrated westward in stories of which the version given above is typical. A consideration of the several versions enumerated by Penzer will give an idea of the diffusion of the motif underlying such incidents in traditional fiction and the transformation of the details woven around it.[14] For instance, it occurs in the *Arabian Nights* in the story of "The Sultan of Al-Yaman and His Three Sons."[15] Here, among other clever deductions made by the three sons, the second son notices that the piece of kid he is eating has the flavor of a dog, and it turns out that the kid had been brought up on dog's milk. In a tale from *The Exempla of the Rabbis*,[16] one of the sources of Jewish folklore, three astute Jewish captives declare, among other things, that the lamb smells of dog—the lamb had been brought up on dog's milk—and that the wine has the odor of a corpse—the grapevine had grown on the grave of the hostess's husband. A version fairly similar to this one is found in Christoforo Armeno's *Peregrinaggio dei tre giovani figliuoli del re de Serendippo*.[17] Here too we have the incident of the lamb brought up on dog's milk and the grapes grown in a cemetery.[18] Closer in details to Sancho's story is the decision of Amleth in the twelfth century *Danish History* of Saxo Grammaticus.[19] At a feast Amleth will not eat or drink but disdains all that they bring before him. He later satisfies the curiosity of his friend by telling him that he had refrained from eating because the bread was flecked with blood—the grain had been grown on a battle field—and there was the stench of human carcass to the meat—the pig had eaten a corpse. As for the liquor, there was a tang of iron in it, and it turned out that the meal for the liquor had been mixed with water from a spring at the bottom of which were found several rusted swords.

All the stories I have mentioned are versions of the tale type listed in the Aarne-Thompson *Types of the Folk-Tale* as type 655, "The Three Wise Brothers."[20] Thompson states that while this tale is primarily a literary one with versions occurring in most of the important collections of artistic tales of the Orient and Europe, it has also been reported as occurring orally from Norway, Denmark, Estonia, Russia, the Sudan, and Indonesia.[21]

It is, of course, not to be expected that the details of the story will remain unchanged from one version to another. The transformations that take place are sometimes considerable. In the versions we have considered the central theme, the motif, remains—a person with marvelous sensitiveness perceives through the senses of smelling or tasting the origin of a thing—but the details of the origin change. In some of the versions the milk on which the person or animal was brought up is the contributing agent: a girl acquires the odor of goat from having been brought up on goat's milk; dog's milk imparts the flavor of dog to the meat—now lamb, now goat. In a parallel manner, rice and bread acquire the odor of corpse because the grain was grown in a cemetery or burning-ghat, depending on the burial customs of the people in whose culture the story appears. Again, the meat-dog-milk and the grain-corpse themes cross, and the meat acquires the odor of corpse—the pig has eaten a corpse. Along with food grown in a cemetery, the liquor made from grapes grown in a cemetery or on a grave acquires the odor of corpse. Then the contributing agent shifts from the plant to something in the water used for making the liquor, as when the liquor has the flavor of iron because of swords in the water; and from that to a small object in the liquor itself, as a key with a leather strap or a leather-headed tack. The last two examples present a version further exaggerated by the presence of two small objects in the liquor, only one of which is perceived by one person through the sense of smell, and the other by a second person through the sense of taste.[22]

The diffusion of such a motif is also an interesting phenomenon. It has been pointed out that the motif under consideration occurs, along with a number of related ones, as an integral part of the tale type of "The Three Wise Brothers." In this context the incidents woven around it are related in a tone in keeping with that of the serious folk tale. Yet an incident based on this motif is distinctive enough to appear as a simple one-motif tale with an independent existence of its own.[23] In a different context, divorced from the serious folk tale, it appears as a humorous tale, as in the American version told as a joke, a German version facetiously reported as a real incident in the newspapers, or in Cervantes where it is used to create a humorous situation and give Sancho an occasion to display his wit.

How this tale reached Cervantes and in what form, it is, of course, impossible to say. Did he come across it, in his readings or from oral tradition, in much the same form as it appears in his book? Or did he take the theme from such versions as those that have been enumerated—for example, the Italian version of the three princes of Serendip, with which Cervantes was probably familiar[24]—and invent the rest? What role did the version in *Don Quixote* play in the further dissemination of this motif? The anecdote which appeared in the German newspapers was, according to H. Fischer and J. Bolte, similar in details to the one in Cervantes.[25] The one told in America differs only in that a leather-headed tack replaces the key on a leather strap. However Cervantes came by this tale, he seems to have been fond of it; for, as most of the annotators have pointed out, it occurs again, with a few minor changes, in one of his interludes.[26]

Closely related in theme to the anecdote about the wine tasters is another incident in *Don Quixote* involving Sancho as a marvelously sensitive person. In this incident Don Quixote and Sancho have come to an inn, both sorely belabored after their encounter with the Yanguesans. Sancho, in order to hide from the inn-keeper's wife and her daughter the humiliating fact that he and his master had received a good drubbing, tells them that Don Quixote had fallen from a cliff. When the inn-keeper's wife remarks that Don Quixote's bruises look more like those received from blows than from a fall, Sancho tells her that the rock his master had fallen on had many sharp points and jutting edges, and each one had left its imprint. Sancho then tells her that when they get through dressing his master's wounds, they can attend to him. Whereupon the inn-keeper's wife says that he must have fallen too. Sancho replies that he had not fallen, but the shock he had at seeing his master take such a tumble makes his body ache as if he had received a thousand blows. The daughter then observes that this could easily be so, since on many occasions she had dreamed of falling from a tower and on awakening would feel as bruised and broken as if she had really fallen. Sancho then adds that he was not dreaming at all but was more wide awake than at this minute, yet he finds himself with scarcely less bruises than his master (I, 16).

Whether Cervantes was aware of it or not, Sancho's story about receiving pain with outward physical results merely from seeing somebody else suffer has an underlying motif of ancient standing. It is listed in the *Motif-Index* as "Marvelous sensitiveness" (F647). In the story of "The Three Wise Brothers," previously cited in connection with clever deduction by tasting and smelling, the experience of the third brother who got up in the morning with bruises received from a hair under several mattresses is an example of the marvelously sensitive person. Penzer calls it the "Sybarite motif" and cites different manifestations of it. Typical is the story of "King Dharmadhvaja and His Three Very Sensitive Wives" in the old Sanskrit *Vetālapañchaviṃśati*. Here the first wife is so sensitive that a flower falling from her ear to her lap so wounded her that she fainted; the second wife was severely burned from a ray of moonlight that fell on her leg; the third had her hand covered with bruises simply from hearing the sound of a pestle pounding rice in a distant house.[27] The experience of the third wife involving pain with physical results from merely witnessing an event or hearing work being done has many analogues in traditional fiction. Thus, a woman gets swollen hands on seeing someone crushing rice; another feels as if her breast were being beaten to bits on hearing a drum played; the wrist of a third becomes tired on seeing someone carrying water; a man said that the sight of farmers digging in the ground had given him a rupture, and his companion said that just listening to this story had given him a pain in his side; another man gets a fracture on hearing someone chopping down a tree. These and other analogues, some of a less delicate nature, are cited by Penzer from Indian and Sanskrit works as well as from several European collections, including some from the third century Greek Athenaeus, who quotes Sybarite stories from Timaeus, Greek historian of about 300 B. C.[28]

It is evident that Sancho's story about receiving bruises from merely seeing his master falling on sharp rocks is in the tradition of the marvelously sensitive men and women of folk literature. This theme is, of course, based on common experience. There is nothing very unusual about feeling a shock on seeing someone else suddenly undergoing a painful experience. The idea is certainly not uncommon in metaphorical language, where it is represented in such expressions as "He has so much energy that I get tired just looking at him go all the time," or "This will hurt me more than it will you." What makes Sancho's story and similar stories of sensitive men and women distinctive is the exaggerated aspect of the experience which they present. Admittedly, the bruises, blisters, ruptures, fractures, etc., that result from merely witnessing an event tax rather heavily the credulity of the reader. But it is precisely this exaggerated aspect that gives the idea enough distinctiveness to cause it to persist in tradition as a folk-motif.[29]

In developing this incident, it is on the incongruity between the exaggeration in the story and the element of common experience which it contains that the author plays. Sancho's ready wit not only furnishes him with a fantastic explanation, but the explanation is such that he gets by with it. For the daughter, it will be remembered, gives credence to Sancho's story. In so doing she is struck not so much by the exaggeration in it, but rather by the analogy which it presents with the more believable dream experience which she relates.[30] That this incident should have escaped the notice of annotators may be due in part to this development in the story, which has the effect of playing down the exaggeration, and to the fact that, while the motif in this episode and that in the analogues are recognizably similar, the details of the plots woven around them and the contexts in which they appear are not.

Somewhat different in character from the popular incidents so far studied are those which appear in the burlesque episode dealing with Sancho as governor of the Island of Barataria. A good part of this episode is taken up with cases brought before Sancho to be judged or with riddles to be solved. For these Cervantes drew heavily on traditional themes.

One of the cases is that dealing with the girl who claimed to have been raped. While Sancho was holding court, a woman with a strong grasp on a man dressed as a hog dealer came in. She accused him of having violated her. The dealer protested that it had been with her consent. The governor ordered the dealer to give the girl his purse, which contained twenty ducats. The girl grasped it hurriedly and went out. The governor then ordered the dealer to run after her and take back the purse, by force if necessary. Presently they reappeared, the girl with her petticoat up and the purse in her lap, shouting at the top of her voice, and proving herself more than a match for her adversary. The latter owned himself beaten. The governor then ordered the purse to be given back to the dealer, and he added that if the girl had shown as much vigor in defending her honor as she did her purse, the strength of Hercules could not have forced her (II, 45).

The comments on this tale by the various annotators have been restricted to pointing out the occurrence of a similar episode in Fray Francisco de Osuna's *Norte de los Estados,* published in the sixteenth century, and speculating on the possibility of the author's having read this work.[31] The popular nature and origin of this theme have been overlooked. For this tale, based on the motif listed in the *Motif-Index* as J1174.3, has a wide distribution in traditional fiction. W. A. Clouston states that its occurrence in Gladwin's *Persian Monshee* and in several Indian story books makes it probable that it is of Asiatic origin.[32] It also enjoyed wide popularity in Europe, finding its way into important exemplum collections of the Middle Ages and many of the tale collections of the Renaissance.[33] Considering its wide currency in traditional fiction, it would seem insufficient to limit the study of sources to a single work which Cervantes may or may not have read.

Another case brought before Sancho to be judged is that of two old men, one of whom had a walking cane. The one without the cane, the plaintiff, presented his case to the governor. He had lent the other man ten gold crowns on condition that he should return them on demand. Later, when he tried to collect, his debtor said that he had never borrowed the money, or if he had he had repaid him. The plaintiff asked that the defendant be put on an oath, and if he swore before God that he had repaid the debt then would he withdraw his claim. The defendant admitted having borrowed the money, but he added that he had repaid it and was willing to swear to it. So saying, he handed his cane to the plaintiff, and laying his hand on the cross of the staff the governor held out to him, he swore that he had borrowed the money but had given it back, and the other not realizing it, kept on asking for it. The plaintiff was satisfied, and the defendant took his cane and left the court. Sancho, after reflecting on the matter for a while, ordered the man with the cane brought before him. When he appeared, Sancho asked for the cane and gave it to the plaintiff saying that he was now paid. Following the direction of the governor, the cane was broken and in it were found ten gold crowns (II, 45).

This incident is constructed on the motif listed in the *Motif-Index* as J1161.4 ("Money in the stick. Before swearing, the cheater hands a stick containing the stolen money to the man he has stolen it from. He then swears that he has repaid it"). This theme enjoyed wide currency in European *exemplum* collections—Latin, Spanish, Jewish, and German—and occurs also in a French collection taken from oral tradition.[34]

The commentators, beginning with Bowle in the eighteenth century, have cited the *Legenda Aurea* of Jacobus de Voragine as the source for this tale, since an incident making use of the same motif appears in this popular thirteenth-century work to illustrate the miraculous power of Saint Nicholas of Bari.[35] It is not unlikely that Cervantes came by this tale from the *Legenda Aurea*. The book was tremendously popular throughout Europe in the Middle Ages and the Renaissance, as shown by numerous manuscripts, Latin editions, and innumerable translations, and it was widely used in sermons.[36] Sancho, after boasting about his power of deduction from observation (reminiscent of the marvelous deductive powers of "The Three Wise Brothers"[37]) admits having heard of such a case in a sermon by a village priest.

Of two other problems brought before Sancho, one is an incident concerning a customer who has been tricked by a tailor, and the other is a riddle. The first one (II, 45), while not listed in the *Motif-Index* as such, is obviously one of the many popular tales dealing with the roguery of tailors, a number of which are given in the *Motif-Index* (X220 ff).

The other is a riddle involving a paradoxical problem. A river separated two domains. Over this river was a bridge at the end of which stood a gallows with a court of justice charged with enforcing a certain law. The law was to the effect that anyone who wanted to cross the bridge had to say where he was going and why. If he told the truth, he was allowed to pass; if he lied, he was hanged on the gallows. A man presented himself and stated that his sole destination and purpose was to die on the gallows. The judges were in a quandary. If they allowed him to pass, then the man would have perjured himself and according to the law he should be put to death. If, on the other hand, they hanged him, he would have told the truth and according to the same law he should go free (II, 51). This riddle involves a paradox that goes back ultimately to the ancient Greek logicians.[38]

Of special interest to us here is Sancho's solution to this problem. His opinion is that the man's statement is half true and half false, and his judgment is that the lying half of the man should be put to death and the truthful half should be spared. When the propounder of the riddle points out that in killing the lying half the whole man will die, Sancho answers that in that case the man should be allowed to go free, because it is always better to do good than harm. He adds that in arriving at this decision he recalled Don Quixote's advice to him, namely that when justice is in doubt, one should always lean to the side of mercy. That Sancho's decision is reminiscent of Solomon's judgment of the divided child (J1171.1) or the divided bride (J1171.2) need hardly be pointed out.[39]

One of the items I have examined is a clearcut folk tale told as such by Sancho, but for a purpose. In the episode of the fulling mills, night has overtaken Sancho and Don Quixote in a valley. While feeling their way in the dark in search of a spring, a terrible din of measured blows and rattling of chains reaches them, all of which strike terror in Sancho's heart. To keep his master's mind off the mysterious adventure so he will not go forth and do battle, he has to resort to his wit. His solution is to hold tightly to Rocinante's saddle, after tying the beast's legs to keep him from walking, and telling the dignified Don Quixote a naïve bedtime story. It seems that the shepherdess Torralba was pursuing her erstwhile lover. He, having reached the bank of the river Guadiana with his goats, arranged with a fisherman to carry them across. But, as the bark was very small, he carried only one of them on each trip, then came for another, and another, and another. Sancho warns his master that he must keep count of the goats, for if one of them escapes his memory, the story will come to an end. And so it does when Sancho, after he has achieved his purpose, asks his master how many goats have been taken over and the latter is unable to answer (I, 20).

This bedtime story, which is akin to the popular concept of counting sheep in order to go to sleep, is classified in the *Motif-Index* as Z11 ("The Endless Tale. Hundreds of sheep to be carried over a stream one at a time. The wording of the tale is so arranged as to continue indefinitely"). Its very wide distribution in European folklore has been noted by J. Bolte and G. Polívka.[40] Rodríguez Marín has correctly pointed out that Cervantes need not have borrowed this tale from any of the suggested sources, such as the *Cento novelle antiche,* the *Disciplina clericalis* of Petrus Alfonsi, or an Aesop collection of the fifteenth century. He could simply have taken it from oral tradition.[41]

The final item to be reported here is an anecdote told by Don Quixote as one of several examples to illustrate his argument that the desire to achieve fame is a powerful incentive in the actions of men. It concerns a shepherd who set fire to the famous temple of Diana in order to make his name live in after ages. Though it was forbidden to name him, lest his object be attained, it nevertheless became known that his name was Erostratus (II, 8).

This is listed as motif J2162.1 ("Burning of the temple to achieve notoriety") and appears in several collections of the Middle Ages and the Renaissance as well as in the works of several classical authors.[42] This item has a more sophisticated tone than the others we have considered and is more in the nature of a classical allusion than of a popular folk element. As such it would be out of place in Sancho's speech. Accordingly, it is Don Quixote, and not Sancho, who tells it.

From this classification and consideration of some of the popular elements in *Don Quixote,* what conclusions can be drawn?

In the first place, the concept of the motif and the arrangement used in the *Motif-Index* permit the easy identification of popular traditional elements in this work, items which would otherwise be difficult to pin down. For, as we have seen, the similarities between the narratives studied here and their analogues in traditional fiction consist not so often in the details of the narratives themselves as in the motifs on which they are based.

Our study of these motifs, however, does not go beyond indicating that the themes around which the narratives are woven are current in traditional fiction and are therefore unlikely to be original with Cervantes. It does not, of course, show that he was aware of the currency of these themes, nor does it establish the sources he may have used. If anything, it points out how tenuous conclusions about sources in this type of material may be, especially when we take into consideration the complex nature of the diffusion of traditional tales and the ease with which they may pass from the written to the oral tradition, and from the oral to the written form.[43]

This becomes particularly significant in the case of Cervantes, considering, from what we know of the man and his life, how numerous were the possibilities of his becoming acquainted with this type of material. What could he not have accumulated of such matter from his close acquaintance with every type of man or woman from all strata and walks of life, his contact with different countries and civilizations, and his wide and indiscriminate reading?[44]

As regards the place these popular narratives occupy in the structure of the novel, a study of the motifs around which they are woven brings into clearer focus the use to which they have been put. It has been pointed out that the humor in *Don Quixote* consists mainly in unforeseen situations which arise from violent contrasts and incongruities inherent in the characters.[45] It is precisely in that context that we find the main popular elements we have studied. Thus, we have humorous situations based on the contrasts of Sancho successively presenting himself as the rough, unlettered rustic; as a connoisseur, descended from a line of ancestors endowed with extraordinary gifts of tasting and smelling; as a marvellously sensitive person in the tradition of the Sybarites; as a man possessing great powers of deduction from keen observation reminiscent of the three wise brothers of folklore; as an astute judge and solver of difficult or impossible riddles not unlike the wise Solomon of tradition. In the endless tale episode we have the incongruous situation of the dignified Don Quixote patiently listening to his squire telling him a bedtime story, which the latter shrewdly uses to achieve his purpose.

Moreover, the accumulation of these incidents contributes to the delineation of the character of Sancho. While the squire is presented as an ignorant, unlettered peasant, he is certainly not without his just share of native cleverness and wit.[46] Cervantes achieved that, in part, by making use of these popular themes. All of those examined here, with the exception of Don Quixote's classical one about the burning of the temple, have to do with Sancho and are presented in such a way as to bring out his natural shrewdness.

Parallel Tendencies in English and Spanish Tragedy in the Renaissance

by
Jean Alexander

THE PATTERNS OF evolution in English tragedy of the sixteenth and seventeenth centuries have been traced in design and in texture by many modern scholars and critics; the structure of French classical tragedy is familiar to most students of drama; but the tendencies of Spanish tragedy in the Golden Age are unknown to most critics who are not specialists in Spanish literature. However, the study of the Spanish Golden Age is fruitful and enlightening for the study of European literature in the Renaissance and seventeenth century, and specifically for the parallels between the drama of England—often thought unique—and of Spain.

The basic similarity between English and Spanish tragedy of the Renaissance is that both were written for a popular theater and both incorporated native dramatic tendencies which were inimical to the neoclassic tendency inherited from the Latin grammarians and developed and expanded by the Italian Renaissance theorists. In England, morality elements persisted even into the period of the decadence of tragedy; in Spain, morality and ballad characteristics were introduced in the early period and soon became conventional. This retention of native elements resulted in a type of tragedy which rejected the classic purity of design—elevated style, unified plot structure, highborn protagonists—by the use of popular speech (and in Spain, popular meter) and by the use of contrasting or parallel plots. The double plot

was used in a variety of ways, but perhaps the essential and profound difference in tragic structure, between the classic and the
"romantic," is due to the potentiality for tragic irony inherent
in the use of a second plot. Departure from the elevated style
was not simply a device for comic relief; in the early phase of
English tragedy—in *Doctor Faustus*, for example—it tended to be
simply that, but by the time *Hamlet* was written it was used both
for ironic contrast and for placing the action on various levels
of tragic attitude. In Spain the use of low style is somewhat different, for popular poetic forms were often used to achieve a
legendary effect. *El caballero de Olmedo* is an example of a
tragedy whose main effect is gained by intensifying the ballad
type of tragedy; *Los Amantes de Teruel* follows the same pattern, somewhat modified. In both, the medieval romance mystery
of destiny provides the tragic theme, and legendary folk songs
and folk meters are used.

Both the spirit and technique of tragedy altered during the
golden era; it changed in both England and Spain, in England
perhaps more than in Spain. However, in both countries there is
a clearly marked division between two tendencies. The first
tendency, that of expansion, is termed Elizabethan in England
(although the point of Elizabeth's death defines the Elizabethan
and the following period a little too sharply) and is identified
with "the cycle of Lope" in Spain; the second tendency, that of
concentration, is characteristic of the Jacobean era in England
and the "cycle of Calderón" in Spain.[1] The second period manifested itself quite distinctly in the two countries, but the great
design of the second period in both countries is one of turning-
back-upon-itself. This second period is the beginning of decadence. The factors involved in this tendency towards questioning
or stasis are difficult to determine: partly they are those of self-
determination of the genre, and partly they are political and
social, for at the high point of the development of drama in both
countries political shock and disintegration began to unsettle
the structure of attitudes which formed the basis of tragedy.
Theodore Spencer shows, in addition to this political unsettling
in England, a triple ideological unsettling, for attitudes towards
nature were thrown in doubt on three levels—the cosmological,

the civil, and the psychological—by Copernicus, Machiavelli, and Montaigne.[2]

But the first period, one of expansion and construction, shows the basic patterns of tragic action; it also shows the wide area within which dramatists were experimenting. In England the great period began with Marlowe and Kyd, and the patterns they established can be traced through the work of subsequent dramatists. Kyd's work represents the constructive influence of Senecan drama, his *Spanish Tragedy* the point of departure for Elizabethan tragedy with its establishment of one of the major themes of tragedy: revenge.[3] Marlowe, on the other hand, represents what was fruitful in the medieval tradition; his handling of the theme of ambition, in *Doctor Faustus* and in *Tamburlaine*, frees the gigantic hero from the *de casibus* theme, from the *contemptus mundi* theme. With these two themes, revenge and ambition, both the early and later phases are concerned. However, there is a vast difference in the handling of the theme, for the defeat of the overreacher, as in *Doctor Faustus*, took place on a great stage, where the natural order could be seen as a firm background for the protagonist's destruction; furthermore, as Willard Farnham indicates, the tragic hero in the early phase was thoroughly noble and admirable—in spite of any question of tragic flaw.[4] It is also noteworthy that much of the tragedy in the early period in England was historical; the result was not only to place the protagonist in a large social and political context of stability—for that stability depended in a sense on the dramatist's making it so—but also to carry over into tragedy a view of life which had dominated the dramatic work of the early sixteenth century. The attitude inherited from the morality play, combined with the historical order, a combination which made it possible to see English history in terms of a great moral-religious destiny, had provided the authors of the *Mirror for Magistrates* with a world-view, and that view had been reflected in the early attempts at tragedy such as *Gorboduc*. Thus in using historical themes the Elizabethan dramatists almost automatically fell into a pattern of attitudes which was, on the political level, optimistic.[5] Within this structure, then, which was viewed as wholesome, the tragic action had to take place.

The Renaissance hero, the result of a new individualism which was also optimistic, was also in a sense glorified. Thus the two affirmative forces—the hero and his society—were both treated on the grand scale, and in the *hubris* and defeat of the protagonist there was grandeur and nobility, even if there was error. This tendency is not, of course, all-pervasive, for a tragedy such as *Soliman and Perseda* (*ca.* 1590) has more of the characteristics of the later period than of the early, and a very early tragedy, *Tancred and Gismund* (1566), is as decadent in its main action as is *'Tis Pity She's a Whore* (1625-1633). But the general pattern perceived by Farnham and Una M. Ellis-Fermor seems to be right, and the early period in England was characterized by an optimism based on the sense of a rational natural order.

Dramatic technique in this period was generally eclectic. Marlowe's *Tamburlaine* has been called a pageant, for its grandeur of spectacle is not disciplined by any concept of dramatic action which might enclose it. His *Doctor Faustus* shows a strong tendency toward the morality structure, using techniques associated with the morality—the contention of vices and virtues for man's spirit, allegorical figures, dumb-shows; the comic element is largely extraneous, relying on simple comic relief, rather than functional. Kyd's *Spanish Tragedy* uses a structure basically Senecan, introduces the Senecan ghost as prologue (although there is a precedent for that in the *Mirror for Magistrates*), and also introduces the chorus; the tricks of madness and of presenting a play within a play, which were used so frequently and so variously in later tragedies, first occur in Kyd's tragedy and probably were suggested by the dumb-show, Seneca, and Belleforest's story of Hamlet. The successors of Kyd and Marlowe in the early period, led by Shakespeare, used techniques from both, developing a more tightly-knit structure—for example, the comic relief or subplot becomes more integral. Kyd himself apparently did not see the structural failure of his use of the chorus, for the same non-functional technique is seen in *Soliman and Perseda*. When Jonson later used the Senecan ghost to introduce his action in *Cataline*, he made it perform an essential function, just as had been done previously in *The Misfortunes of Arthur*, for the ghost provides both the context and the cause of the subsequent action and establishes the tone of the tragedy. Most of the dramatists after Kyd, however, were not concerned with conforming to a classic pattern, and they abandoned the use of the ghost as a formal prologue as well as the formal use of a chorus.

In technique, the early Elizabethan dramatists—that is, from 1587-99—show a process of experimentation, freedom, and a certain looseness of structure. Incorporating elements from Seneca, from the *Mirror for Magistrates*, from the morality plays, and from history, they gradually abandoned, altered, and fused the elements into a dramatic type which abandoned most of the classic characteristics except the act-division and the moral sententiousness.

Some of the same tendencies can be seen in the development of the first phase of Spanish Golden Age tragedy. The force that impelled the Spaniards in the New World to conquer in the name of God and "los Reyes Católicos," uniting the desire for crude national power with a crusading spirit and with a sense of royal sanctity far beyond that of the English, also impelled the dramatists to evolve a national drama.[6] The Spanish dramatists rejected the prevailing notion of tragedy, for, as they understood the classification, it was an artificial hierarchic distinction rather than a concept of human action. This attitude led to an eclecticism which progressed more unevenly towards an integral tragic structure. The tragedies of Guillén de Castro will perhaps illustrate. His *Progne y Filomena*, like Kyd's *Spanish Tragedy*, seems to represent an early phase of grappling with a classic theme to make it conform to a native pattern. In neither tragedy is there much hint of an intellectual subtlety which would see the destructive action as essentially moral; both plays are superficial and spectacular. The potential moral conflict suggested in Guillén de Castro's first act, in which we are led to expect that character and event will have some degree of causal relationship, is completely abandoned, giving way in the final act to pure sensational event. Yet the same dramatist—unlike Kyd —was capable of writing another tragedy, *Dido y Eneas*, in which event, fate, and character are inevitably interwoven. Furthermore, in that tragedy he used techniques which were being used

by Lope de Vega in another pattern; for example, the lyric theme
in place of the classic chorus. This device is characteristic of the
early period of Lope and apparently abandoned in the second
period. In *Dido* it is used most effectively in the crucial scene,
that is, the scene in which the moral conflict is made explicit
and in which the crisis occurs; it is used to present one attitude
involved in the conflict, while sounds of war in the background
provide the other attitude. In other tragedies which are not
concerned with classic themes or plots, a similar intention is
discovered in the use of lyric. In Vélez de Guevara's *Reinar después de morir*, songs are used thematically, reinforcing thematic
imagery as a commentary on the action and as a device to convey
an attitude toward the action. In Lope de Vega's *El caballero de
Olmeda*, as already suggested, song is used to "place" the action
in the mysterious world of the ballad. In Tirso de Molina's
La venganza de Tamar, as in Guillén de Castro's *Dido*, song
occurs at the action's turning point, but Tirso's use of this
device is a great deal more sophisticated and subtle than the
latter's, for in *La Venganza* it provides a thematic contrast. The
action to follow is the catastrophe, the act of vengeance; the delicate pastoral lyric, comparable to Perdita's telling of the flowers
in *The Winter's Tale*, provides both the idea of the wholesome
order which has been violated and a dark hint of the violence
to ensue. This lyrical tendency is found also in English tragedy,
in Ophelia's song, for example, but it seems to be more important
structurally in Spanish tragedy. It may be simply another aspect
of the very important relationship between Golden Age tragedy
(and comedy) and the *romancero* tradition.

In addition to the tendency, in this first cycle, to adapt classic
plot and theme and to use poetic structures of song and imagery
complementing plot structure, several distinct native traditions
of drama were being used experimentally. A highly Christian
version of Boccaccio's *de casibus* theme survives in Mira de
Amescua's *El ejemplo mayor de la desgracia*, but this is largely
an anachronism and is not characteristic. Calderón used the
same theme once later in *El mayor monstruo los celos*, but less
superficially, for it is so firmly imbedded in the larger structure
of *hubris* and fate, of honor and revenge, that it ceases to be the

mechanical fortune-theme. The major tendency in plot and theme is of course Lope de Vega's, and its dominance tends to obscure the other attempts, which had few progeny.

The nationalistic tendency of Lope's tragedy, like that in English tragedy, is not chauvinistic; "nationalism" is thoroughly involved in a world-view which provides a context for the tragedy. This can be seen most clearly perhaps in *Fuente Ovejuna* (which is not really a tragedy, although it has been so considered), in which there is a fairly explicit intention to exalt *res publica*; a social structure which has its link with divinity in the king is shown flawed but finally triumphant. In *Porfiar hasta morir* the element which is considered the major one in Spanish drama—the code of honor—appears as a symbol of the social structure. A parallel in attitude can be drawn between this tragedy and, say, *Doctor Faustus*, not because the tragedies have the same theme, but because both the world-view and the rebellious protagonist are nobly conceived and drawn. Macias, in *Porfiar hasta morir*, violates the code of his society; in part, he is an individualist following his own destiny—at the same time epitomizing the concept of courtly love—and as such he suffers defeat. Yet there is no attempt to destroy what he represents, for his intention is never presented as less noble than the idea of Spanish aristocracy implicit in the honor code; two systems of idealism are shown in conflict, and each code is allowed full play. Perhaps for that reason, *Porfiar hasta morir* has some of the elegiac quality of acceptance of Racine's *Bérénice*.

Even when there is considerable tension between the world-view, as exemplified in the social structure, and the forces of individual destiny, the basis is never challenged by Lope. One of the most closely constructed tragedies on national themes, *La estrella de Sevilla*, shows the social order defective at the core in that the king is unjust. He follows standards of individual appetite rather than those of royal responsibility, and yet the great chain is impaired scarcely more than it was in *Fuente Ovejuna* by the defection of a lesser nobleman. This is really a major dramatic achievement, since most Spanish tragedies rely upon an idea of kingship as the emblem of social order; but *La estrella de Sevilla* shows the idea functioning above and beyond the king

himself. The conflict becomes an inner one, and the drama gains
its power partly through the adherence of the protagonists to
the ideal in spite of desire and in spite of justice. An interesting
parallel to this use of national theme is seen in one of Lope's
tragedies which uses an Italian plot, *Castigo sin venganza*.[7] In
both plays the ruler is shown, in the first scene, pursuing his
lusts rather than his duties; in both cases his defection is the
cause of subsequent catastrophe, and in both cases other characters suffer tragic defeat because of the course of action begun
by the ruler. *Castigo sin venganza* shows its Italian ancestry in
the perversity of the love-theme, for in his plays which draw
upon national themes Lope tends to present the protagonists as
idealistic and chaste; but the resolution brings justification of
the social order and punishment of the violation of the hierarchical relationships. The difference is that when working with
national themes there is a very real affirmation of the social
order; while the treatment of Italian themes seems to us to have
more psychological realism, the basic structure is less coherent,
and the final justification of hierarchy is less thoroughly prepared for.

Thus in the early phase, the tragedy of both England and
Spain was firmly based in a sense of national destiny (not necessarily explicit, but as a context of attitude) and in a tragic vision
which might see the individual and society engaged in an irreconcilable conflict, but saw them as essentially sound and noble
forces. Even Tirso de Molina's Don Juan, who is as thoroughly
destructive of his society as any character in the decadent phase
of English tragedy, has a grandeur of *idea*, single and self-con-
sistent, which in no way corresponds to the destructiveness of
the hero-villain in a tragedy such as Tourneur's *Revenger's
Tragedy*. Tirso's Don Juan is most comparable to Marlowe's
Doctor Faustus. Although Tirso's protagonist is colder and
more intellectualized than Marlowe's, in the sense that his destructiveness is completely calculated as an opposition to his
society, both are aspiring above the materialistic, opportunistic
level of the later "Machiavel."

The second era of Golden Age drama in Spain is considered
to begin with the death of Lope (1635) and to be dominated

by Calderón. In this period the minor tendencies in tragedy have more or less dropped out, although Calderón does use Roman historical material in *El mayor monstruo los celos*, and themes and plots are drawn largely from national legend and develop national themes. In this period also there are fewer tragedies and fewer dramatists who are worthy of notice. Whereas the era of Lope included Guillén de Castro, Mira de Amescua, Tirso de Molina—all original even though uneven—the era of Calderón has largely second-rate dramatists,[8] proficient technically but lacking in originality; furthermore, the secondary figures wrote comedies, largely of the intrigue type. The two dramatists who attempted tragedy are, however, very interesting. Calderón represents one tendency or set of attitudes in developing the dramatic themes and conventions of Lope, and Rojas Zorrilla represents a contrasting tendency.

Calderón elicits a great deal of antipathy in many critics because of the "barbarity" of his treatment of the national theme of honor; he has been branded, in fact, as the "poet of the Inquisition."[9] While it is true that he inclines to fix and emphasize the tendency, already seen in Lope's drama, toward glorification of the hierarchical concept at the expense of the individual, at its best his tragedy of honor is not limited to social justification and does not falsify the issues. The idea of honor and the sacrifice made to it is not essentially more barbaric, I think, than the idea of destiny on which *Oedipus Rex* is founded; both tragedies demand reading on the symbolic level.

The changes Calderón made in the honor convention, causing a totally different attitude towards it, justify calling his cycle one of "concentration." He has (using the term broadly) classicized the theme; the great stage on which Lope's tragedies of honor were acted has been narrowed almost as much as Racine's stage restricted the area of action of Corneille's. The result is that the issues are sharper although more limited, extending themselves to the larger world only by implication. Calderón's tragedies of honor are not all as limited in scope as *El médico de su honra*. For example *El Alcalde de Zalamea* is broader, in that it explicitly includes the political concepts which are the counterpart of the domestic concepts of the honor code, and for this reason the play is generally the favorite of critics. Even there, however, the conceptual basis is intensified and made explicit; it is intensified in somewhat the same way that Racine's is also—by eliminating potential areas of development which might impair the searchlight power of the central conflict.

Calderón's technique in this respect is illustrated by his handling of the clown. Lope had given the *gracioso* an inalienable right to exist in tragedy, and Calderón, in accepting Lope's structure and the rationale behind the structure, accepted the fool. However, the *gracioso* in the first period has an exuberance entirely lacking in Calderón's tragedy. In Vélez de Guevara's *Reinar después de morir* the *gracioso* provides some stringent commentary on the hero's love-lyricism, and this in spite of the fact that love is glorified and is not treated at all satirically; similarly and more extensively, the *gracioso* comments on the courtly love of Macías in Lope's *Porfiar hasta morir*. This use of the *gracioso* in his drama approaches the choral function and the license of the fool in *King Lear*, though with nothing approaching the profundity of the fool's commentary. The *gracioso* in the cycle of Lope could function as chorus or as foil for the protagonist;[10] but he has vitality and existence aside from the central theme of the drama. Calderón's *gracioso*, on the other hand, lacks the wit that Lope's has, and he trends to function in a very limited way. For example, in *El médico de su honra*, the *gracioso* is merely an attendant except in one episode; instead of providing a constant parallel in attitude to that of his master, he provides, in an isolated episode, a symbolic parallel to the entire action of the drama. The *gracioso*, meeting the king, tries to escape unseen, is caught, is made to tell his business—that of professional wit, and is ordered to make the king laugh within a month, at the risk of having his teeth extracted if he fails. The fact that this is intended as a commentary on the main action might be missed if the *gracioso* did not point it out. Again in revealing to his master his intention to escape, when they are both honor-bound to return to prison, he indicates his disinclination to conform to the code of honor, which is categorized indirectly as vainglorious concern for appearances, because it is artificial and unnaturally destructive; there is then a rather bitter irony in the imposition of duty by the king. But—whether because of external pressures for conformity or because of inner allegiance it is difficult to determine—this ironic contrast is subtly handled and ambiguous, like an iceberg just barely showing above the water. At any rate, this is the only time the *gracioso* is permitted to act as a contrast to the central attitude.

Another technique for concentrating issues that were diffuse in Lope is that of limiting the actors and relying to a larger extent on introspective monologue—again like Racine and also like Ford— with the servant as confidant. One of the major differences between Lope and Calderón as dramatists is the difference between action and intellection, but the difference cannot be explained simply by reference to the audience. Calderón, it is true, was patronized by court circles which would not have grown restive during long discursive analyses of motive and idea. That is a factor, but it does not explain the reason for Lope's failure to be intellectual as well as spectacular, as Shakespeare was. One is tempted to explain Calderón's subtle theorizing about honor and self by seeing his drama as an attempt to stabilize and to justify a disintegrating society, while Lope felt free not to think and to let the destructive forces have full play because the order was still secure. The reason is uncertain, but the dramatic fact is not: Calderón avoids full statement of the position of the force opposing social order. For example, the seducer (or abductor) Don Juan in *El Alcalde de Zalamea* is shown entirely in the role of villain, a creature of appetite and a spoiled brat of the aristocracy, whereas the anti-social action of Tirso's Don Juan has its source in idea as well as appetite. Similarly, the would-be seducer in Lope's *Peribáñez* is shown suffering a tragic conflict between desire and duty, so that he is not simply a villain, certainly not callous as is Don Juan in *El Alcalde de Zalamea*. The same pattern is formed by the dramas which are purely tragedies of honor: *El pintor de su deshonra, A secreto agravio, Secreta venganza, El médico de su honra*. And it proved a handicap, for in spite of Calderón's skill as a dramatist, only one of the tragedies of honor can be considered a great tragedy.

In contrast to Calderón, however, Rojas Zorilla treated the inherited themes and conventions rather cavalierly. Instead of

intensifying the idea of fixed and almost mystical hierarchic relationships, Rojas undermined them. His tendency was to question the scheme of things, and in some respects his technique
is similar to that of the Jacobeans, particularly Webster. Although
comedy is not under consideration here, it is significant, I think,
that Rojas' comedies tend to make the *gracioso* the protagonist,
thus leading tragedy towards realism. In his tragedies the role
of the *gracioso* shows the influence of "Machiavelli-misunder-
stood." In the cycle of Lope the *gracioso* often provided a realistic contrast to the idealistic attitude of the master, but he remained a loyal servant and his commentary was benevolent and
salutary; in contrast, the *gracioso* of Rojas Zorilla's tragedy is
no longer loyal, but pursues his own goals separately from those
of his master and frequently to his master's destruction. This development indicates not only a breaking-up of the social code,
but in terms strictly of dramatic structure indicates less plot integrity. The inseparability of master and servant in Lope's drama
and the coherence of their interests, even if their attitudes were
different, makes the dual attitude seem unified; the two attitudes are in harmony. The two attitudes in Rojas' tragedy are
in dissonance. The self-interest of the servant in *No hay ser
padre siendo rey*—the servant betrays his mistress for money
by giving the prince entrance to her house—is a reflection of
the same pressure of doubt and disillusion found in Flamineo's
behavior in *The White Devil*.

Questioning of the traditional world-order and traditional
values did not result in cynicism or moral anarchy, however, for
Rojas; in part it led to his turning the tragedy of honor into a
thesis play. *A Cada cual lo que le toca*, for example, is difficult
to categorize, for in spite of the moral conflict and the strong
emotional current underlying the revenge theme, the final effect
is not tragic. Rojas is obviously upsetting the order of things
according to a theory. Likewise, in *No hay ser padre siendo rey*,
there is tragic conflict and tragic rhythm in Act II, but it is re-
versed by a non-tragic resolution, the avoidance of a seemingly
insoluble tragic knot by means of a trick. The device is, dra-
matically speaking, as spurious as that of Beaumont and Fletcher
in *A King and No King*, but the purpose is different; again,

Rojas is writing a thesis play, criticizing the concept of duty and the hierarchic role of the king, in which he is ideally supposed to function as king and not as man. Thus in spite of his perhaps greater originality and intellectual vitality—greater, that is, than Calderón's—Rojas Zorilla's tragedies tend to be tragicomedies, with the exception of *Casarse por vengarse*.

It is perhaps unfortunate that Lope de Vega was such a monumental figure, for his successors might otherwise have been able to alter the dramatic structure he bequeathed to them. If there had been even a few large-scale figures, his successors would have had a variety of precedents for dramatic structure, comparable to the choice that Shakespeare's successors had. But Lope's followers were committed to one national tradition and, if they chose not to imitate slavishly, took the the two divergent paths of Calderón and Rojas. Most of Lope's successors imitated him until his form of drama was enervated.

For reasons which are usually seen as political, English drama followed an entirely different pattern in its second period. Literary historians ascribe the degeneration of Spanish drama in the cycle of Calderón to the repressive influence of church and state, which refused expression to the intellectual currents which "cast all in doubt."[11] Whatever the reason, it is interesting that the great period in English tragedy occurs in the Jacobean rather than the Elizabethan era—that is, in the era of doubt rather than the era of affirmation. Perhaps there was more freedom in the circulation of ideas, so that the skepticism of Montaigne and the amoral self-determination of the Machiavellian hero could be found overtly conflcting with traditional values; certainly the great targedies show this conflict.

Although Tourneur and Webster use the themes of revenge and ambition established by Kyd and Marlowe and developed in the last years of Elizabeth's reign, attitudes have altered. The change has been illustrated by Fredson Bowers in tracing the evolution of the revenge theme in tragedy,[12] and by Willard Farnham in tracing the evolution of the Shakespearean tragic hero. In both cases the development has been based on a theory about the philosophic and moral attitudes underlying the idea of tragedy, so that the second phase questions, seriously and profoundly, the assumptions upon which the tragedy of the first phase rested. Instead of a stable world-order taken for granted as a field for action, testing of the world-order is part of the action. In Webster's *The White Devil* we find the dramatist repeatedly pointing out that conflicting attitudes about the basis of man's relationship to his society provide one of the themes of the tragedy. In addition to the conflict between reason or duty and desire, which takes place in the main action involving Bracciano and Vittoria, there is a parallel subplot conflict thoroughly involved with the main plot, and that conflict is made almost allegorically pointed at the end of Act I and again at the end of Act II. Flamineo's Machiavellian attitude towards the world, which considers only self-advancement and expediency in materialistic terms, is contrasted first with the attitude of his mother, who represents the old order in which the individual preserved integrity and honor by fulfilling his proper social role and by meeting ideal standards of conduct; then contrasted with the attitude of his brother Marcello, who also represents the idealistic rather than the materialistic value system, but provides a more intense contrast because his situation is identical to Flamineo's. The two attitudes are given equal representation, in that no moral judgment is made by Webster and justice is done to the code of conduct which Flamineo represents, but the balance finally goes down for the old order. In effect, the mode of conduct based on moral concepts is affirmed but defeated; Webster's tragedy is nihilistic because both of the conflicting forces are defeated, in both subplot and main plot. There is a semblance of order, a view of a sane world, in the Cardinal, but his conduct as well as Lorenzo's is tainted by the code of the Machiavel. In Tourneur's *The Revenger's Tragedy*, the nihilistic tendency is almost all-pervasive and the world is shown as corrupt not only in the action, where motive is all lust (for power, for wealth, for sex, for destruction) but in the imagery as well; Tourneur's tragedy is noted for the power of its pejorative imagery, which reduces man to the simply organic level. An attempt is made to resolve the tragedy in regeneration, but it is hardly more than a gesture, and it gives us no more than a glimpse of a sane order; it lacks conviction. The tragedies of Webster and

Marston represent the extremes to which tragedy can go in questioning the world in which it exists.

The progress from affirmation in the early phase to denial in the second phase ended perhaps inevitably in the easy affirmation or false solution offered in the type of drama Beaumont and Fletcher made popular, since even Shakespeare found no way back to the stage of affirmation. It is true that he resolved the conflict between the Machiavellian attitude and the moral attitude in *King Lear* and *Othello*, but his last tragedies do not achieve an affirmation of the social structure; on the contrary, *Coriolanus* and *Antony and Cleopatra* indicate a final denial of the order. This spirit of denial has been seen by Alfred Harbage as the work of "coterie-dramatists," with the implication that the court coterie patronizing the type of drama written by Marston, Jonson, and Beaumont and Fletcher was a degenerate society, seeking thrills in perversion; consequently, in these dramatists there is a dwelling upon evil and perversion.[13] According to this view, the popular theater, represented dominantly by Shakespeare, was not concerned with the perverse but with refuting the "Machiavellian" and with reaffirming the traditional social values. There is probably a good deal of truth in the distinction between popular and coterie theater, not because the coterie was corrupt, but because the popular element is always more conservative and new ideas begin with the select groups. It is true also that Shakespeare rejected the Machiavellian theories and affirmed the old values, but not as an easy fulfillment of the popular demand—as the profundity of exploration in *King Lear* proves.

The satiric tendency of the tragedy of the early Jacobean era is the result, in part, of Ben Jonson's powerful influence, and in part another facet of the English tendency not to have tragedy pure. One of the effects of the introduction of classical drama in the sixteenth century had been to keep tragedy and comedy distinct, and even though comic elements were retained in the tragic structure, they were forced to serve tragedy—at least Shakespeare's tragedy. Jonson, however, classicist though he was, allowed non-tragic elements to obtrude at times. No doubt it was partly because of his wholehearted acceptance of the classic idea, with its emphasis on didacticism, that his tragedies are impelled towards the satiric. This is true not so much of *Sejanus*, where the didacticism is fairly directly presented by the choral figures, as in *Cataline*, where the action digresses in order to satirize the vices of courtesans and of women politicians. The same flaw in structure is evident in *The White Devil*, when Webster permits the effect of the catastrophe to be threatened by the satiric scene in which Flamineo tests his sister's loyalty by giving her an opportunity to shoot him. It is possible, of course, that Webster intended to undermine the character of Vittoria, which until that point had been consistently great although evil in its following the impulse of the blood rather than the dictates of reason, by showing her engaged in treachery and petty motives of self-interest like an ordinary courtesan. However, the fact that he returned to the exalted view of Vittoria in the resolution would seem to indicate that he included the satiric episode because at the moment the idea behind the tragedy mastered the internal organization of the play.

Although it may have been a period of decadence, in that the old world was disintegrating, the early seventeenth century produced great if irregular tragedy. The true era of decadence in English drama is the period just preceding the closing of the theaters, and is represented by Ford and Massinger. These two dramatists are considered decadent largely because, like Calderón, they are simply reworking old themes and plot-types. Furthermore, their dramatic world is also a narrowed world, for Ford has been criticized for his inept handling of the comic subplot, just as Calderón has, and in a tragedy such as *'Tis Pity She's a Whore* the erotic world of *Romeo and Juliet* has not only excluded the political world and almost excluded the domestic world, but in the incest theme has turned back upon itself completely.

A different kind of atrophy of the dramatic form occurs in Massinger. In *The Duke of Milan* we see a late version of the revenge theme, which proved itself remarkably versatile, and what is in a way a powerful drama. The disintegration of one of the important tragic conventions, that of the final speech in the grand manner, gives a striking illustration of the death of a

genre. In Othello's last address he recaptures his noble stature
and thus permits the tragedy to end in reconciliation; in *Hamlet*, the last brief speech of Hamlet, combined with the vale-
dictory statements of Horatio and Fortinbras, functions to the
same purpose; even in *The White Devil* and *The Duchess of
Malfi* the conventional nobility of the protagonist is recaptured
in the final scenes. In Massinger's *The Duke of Milan*, however,
we are given what amounts to a parody of the speech of Othello,
for the Duke ends the play by saying "let my epitaph be—." The
revenge structure, which hinges largely on the character of the
revenger, is also altered. The original pattern of the revenge
tradition placed the revenger in the role of hero; the revenger
had to be punished, of course, but he was sympathetically presented. Later, in Tourneur and Chettle's *Hoffman*, he became
the villain. Massinger presents him first as villain, then as hero,
finally as villain again, and he manages to do so by keeping hidden until late in the play one element in plot. As far as Renaissance drama is concerned, that device for suspense represents degenerate tendencies, a counterpart of the tendency seen in *A
King and No King* to save the issue by a last minute disclosure,
to hover dangerously on the edge of the incest theme but not to
explore it.

Corresponding to the lack of new techniques or new plots and
themes in this period is a failure to renew or recapture the
Elizabethan and early Jacobean richness of language and imagery. The imaginative vitality of the earlier dramatists reveals
itself in a plenitude and flexibility of language in both the
romantic or traditional school and in the satiric school, except
perhaps for Chapman, and his tortured style has its own kind
of power. In Ford and Massinger the language of tragedy tends
toward abstraction, and in Beaumont and Fletcher it tends
toward softness and gracefulness. In both cases the language is
appropriate for the kind of drama being written, but it is also
indicative of the falling away from the high point of dramatic
achievement.

It is interesting that the same kind of distinction is made between the style of Calderón and the style of Lope. For example,
Lope uses descriptive and metaphoric imagery thematically, to

establish the tone of the drama as a whole or to convey an attitude towards a specific character. Thus in *El castigo sin venganza*, horse imagery is used, not to debase the character who is metaphorically identified with the horse, but to convey a general impression of eroticism. Calderón's imagery is never that specifically applicable: he has a set system of analogies, in a series of three, which he uses for any lover's statement; their application is extremely abstract, in that a flower, a bird, and one other element serve as analogies for the lover's situation. The beauty of Calderón's verse resides in this kind of rhetorical patterning rather than in sensuous evocativeness or flexibility and ease. A uniform tone pervades his speeches, except for the speeches of the *gracioso* which are intended to serve as contrast, such as the example given from *El médico de su honra*, and it is a tone elevated, dignified, and conceptual rather than passionate. The slackening in dramatic tension in the late English dramatists is not of the same type; Massinger's diction can be highly responsive to the particular dramatic situation and character, and the difference between his style and that of the earlier dramatists is not necessarily derogatory to him, even though it is *poetically* less vivid and rich.

This analysis has not, of course, attempted to define the nature of either English or Spanish tragedy; it has attempted to show their similarity in the use of dramatic devices. It must be said that English tragedy is not as simply unified as Spanish tragedy, because there were more original dramatists following their own visions within the structural and conventional patterns established by Kyd and Marlowe, while Spanish tragedy, like Spanish comedy, was largely determined by one man in a pattern that glorified a convention which was accepted as a national theme.

A Review of Scholarship Dealing with the Problem of a Spanish Source for *Love's Cure*

by
Martin E. Erickson

OF ALL THE problems involving questions of possible Spanish sources for Elizabethan plays, possibly none are beset with greater obscurity or controversy than those involving *Love's Cure*. The relationship between English and Spanish literature have never been satisfactorily or thoroughly investigated, although a great deal of debate has taken place over alleged borrowings.

When we come to the vast body of dramatic literature in Spanish, it is all too evident that its contents are unknown, even among Spanish scholars. Felix E. Schelling, writing of the relations between English and Spanish drama says: "If we consider, however, the almost incredible mass of writings of Lope de Vega (to mention him only), unread by English and even by Spanish scholars, and further keep in mind that those conversant with Spanish drama are not always conversant with English and *vice versa*, it would be rash to affirm that a last word has been said on a topic which as yet has not been seriously opened."[1] The same thought was expressed many years before by Rudolph Schevill[2]—in a study which has been undeservedly neglected—and the wonder is that his study has remained so long unconsulted by scholars in English.

The prejudice against Spanish sources is further complicated by lack of definite knowledge of direct borrowings. English playwrights in the early seventeenth century had access to trans-

102

lations of Spanish stories and novels, often basing dramas on them rather than on plays. Schelling makes much of this tendency, but why such second-hand borrowings should lessen the Spanish influence in the English plays is difficult to understand. Schevill mentions the fact that many Spanish plays came into English through French, which indeed is true; but this fact should not make the original source less worthy of study. Schelling further asserts: "We may not feel sure that a Spanish play has actually influenced an English play by direct borrowing until we reach Shirley, who is reported on credible authority to have utilized a comedy of Tirso de Molino in *The Opportunity,* and another of Lope de Vega in *The Young Admiral.* Fitzmaurice-Kelly skeptically observes even as to these examples: 'A minute demonstration of the extent of Shirley's borrowings would be still more satisfactory!' "[3]

To complicate matters, we do not know who among the English Jacobean dramatists read Spanish. Almost every critic has his own ideas, but no one has ever given the matter detailed consideration. James Fitzmaurice-Kelly asserts that " at the present stage, [the] balance of probabilities is against the view that Fletcher knew Spanish."[4] This observation is quoted with approval by Schelling. Schevill, with perhaps more authority, says: "Ward [*History of English Dramatic Literature* (3 vols.; London, 1899), II, 753] has certainly no ground for saying: 'Thus [Beaumont's and Fletcher's] acquaintance with the Spanish language, and later Spanish literature is removed beyond all doubt.' "[5] But T. P. Harrison, Jr., quoting part of Ward's statement, unequivocally attributes a knowledge of Spanish to Beaumont and Fletcher. He writes: "That Beaumont and Fletcher were acquainted with the Spanish language 'beyond all doubt' does not make it more likely that they knew the English *Diana,* since Bartholomew Yong's translation, completed in 1583, was unpublished till 1598; but that they almost habitually depended upon Spanish sources, convinces one of their peculiar interest in the literature of the peninsula."[6]

Presumably Harrison did not know of Schevill's study or he would not have been so emphatic in his assertion. Baldwin Maxwell, too, ventures his opinion that Fletcher knew some

Spanish for he says: "I am not so certain as some critics have been of Fletcher's small knowledge of Spanish . . . ."[7] Suffice it to say that scholars in English have not brought forward evidence beyond dispute either one way or another that Jacobean dramatists could read or not read Spanish.

The problem would be much easier of solution if we knew more about possible Spanish sources. But Spanish drama is practically undiscovered even at this date; titles, authors, and even dates of printing are often obscured, so that too much reliance cannot be placed on such data. Schevill, perhaps too pessimistically, writes:

> The study of the sources of innumerable Spanish comedies is as yet in its infancy and all investigation is confronted here and there with insurmountable bibliographical difficulties. And it is these difficulties which make a thorough presentation of the influence of the Spanish drama upon that of England before 1630 so impracticable at the present state of knowledge. They consist in insufficient data on the novelistic literatures of southern Europe and their inter-relations up to the time of Lope de Vega and Shakespeare. Especially does an acquaintance with the *comedia* convince one that it is impossible to go far beyond the work already done on Spanish sources in other literatures until the history of fiction, chiefly of Italian and Spanish stories, and of the sources or *motifs* and episodes —dating from ancient or medieval times—has been further investigated. It is, for instance, of little service to call some Spanish play the source of a similar English one, if the near future should reveal as the common source a novel hitherto overlooked.[8]

Objection can be made to this attitude toward such literary investigation, for if one must wait for a final solution to a problem, he may wait forever, without either advancing toward a final solution or having aided in its eventual bringing about.

Having reviewed the general problem, let us now examine a specific example in the case of *Love's Cure*. First of all, it must be apparent that a play which has caused so much confusion is worth looking at. Therefore I will give the history of the Spanish source first in order to show what vogue it had in Spain and its subsequent history there.

II

Strangely enough, little comment exists in Spain on *La fuerza de la costumbre,* by Guillén de Castro y Bellvis. Ernest Mérimée and S. Griswold Morley[9] do not mention the play among Guillén de Castro's; Miguel Romera Navarro [10] cites it without further ado; Juan Hurtado and Angel González Palencia[11] do not mention it, nor do George Tyler Northup,[12] Angel Valbuena Prat,[13] or George Ticknor.[14] Julio Cejador y Frauca remarks that *"La fuerza de la costumbre,* de Castro, pudiera ser la fuente, segun Stiefel, de *Love's Care* [sic] de Fletcher."[15] Ludwig Pfandl[16] makes no mention of the play. From the historians of Spanish literature, then *La fuerza de la costumbre* has received at most only passing mention.

Turning to historians of the stage and actors' lists, we find that Cayetano Alberto de la Barrera in his *Catálogo bibliográfico y biográfico del teatro antiguo español* lists the play as being in a manuscript in the library of the Duke of Osuna but without the author's signature.[17] Antonio Paz y Mélia mentions the play in his *Catálogo de las piezas de teatro.*[18] A. Schack does not mention the play.[19] Not even in such a great work as Menéndez y Pelayo's *Origenes de la novela* is the play named, although don Marcelino usually took care to mention possible foreign influences in Lope de Vega, for example.

The first edition of the *La fuerza de la costumbre* was printed in Valencia by Miguel Sorolla in 1625. In the foreword to this edition, Guillén de Castro says that one reason for the publication of the second volume of *comedias* is that a spurious edition of the first twelve plays had been issued during his absence, making it necessary for him to print a new one free from errors. This assertion is now generally discounted. Eduardo Juliá Martínez, the editor of the Spanish Academy edition of 1927, says: "Entendemos que se ha dado demasiado crédito a este prólogo; es falso lo de que se imprimió la Primera Parte durante su ausencia y de modo furtivo, pues ya hemos visto que negoció él cuanto pudo sobre la base de la mencionada edición y por consiguiente debe mirarse con reserva el resto de las afirmaciones. La cronología de la producción de Castro debe estudiarse, a nuestro juicio, desde otro punto de vista, apoyándose en otros datos. Cuando el poeta hablaba de si mismo, facilmente incurría en errores que no parecen involuntarias."[20] However, there still remains the possibility that the play was printed earlier or at least acted on the stage long before. The same editor adds: "Debe advertirse que el éxito y popularidad de los autores dramáticos no está en relación con la publicación de sus obras, sino con la representación de las mismas."[21] Moreover, he remarks: "Una dificultad se opone a que pueda estudiarse de un modo exacto la evolución de nuestro escritor: la falta de datos para establecer el orden cronológico de sus obras."[22] Juliá divides the plays of Guillén de Castro into three periods, according to their ideology, technique, and versification.

These three periods are, first, the initial stage in which the playwright is dependent upon the Valencian school and especially influenced by Cristóbal de Virués. Also characteristic of this period is "la tendencia métrica a las estancias sobre la base de dos heptasílabos y otro endecasílabo en los monólogos en que se expresa la desesperación del héroe. . ."[23] The second dramatic period is devoted to subjects national in character such as *Las mocedades del Cid,* while the third period is devoted to intrigues "con las que ya intenta renovar los aplausos alcanzados en la primera manera de construir, como en *El nieto de su padre,* o forja, ya conflictos tratados de una manera enérgica y rápida, cual ocurre en *La tragedia por los celos—.*"[24]

A second printing of *La fuerza de la costumbre* was issued in 1857 when Mesonero y Romanos edited it for the Biblioteca de Autores Españoles, along with six other plays, including the two parts of *Las mocedades del Cid.* Evidently Mesonero y Romanos thought this play worthy of another edition along with the author's best; and in order to justify its inclusion he quotes Gracián, who says: "Por la bizarría del verso y por la invención merece el inmortal laurel."[25]

The third and latest edition of *La fuerza de la costumbre* is that of the Real academia española, 1927. The complete history of the play is given by Eduardo Juliá Martínez, editor of the Spanish Academy edition of Guillén de Castro, but he does not mention the controversy concerning the likeness of *La fuerza de la costumbre* to *Love's Cure.* The following comment, however, is of some interest: "Es curiosa comedia en la que, quizá como en ninguna, se sostienen los caracteres con una evolución perfectamente gradual y propia, y en la que se plantea el problema de la educación como medio de contrarrestar la costumbre, no a la manera como lo hubiesen planteado un Terencio o un Alarcón, sino en la forma genuina de nuestro más español teatro: por medio de la acción."[26]

One can readily see, from the foregoing summary, that *La fuerza de la costumbre* has not caused much comment in Spanish criticism, although the play is certainly better than a good many of its day. Of the critics mentioned, only Cejador y Frauca seems aware of the English play which is said to have been based on this play.

Among the French critics, Henri Mérimée has shown most interest in Spanish drama, devoting two books to the study of it; Guillén de Castro figures prominently in these studies, although one will look in vain for an answer to our problem or even a casual reference to it.

In *Spectacles et Comédiens à Valencia,* Mérimée mentions among many in an actor's list of plays belonging to Jerónimo Amella, one called *La fuerza del ejemplo* which he says was played in February 1623. This information he learned from Antonio Restori, who says: "Nella lista originale le commedie si seguono si quattro gruppi, secondo il presunto autore; 19 attribuite a Lope; 15 a Mira de Mesaua, 23 promiscuamente al Castro o al Vélez, le ultime al Claramonte. Io credo più vantaggioso disporle in ordine alfabetico, ponendo tra parentesi quadre il nome d'autore indicato dall'Almella."[27] *La fuerza del ejemplo* is listed as follows: "Fuerza del ejemplo (la) — (Lope) Ignota; rappr. a corte nel febraio 1623."

This play, from the title, at least, sounds very much like *La fuerza de la costumbre,* but if the latter is based on it, one wonders how Guillén de Castro would have dared to stage a play patterned so closely on one of Lope's, if indeed, the play is by Lope. I am unable to find it in any Lope collection. Mérimée does not remark on the similarity of title between these two plays.

In his other book, Mérimée makes mention of *La fuerza de la costumbre* only in passing in his long chapter on Guillén de Castro, calling it a play of the second period, and therefore a thesis or moral play. He does, however, call attention to the very marked Italian influence in the Valencian school of drama, an influence for the most part in story and plot which the Spaniards got from the Italian *novelle*. He likewise notes that Menéndez y Pelayo has treated this influence "si admirablement . . . au début du tome second" of the *Orígenes de la novela*.[28]

III

When we examine English criticism dealing with the possibility of a Spanish source for *Love's Cure,* we find the utmost confusion. Instead of one problem we now have two, the second problem arising from the fact that no one can say for certain who wrote *Love's Cure*.[29] Most scholars are now agreed that Massinger had the largest share in the play,[30] but strong reasons are still adduced for Beaumont's authorship. Let us review some of the remarks of English scholars and then take up in detail the chief Beaumont and Fletcher experts.

G. C. Macaulay, writing his chapter on Beaumont and Fletcher in the *Cambridge History of English Literature,* says regarding their use of Spanish sources: "The contemporary Spanish stage might have supplied him [Fletcher] with abundant materials, and its methods in comedy were not very unlike his own; but Spanish plays were not very accessible to English readers; and, though the assumption has frequently been made that the Beaumont and Fletcher plays are partly founded upon Spanish dramas, it is to be noted that this has in no instance been actually shown to be the case. A recent attempt to prove that *Love's Cure* is taken from a comedy by Guillén de Castro can hardly be regarded as successful."[31] In an appendix to his chapter Macaulay adds: *"Love's Cure* or *The Martial Maid,* date uncertain but not earlier than 1622 in its present form. No scene can be attributed to Fletcher; Massinger probably wrote acts I, IV, V, scenes 1, 2. There is no real ground for the suggestion (by A. L. Stiefel), that this play is taken from the Spanish comedy by Guillén de Castro, *La fuerza de la costumbre*. The two dramas are founded on the same story but the treatment is entirely different."[32] Macaulay does not state what the differences are or why or on what he bases his assertion.

In another chapter of the *Cambridge History of English Literature,* Felix Schelling undertakes the difficult task of treating foreign influences in English drama of Elizabethan and Restoration times. Unfortunately, his material is practically the same as that in his *Elizabethan Drama* (1908), which in turn furnishes the bulk of his observations in *Foreign Influences in Elizabethan Plays* (1923). There was much material that Professor Schelling could have used for the improvement of his deductions. Speaking of Fletcher's use of Spanish sources, he observes that "not one of these originals is a play, nor need Fletcher have read a word of Spanish to have become acquainted with them, for all had been translated into French or English and were readily accessible to his hand. About two only of the Fletcherian plays has any question on these points arisen. *Love's Cure*, first printed in the folio of 1647, but commonly dated back to the early years of King James, has been referred to a comedy by Guillén de Castro, written at so late a date as to make it quite impossible that Fletcher could have seen it."[33] Schevill and Fitzmaurice-Kelly are quoted to show that Fletcher did not read Spanish.

More detailed comments on the possible Spanish source for *Love's Cure* appear in Schelling's *Elizabethan Drama:*

> *Love's Cure* or *The Martial Maid* was first printed in the folio of Beaumont and Fletcher in 1647, and has been variously regarded as an early production of Beaumont's rewritten by Massinger, as Fletcher's revised by Massinger, or as Massinger's alone. The story of *Love's Cure* turns on the bold idea of a girl reared in the camp and inured to martial deeds, and a boy, her brother, contrastedly housed and effeminated. In both the power of love works a regeneration to the more appropriate temper of each sex. It now appears that this striking plot is an adaptation of the *Comedia de la fuerza de la costumbre* by Guillén de Castro, a production licensed for print at Valencia, February 7, 1625, and published about three months

later. We may allow, with Stiefel, some eight weeks for the
arrival of a copy of this play in London. That would make it,
say, July. Now as Fletcher died in August of this year, had he
a hand in *Love's Cure* it must have been written within the
period of one month. Stiefel accepts this with its corollaries,
that Fletcher read Spanish, and that this was the latest of his
works. Rosenbach, on the contrary, combats this view, calling
attention to the fact that *Love's Cure* exhibits a closer familiarity with the Spanish tongue and a more frequent and natural employment of Spanish words than are to be found in any
other play of the Beaumont and Fletcher folio. Besides this,
he finds the blank verse of this comedy totally unlike Fletcher's,
as is the author's free method in treating this borrowed plot.
On the strength of these premises, together with the likeness
of the verse to Massinger's and the similarity of certain characters of that poet to characters in *Love's Cure*, Rosenbach accepts Bullen's ascription of the play to Massinger, and denies
Fletcher even the slightest part in it.[34]

Schelling thus closes his discussion without considering the
possibility that the two plays in question could have been almost identical in dramatic treatment and *Love's Cure* could
have been written by someone other than Fletcher. He is wrong
in his assertion that A. L. Stiefel's argument for a Spanish source
is based on Fletcher's authorship. Stiefel was well aware of the
controversy over the multiple authorship of *Love's Cure* and
made some attempts to solve it, though he was no doubt mistaken in accepting Fletcher as the author. What he was concerned with was pointing out that the English play, whoever
wrote it, had a base in Spanish. We shall come to Stiefel later.
Likewise Rosenbach's refutation does not affect Stiefel's argument except for the point of Fletcher's authorship, but rather
supplements it, as we shall see. It is a pity that Rosenbach's
studies have not been published, as A. H. Cruickshank has remarked: "Much interesting information on the great debt which
Fletcher and other dramatists owed to Spanish literature will
be found in F. E. Schelling's *Elizabethan Drama*, vol. II, pp. 205-
218 and 530. Schelling comes to the conclusion that Fletcher did
not know Spanish; but he quotes an unpublished dictum of his
friend Dr. Rosenbach, who holds it as certain that Massinger

knew Spanish . . . . Further, *Love's Cure* is based on the *Comedia de la fuerza de la costumbre,* by Guillén de Castro, licensed at Valencia, Feb. 7th, 1625, and published three months later. Fletcher died in August, 1625, and Stiefel thinks that he read Spanish, and that this is his last work. Rosenbach and Bullen assign the play to Massinger. It is highly desirable that the grounds which lead Dr. Rosenbach to believe that Massinger knew Spanish should be made public."[35]

We may now turn to a specialized study of Beaumont and Fletcher to see what has been done to clarify the problem. E. H. C. Oliphant in a very detailed study has tried to account for dates and authorship of all the so-called Beaumont and Fletcher plays. Of *Love's Cure* he has this to say: "This amusing and much underrated play affords one of the most difficult problems of all. One need only mention the varied views held regarding its authorship to make that fact quite plain."[36] He then reviews what others have said concerning the authorship, enumerating no less than thirteen scholars besides himself who have tried to account for each scene in the play.

Pertinent for us is a further argument relating to the date, authorship, and Spanish source. Oliphant writes:

A much more serious argument for a late date is that advanced by Stiefel, who asserts that it must be the very latest play of Fletcher's since it is based on a drama by Guillén de Castro, licensed for printing in Spain, Feb. 7th, 1624-5, and published some three months later. As one who had been arguing for an early date for *Love's Cure,* I had to admit the important bearing of this discovery upon my views; but I held those views so strongly that even then I was prepared not to abandon them. I failed to understand how, if it was a post-Fletcher play, it had found its way into the first folio, and how the prologues [*sic*] definite attribution of it was to be accounted for. So, writing in "Modern Philology," January, 1911, I argued: "is it not possible that Massinger incorporated in his version of the Spanish play some scenes out of an early play by Beaumont? I do not know the Spanish play, or how much of the English comedy is derived from it, and so this suggestion may be utterly opposed to the facts of the case; but I shall be surprised to learn that the Spanish original shows any sign of the humors of Lazarillo (a distinctly Beau-montesque character) or more than a little of the contents of Act III. If it do, I shall not be ashamed to confess myself mistaken." That my attitude was not without justification seems to be shown by the fact that I am now given to understand that Guillén de Castro's drama is not the source: The story is the same, but the treatment is very different.[37]

It is plain, therefore, that Oliphant believes *Love's Cure* is not based on *La fuerza de la costumbre,* principally because Guillén de Castro's play was not printed until 1625, which means that neither Beaumont nor Fletcher could have had a hand in *Love's Cure,* as Oliphant himself points out. But why does he, then, in the quotation from his earlier article, argue for the possible inclusion of a Spanish source by Massinger? In any case the Spanish source is there, regardless of who wrote the English play. On the one hand Oliphant says that if the play is Fletcher's, it cannot have a Spanish source; on the other, that if the source is Spanish, Massinger must have added the Spanish element. What is only too clear is that, on someone else's word, Oliphant has assumed that Stiefel was wrong, acknowledging that he has not read the Spanish play. Yet on hearsay evidence he dismisses the Spanish source.

It is evident that all the arguments so far brought forth by scholars in English literature against a Spanish source are founded wholly on supposition. Macaulay had stated that the two plays in question were "founded on the same story, but the treatment is entirely different," which Oliphant has changed to read, "the story is the same, but the treatment is very different." Neither investigator offered proof for his assertions. In fact, their arguments prove nothing except a complete lack of knowledge of the Spanish play. Schelling alone quotes both Schevill and Stiefel as to the possibility of a Spanish source; yet had he read either Spanish scholar carefully he could not have arrived at any conclusion other than that *Love's Cure* follows very closely *La fuerza de la costumbre.*

Oliphant's concluding remark's on his study of *Love's Cure* are as follows: "To summarize, I regard *Love's Cure* as originally written by Beaumont, for Paul's boys not later than 1605, revised by Jonson and another in 1622, for Lady Elizabeth's and revised once again, this time by Massinger."[38] No mention is made of Fletcher as the author, which is in accord with general opinion. Yet Oliphant clings to Beaumont as the original author, with Jonson and Massinger as later revisers; when on the evidence laid before us it is plain that Massinger's hand is the clearest of all, which is the conclusion reached by Rosenbach and others. An early date would preclude Guillén de Castro as a source of the play as "originally written," but it would allow for a later interpolation by Massinger using material from *La fuerza de la costumbre*. Oliphant admitted this possibility in his 1911 article. How much *Love's Cure* might owe to *La fuerza de la costumbre* he was in no position to say either in 1911 or in 1927, never having read the Spanish play.

A further complication of the problem was made by Bond in 1935. He sets forth his ideas on the Spanish influences on *Love's Cure* in clear terms, and it is a pity that he did not do so years before, for it would have saved much useless bickering. His argument is brief and convincing because he has read the Spanish play in the original. He writes:

> The main action, the correction by love-passion of natural sex-instincts perverted by habit, is closely borrowed from a comedy *La fuerza de la costumbre* of the Valencian poet Guillén de Castro, author of two dozen plays. . . . Of these plays twelve were published at Valencia in 1621 and the rest at the same place in 1626. *La fuerza* offered originals for all our leading characters save Malroda, and some suggestion even for Bobadilla and the Alguazir, as will be apparent to those who will compare the English play in Dyce's edition of Beaumont and Fletcher with the following *precis* of the Spanish by me in 1905-6 for Bullen's edition. Struck by the inadequacy of suggestions of source then known to me, and aware of the Spanish sources for other of the plays, I began to ferret, and in Aribau's collection on the shelves of the Reading-Room noticed the very promising title of this play by Guillén de Castro. Though no Spanish scholar, I attempted it with the aid of a Spanish dictionary, and copy here what I then wrote with the addition only of a few further parallels with the English play. Later, about July, 1908, I chanced to

meet a Mr. J. A. Jacobi, then I think composing a doctoral thesis on Beaumont and Fletcher, who informed me that my discovery had been anticipated by A. L. Stiefel. Neither then did I, nor since have I consulted Stiefel's essay, which I learn from the *Cambridge History of Eng. Lit.* VI, 540, is in Herrig's *Archiv für die neueren Sprachen,* vol. XCIX, pp. 271-310, (1897) : nor have I anywhere seen any detailed account of the Spanish play. I already knew that Stiefel was right, and quite fail to understand the *Cambridge History's* view that there is "no real ground for the suggestion . . . the two dramas are founded on the same story but the treatment is entirely different."[39]

Bond adds: "The resemblances are too numerous and close to be denied; though it is equally plain that *Love's Cure* has enlarged and improved the Spanish material . . . . This obvious improvement and strengthening certainly need not rob Stiefel of the credit of first discovering and announcing the main source, which credit I had promised myself but must now renounce. Here is my own account of the Spanish piece which I have not seen since 1905-6."

Bond then summarizes the plot. For a man not claiming to be a Spanish scholar, he does very well. His *précis* is accurate as well as complete. One wonders why he did not make known his findings in 1906 instead of waiting thirty years, during which time the same errors were being repeated and passed on from one scholar to another. Yet the answer was there all the time if the right investigator had found it. Bond's statement should clear at last the haze that centers round the Spanish source for this much-discussed play. Unlike Stiefel, though, Bond can see the hand of neither Beaumont nor Fletcher in the play and takes for granted that 1626 (his date for the Spanish play) would prevent or preclude Fletcher's partnership. In conclusion he states that "Beaumont's claim, seriously weakened by its advocates' discrepancy on metrical marks, is now definitely negatived by the discovery of the play's close connection with the Spanish *La fuerza de la costumbre* of February, 1625."[40]

Whereas Oliphant could not see a Spanish source because of his desire to attribute the play to Beaumont and his belief in an early date, Bond cannot see either Beaumont or Fletcher in the play because he prefers 1626 as the date. Bond is partly right and so is Oliphant, but each in different spheres. What Bond refused to see was that it was quite possible for Massinger to have written a play around bits of an old Beaumont and Fletcher play. Bond should get credit, however, for having confirmed the Spanish source for *Love's Cure*.

Not to be outdone, Oliphant offers a rebuttal of Bond's contentions. In arguing for an early date for *Love's Cure* he remarks:

> It is all too readily assumed that this play "cannot date before 1625"—Bond's assertion—I agree that Macaulay's statement in the *Cambridge History,* that there is no ground for the suggestion that *Love's Cure* is founded on a play by Guillén de Castro, is unwarranted, though I myself was misled by it. The likenesses between the plots of the two plays are too marked to be the result of coincidence; but it does not follow that the whole English play dates later than 1624-25, when *La fuerza de la costumbre* was licensed. May I be permitted to quote from an article I wrote a quarter of a century ago—an article which appeared in *Modern Philology,* January 1911? [He proceeds to quote himself again, as he had done in his 1927 book.] It may be only coincidence; but professor Bond's resumé of the Spanish play seems to bear out completely the specific exceptions I advanced to the theory of entire indebtedness to *La fuerza de la costumbre.*[41]

Oliphant then goes on to say that he prefers to consider the subplot and the humours of the Alguazir and others as relics of an early play which the reviser used in *Love's Cure*. In that regard Oliphant may be right.

Oliphant, it will be remembered, refused to consider any likenesses at all between the two plays in 1927. Why did he change his mind? Was it because Bond's study revealed to him the plot of the Spanish play, or did he have recourse to the Spanish play in the meantime? Certainly in 1927 he did not know the Spanish play nor had he paid too much attention to Stiefel, who gives a very careful summary of both the English and Spanish plays, act by act. Moreover, Stiefel presents parallel passages—"the deadly parallel" of which Schelling speaks so disdainfully—to demonstrate wherein the plays are alike and wherein they differ. No one reading Stiefel could help being struck by the tremendous similarity between the English and Spanish play. One cannot help wondering why the whole problem was not clear to Oliphant and to Schelling long ago.

Bond's rebuttal to Oliphant is brief and pointed. Of most interest to us is his statement concerning the authorship of *Love's Cure:* "Massinger's hand in the play we have is abundantly clear from the parallels observed by Boyle in *New Shakespeare Society Transactions,* 1880-6, pp. 579-80; and his close Spanish original, *La fuerza de la costumbre,* was only printed in 1626 or (Mr. Oliphant) 1625."[42]

The polemic concerning the prologue and epilogue need not concern us here. Suffice it to say that the critics seem to be agreed that Massinger did rewrite the play, that others too wrote parts, and that perhaps Fletcher did not write any of the play.

The latest commentary on *Love's Cure* that I am aware of is that by Gerald Eades Bentley.[43] He prefaces his review of the scholarship on *Love's Cure* by saying, "Nearly everything about the play is in a state of confusion." His comment that "perhaps a more detailed examination of the relationship between *Love's Cure* and *La fuerza de la costumbre* and Gerardo would be illuminating" is justifiable but solves nothing. The two sections of the Gerardo story that Dyce cited as the source for *The Spanish Curate*[44] are also the source for two scenes in *Love's Cure,* as Bond demonstrates,[45] but the principal source for *Love's Cure* is undoubtedly *La fuerza de la costumbre.*

IV

The only commentator on *Love's Cure* who read the Spanish play which furnished the plot of the English play was A. L. Stiefel. He begins his study with a brief discussion of the authorship of *Love's Cure* together with the confusion among scholars concerning it.[46] He then gives a detailed summary of *La fuerza de la costumbre,* after which he suggests that Guillén de Castro got his plot from the comedy of Luca Contile, *La Cesarea Gonzaga,* which was printed at Milan in October 1550.[47]

Hatte ich in meinem ersten Aufsatze das Verhältnis James Shirleys zum spanischen Drama an einem Beispiele gezeigt,[48] so wähle ich heute in gleicher Absicht ein Lustspiel des John Fletcher, das unter dem Titel *Love's Cure or the Martial Maid* zum erstenmal in der Folioausgabe 1647 gedruckt wurde. Sowohl über die Autorschaft des Stückes, wie über die Zeit seiner Entstehung herrscht grosse Meinungsverschiedenheit unter den Gelehrten. . . . Das englische Lustspiel ist die Nachahmung einer Comedia des berühmten Guillén de Castro, die unter dem Titel *Comedia de la fuerza de la costumbre* zum erstenmal in der *Segunda Parte* seiner *Comedias* (1625) erschien. Beschäftigen wir uns sogleich mit dem Inhalt des spanischen Stückes.[49]

Stiefel also gives a brief summary of Luca Contile's play, or rather enough to demonstrate the disguise motive and the reason for it. He remarks:

Wie man sieht, ist die Verkleidung ähnlich, sogar ähnlich motiviert, nur ist sie auf zwei Familien verteilt. . . . Überhaupt spielt ja in unserer Comedia weniger die komische Verkleidung als die damit verknüpfte verkehrte Erziehung die Rolle, und ein kriegerisches Mädschen auf der einen Seite und ein weibischer, feiger Jüngling auf der andern kommen in keinem mir bekannten italienischen Lustspiel vor. Die kriegerische Dame findet sich freilich im Epos und Roman nicht bloss Italiens, sondern auch Spaniens. Ob aber Guillén de Castro, als er sein Stück schrieb, gerade an Bradamante, Clorinde, Felismena und ähnliche Gestalten dachte, steht noch zu bezweifeln. Eher liesse sich noch annehmen, dass ihm Ricardo de Turias Comedia *La belligera Española* (gedruckt 1616), vielleicht auch Montalvans *La Monja alférez* oder, da dieses Stück möglicherweise erst nach 1625 entstanden ist, Montalvans Quelle selber—die Geschichte der *Monja* soll auf einer wahren Begebenheit beruhen—bekannt war.[50]

A closer resemblance to Guillén de Castro's play is found in a play by Mira de Amescua called *Cuatro milagros de amor.* Stiefel writes: "Dieses Lustspiel berührt sich mit dem seinigen in der Idee: Mira de Amescua führt das Problem durch, dass die Liebe vier Wunder wirkt, dass sie einen Feigherzigen mutig, einen Geizigen freigebig, einen Einfältigen gescheit und einen

Schlampigen sorgfältig macht. . . . Ferner macht das ganze Stück den Eindruck, als ob es die Dichtung des Castro überbieten wollte—hier vier, dort nur zwei Wunder—und so glaube ich, dass Mira de Amescua der Nachahmer ist."[51]

That Mira de Amescua imitated Guillén de Castro is evident from the description of the former's play by Stiefel, who had access to one of the two known "ejemplares sueltos" of this play. Emilio Cotarelo y Mori says of Mira de Amescua's play: "Esta divertida y original comedia se conservó hasta hoy en ejemplares sueltos, de los que se conocen actualmente más que dos: uno en la Biblioteca Nacional de Munich, y otro que debería hallarse en la nuestra, por haber sido adquerido con los demás de Durán y estar registrado en el Catalogo que se imprimió poco después (pag. 88)."[52] Mira de Amescua had collaborated with Guillén de Castro earlier in life and later had written his *El Conde Alarcos* using the latter's play of the same name as a model. Cotarelo y Mori makes no mention of the similarity between the two plays, although he does mention Stiefel's description of Mira de Amescua's play in the Munich collection, and he says that *Cuatro milagros de amor* "es de las ultimas y mejores obras del autor."[53]

Cuatro milagros de amor closely follows the Guillén de Castro plot even to including the return of the father from Flanders and the wars to find his son dressed as a woman just as Felix is in *La fuerza de la costumbre*. In this, the two Spanish plays differ from the Italian model suggested by Stiefel. There is no disguise in the Spanish plays. Everyone knows who the characters are, whereas in the Italian play two characters have masqueraded as members of the opposite sex without anyone's being aware of it, thus furnishing the plot with some unexpected turns and dramatic highlights.

In *Love's Cure* likewise there is no disguise, since everyone recognizes at once that the man has dressed as a woman because of his mother's wishes. In the Spanish plays, the boy is dressed as a woman to keep him from learning the soldier's art, whereas in the English and Italian plays the boys are dressed as women to preserve them from the vendettas which have taken their fathers' lives. Otherwise, the plot of *Love's Cure* is the same as that of *La fuerza de la costumbre*.

Moreover, the Italian play does not have a martial maid, as do both the Spanish and English plays. The double disguise in the Italian play is common to others of its type. The Spanish and English plays have two sets of lovers as in the Italian play, but the latter depends on disguise for its plot and the ensuing dramatic suspense, whereas the other two plays do not. It is quite possible that Guillén de Castro knew the Italian play because of his long stay in Italy, but the only resemblance between his play and Contile's is the double pair of brother and sister lovers.

The sources suggested by Schevill[54]—Bandello, II, tale 36 and Belleforest, Book IV, tale 63—contain the disguise element but not, in my opinion, to the extent of furnishing a plot for Guillén de Castro; nor do I find a plausible source in Straporola or in Cinthio.

There is a good chance that the plot of *La fuerza de la costumbre* may be Spanish in origin. Four titles mentioned by Stiefel may possibly have suggested important themes in Guillén de Castro's play. They are: *La belligera enpañola* by Ricardo de Turias; *La monja alférez* by Montalván; *La bandolera de Flándes* by Baltasar de Carvajal; and *Forsa militar* by Diego Sánchez de Badajoz. The first three, from their titles at least, suggest the martial maid, and the last play has an effeminate man.

In closing I wish to add my conviction to that of Stiefel and Bond that *La fuerza de la costumbre* is the source for *Love's Cure*. Since the Spanish play was never translated into English or French, the dramatist who took the Spanish play for a model —probably Massinger—must have read it in Spanish.

Voltaire's Letters and Notebooks in English (1726-1729)

by

Kenneth R. Wilson-Jones

THE RECENT REVIVAL of interest in Voltaire studies in the past decade has illuminated many hitherto dark corners and shed new light on problems which long vexed students of the eighteenth century. New editions of the correspondence and the notebooks have provided scholars with materials which were formerly available only in partly emended, corrected, or otherwise inaccurate texts.[1] These editions have likewise presented the texts of Voltaire's letters and personal notes in easily accessible collections instead of scattered through numbers of journals many of which are unobtainable in the average library.

The publication of these new editions has revealed the need for re-examining and revising past scholarship based on these texts. Certainly, despite the somewhat inaccurate texts at their disposal, writers of the past have made lasting contributions for which all who are interested in Voltaire must be grateful.[2] It is not my intention to belittle in any way the value of that work, but rather to examine one small corner of the world of Voltaire which in recent years has been left fallow by those who have been cultivating more fertile gardens.

Voltaire's visit to England has always been a subject of considerable interest both because of its importance in the development of his literary taste and philosophy as well as its subsequent significance in the popularization of English letters and ideas on the Continent. The main episodes leading to the visit are well known: Voltaire's acquaintance with Lord Bolingbroke in the early 1720's; his plan for a visit to England several years later; his quarrel with the Chevalier de Rohan-Chabot leading to imprisonment in the Bastille; and finally his voluntary exile in England lasting from June 1726 to the winter of 1728 or the spring of 1729.

It has by now been fairly well established that Voltaire was not merely saving appearances after his final return to France when he insisted that before the Rohan affair he had planned to visit England in order to publish an edition of his epic poem *La Ligue* (later *La Henriade*). The letter to George I of October 6, 1725, has been cited as among the first documentary proofs of that intention. Voltaire begins by saying, "Il y a longtemps que je me regarde comme un des sujets de votre majesté."[3] He then asks the king's permission to come to London to complete the publication of the *Henriade*. The fulsome praise of the boorish Hanoverian king may have had some influence on Voltaire's subsequent successes in soliciting the patronage of the English court for subscription to his poem. But a more likely influence is the support of Lady Bolingbroke, a French lady secretly married to the Tory exile. She was a close personal friend of Caroline, wife of the Prince of Wales who became George II.

Voltaire's personal acquaintance with the Tory exiles living in France may be documented by the correspondence as early as 1718.[4] His closest relations appear to have been with Henry Saint John, Viscount Bolingbroke and his French wife, the former Marquise de la Villette. Through them Voltaire became aware of English literary and political figures of the reign of Queen Anne, including Bolingbroke's intimate friends Swift, Pope, Gay, and Lord Peterborough.[5] Whatever Voltaire's later opinions concerning Bolingbroke and his writings may have been, the Tory Lord's strong and complex personality made a lasting impression on the young French poet and was quite likely the most potent stimulus to his interest in England and things English.[6]

Evidence of the close ties maintained by the Bolingbrokes with their literary friends in England survives in the correspondence of this group. In a passage of a letter to Pope, Bolingbroke describes his calm life at the country estate he has purchased near Orleans, La Source. At this retreat he has only two guests, one of whom is his "Imagination," Voltaire.[7] The answering letter of Pope, who has been sent a copy of Voltaire's *Ligue* as well as the unsuccessful tragedy *Mariamne*, is a lengthy appreciation of the talents and capabilities of France's newest epic poet.[8] Two years later, writing to his friend Caryl, Pope mentions an earlier exchange of letters with Voltaire. None of this correspondence —if it may be called such—has been discovered, but the phrase of Pope clearly shows that he and Voltaire had at least exchanged literary courtesies a year before Voltaire's letter to George I in 1725.[9] The letters between Pope and Bolingbroke of 1723-24 may have been the beginning of the correspondence. Whatever the nature of this lost correspondence, it is clear that Voltaire was thinking of an English journey as early as three years before the crisis which led to his crossing the channel in 1726.

Shortly after the authorities decided on imprisoning Voltaire in the Bastille as a means of calming his indignation against the well-connected Chevalier de Rohan, Voltaire made plans to carry out the English journey he had talked of earlier. Hampered by laws against duels, by close police surveillance, and eventually by detention as the King's guest in the Bastille, Voltaire had been unable to obtain a gentleman's satisfaction by means of a duel with his haughty but cowardly antagonist.[10] Thus placed in an impossible social position and aware of the strict censorship which made the official publication of his epic poem so difficult in France, he naturally turned to England as a refuge where he could escape social ridicule and at the same time carry out his projected publication.

Writing some years later to one of his most intimate and trusted friends, the lazy and fickle Nicholas Claude Thiriot, Voltaire mentioned that he had requested permission to have books and writing materials sent to his rooms in the Bastille. After his request was granted, he asked Thiriot to bring him a crate of English books.[11] Perhaps he had collected them under the guidance of Bolingbroke. In any case these "English books" are the first indication of Voltaire's active interest in mastering the English language, an accomplishment which was to prove diffi-

cult, but profitable, and almost unique, for a Frenchman of the
1720's. The mention of these books is further proof that Voltaire
was making serious preparations for a stay in England, a stay
whose duration he could scarcely foresee when he sailed from
Calais in the late spring of 1726.

Once in England, Voltaire seems to have gone into seclusion.
Firsthand evidence of his comings and goings in the early months
is scanty, but the surviving correspondence of the first five months
of his residence does not confirm older impressions of the brilliant young French poet entertaining, and being entertained by,
the wits of the Pope-Bolingbroke circle. Certainly Voltaire had
connections in high places, both in the Tory group and among
the Whigs of Walpole's cabinet. He was with Bolingbroke occasionally at his country seat at Dawley near Twickenham and
in his town house in Pall Mall, probably after late August or
early September. But these visits occurred at intervals during
the months of exile. Voltaire's early months abroad were anything
but idyllic; rather they were full of hardships and suffering which
drove him to avoid the company of the great and to seek a retreat
far from the social whirl.

There is every reason to accept the surviving letters of 1726-27
as the sincere expression of Voltaire's reactions to his situation.
Written to the most intimate of his friends in France, these
letters convey a tone of deep pessimism. Physical sickness, mental
anguish, and the threat of bankruptcy all contributed to the
distress of the sensitive exile. In addition to all these difficulties
was the problem of language, a problem which lends some
credibility to the doubtful legends of Voltaire's social blunders
and difficulties with spoken English.[12] It comes as no surprise
to find that for more than four months after his arrival in England, Voltaire had spent hardly any time in the city of London
but had rather retired to the seclusion of the outlying villages
of Hampstead and Wandsworth. There, in a secure retreat referred to as his "den," he lived in almost complete seclusion in
the home of the only Englishman to remain his personal cor-
respondent after his return to France, the wealthy merchant
Everard Fawkener.[13]

Periodic retirement from society, especially during times of physical illness or psychic depression, was a habit of Voltaire's already developed before his arrival in England.[14] Once there he easily fell into it again. It seems to have paid off handsomely, as it usually did. One result was Voltaire's mastery of English, at least in writing the language. He may have been able to read it with some ease before leaving France, but his comments to French correspondents about the impossibility of learning English pronunciation outside of England are sufficient proof that he was not exempt from the foreigner's common struggle with the spoken tongue.[15] The numerous phonetic spellings of English words in approximately French versions in the letters and notebooks offer examples of Voltaire's far from perfect speech. For example, he wrote "Popp" for "Pope," "Suiff" for "Swift."

A letter to Thiriot of October 26, 1726, is the first composition in English of any length which can be dated accurately.[16] It is of capital importance for an understanding of Voltaire's early experiences in England, his impressions of the English nation and its inhabitants, his fondness for Pope's poetry, his sickness and financial troubles, his retirement to Fawkener's house at Wandsworth instead of accepting the hospitality of the Bolingbrokes ("because they are lords . . . and he is a single gentleman . . ."), and finally the deep effect on him of the death of his sister. This passage has been called an echo of the "To be or not to be" soliloquy in *Hamlet:* "Life is but a dream full of starts of folly, and of fancied, and true miseries. Death awakens us from this painful dream, and gives us, either a better existence or no existence at all."[17]

This letter is also of great interest as an example of Voltaire's command of written English during the early months of his exile. In spite of the awkwardness of certain expressions and afterthoughts, an uncertainty revealed by added words, strikeouts, and other revisions (some possibly added by a later English hand), Voltaire's sense of English idiom and the rhythm of English prose is already considerably advanced. Many of his difficulties are of a technical nature: spelling (a problem for many Englishmen of the eighteenth century), prepositions, pronouns. His difficulties are those of most beginners in a new language: "I went again in England" is replaced by "I came again into England"; ". . . going at London" becomes ". . . going to London"; "My lord and my lady Bolingbroke were into their country" is replaced by ". . . in the country"; ". . . a nation fond of her liberty" is changed to ". . . fond of their liberty"; "English wisdom and Honesty is above your" is corrected to ". . . is above yours." All of these mistakes, and several others in the letter, are obvious Gallicisms understandable in one whose knowledge of English was so recent. A possible explanation is Voltaire's habit of rapid composition in French, a habit he may have carried into English. Although the minor errors which have been observed in this early letter in English became less frequent in the later correspondence, his English was never free from an occasional blunder. But there is more than ample compensation for this in the lively English prose style achieved by Voltaire.

Other examples of Voltaire's early compositions in English are two notebooks: one almost entirely in English dating from the first months of his stay; the other partly in English, partly in French and other languages, apparently written during the latter part of his stay and after his return to France.[18] These notebooks contain the first expressions of many ideas which later found their way into the author's finished works, among them the *Lettres philosophiques* (first published in an English version as *Letters upon the English Nation*), the *Essai sur la Poésie épique,* as well as later "philosophical" essays and histories.[19]

Though a fragmentary and emended edition of the first notebook has been known to scholars for some time, the "Small Leningrad" notebook was not published in nearly complete form until 1929; the second or "Cambridge" notebook was not published until 1952.[20]

Both notebooks are very personal and informal in arrangement, containing extracts from English authors (principally Pope, Dryden, Swift, Rochester, and Addison) ; newspaper accounts and articles rephrased by Voltaire; anecdotes gathered from conversations in the drawing rooms and coffeehouses; and finally Voltaire's personal notes on the English scene and on the subjects that particularly interested him. A close examination of these journals and commonplace books can be rewarding for those interested in the development of Voltaire's literary taste and philosophical ideas, and in the genesis of his works written or planned in England.

The earlier (Small Leningrad) notebook is written almost entirely in English. Although dates may be misleading and the order of entries may be insignificant, the opening pages provide several indications that Voltaire wrote them during the summer and autumn of 1726. Even if the three passages dated in Voltaire's hand were added later, the similarity of the English prose to that in the letter to Thiriot may be a further if not entirely convincing indication of this early date. An example of this early composition is a prose passage containing a well-developed series of observations comparing the character of the English and the French.[21] The vocabulary and the phraseology are rather skilfully handled, but the last sentence contains Gallicisms similar to those in the letter to Thiriot mentioned above. "The English man is sparing of words, openly proud and unconcerned. He gives the most quick birth, as he can, to his taughts [*sic*], for fear of loosing his time."[22] The phrase "the most quick birth, as he can" is an obvious Gallicism. The word "taughts" may be a simple orthographic slip of the pen, but it could be a phonetic transcript of Voltaire's defective pronunciation of "thoughts."

Although this passage is based on a passage from the *Spectator* of August 4, 1711, like many other similar entries in the notebooks it is not a copy but a rewriting in Voltaire's own words. This habit of memorizing and assimilating passages of prose and poetry was a lifelong practice of Voltaire's, a habit acquired during his humanistic education under the Jesuit masters of Louis-le-Grand. It helps to explain Voltaire's rather amazing mastery of English and his ability to quote from their poets to his English guests at Ferney forty years after his stay in their country. It also explains the variants which occur in the poems and the peculiar French constructions which appear in his early compositions.

Another example of this assimilation and rewriting is a passage based on a composition in *The Independent Whig* (London, 1721). The following sentence illustrates Voltaire's mastery of the cadence of English prose as well as the peculiar Gallicism resulting from his transitive use of the verb "to be born" like the French verb "naître." "How very few are wise enough to admire the daily birth of ligth [*sic*] and the new creation of all things wich [*sic*] born every day with light; the everlasting regulation of the stars, the perpetual miracle of generation, effects of load-stone, of lime burned with water."[23]

The entries following this passage, dated July, 1726, seem to confirm the early date of such compositions. Succeeding passages such as the contrast of the characters of Bolingbroke and Pope may have been written in the late autumn of the same year, when Voltaire at last made his *début* in London society.[24]

The second (Cambridge) notebook appears to be of later composition. It is similar to the earlier notebook in being a combination of observations on readings, collections of anecdotes, and extracts from authors. Far more polyglot than the first notebook, the second contains passages and extracts in English, French, Italian, and Latin. The opening pages are principally in English and French. Voltaire's return to composition in French may have preceded or been contemporary with his return to France. Some of the entries clearly refer to events in France after his return. Only approximate dates could be assigned to most of the entries.

In the Cambridge notebook are found notes or drafts for at least two of Voltaire's finished works. One of these works is the *Lettres philosophiques,* for which the earlier notebook also provides source material. Comments on Newton and Descartes later found their place in Voltaire's campaign to introduce Newtonian physics in France. The brief sentences in French under the title "Sur les belles lettres des anglois" are topics later elaborated in Voltaire's letters on England.[25] Among the most interesting of these preparatory notes are translations of English poets including Rochester, Dryden, and Pope together with a translation of a bit of jingly verse by Lord Hervey shown by the author to Voltaire in Paris in 1729.[26] These translations into French verse were later printed, with interesting minor changes, in the first French edition of the *Lettres philosophiques.*

Two brief sentences in the notebook give definite information on the composition of other works begun in England. "In two months Brutus was framed, not writ in two years. The King of Suden [*sic*] was finished in 3 months."[27] The second sentence refers to Voltaire's *Histoire de Charles XII, Roi de Suéde* which he actually completed in France. The first refers to his tragedy *Brutus,* staged and published in 1731. It is an ambiguous sentence admitting of two readings: The play was outlined in two months, not in two years; or, the play was outlined in two months but remained incomplete for two years. The first reading seems more accurate, for the two sentences occur in the midst of notes in English for the preface to the play.

In the finished French version of the preface to *Brutus,* a dedicatory epistle to Lord Bolingbroke "Sur la tragédie," Voltaire says that after more than two years in England he became so accustomed to thinking and writing in English that he had difficulty expressing himself in French when he returned to his own country. He then states that the first act of his play was originally written in English.[28] The entries in English in the notebooks under the heading "To my lord Bolingb." show that the topics later elaborated in his comparison of English and French tragedy were originally jotted down in short sentences and phrases, probably during the last months of his stay in England. The following are typical: "Scenes in Schakespar [*sic*]. No plays./ We want action./ We deal in words./ We are naturals [another Gallicism], so was Virgil, Horace./ English seem to go beyond nature./ We are slaves to good breeding." Further in his notes Voltaire comments on the difficulty of continuing to write under neoclassical restrictions and on the forced style of many contemporary French authors. "The same subject, new turns, quaere [*sic*] phrases, bad stile, whipt creame."[29] There are interesting comparisons of the ancient Greek tragedians with English playwrights. Almost all the topics of Voltaire's later criticisms of English and French tragedy are here in embryo in these sentences jotted down in English.

In addition to settling some hitherto uncertain episodes of Voltaire's stay in England, the publication of these notebooks has given further proof of Voltaire's command of English idiom and style and of his impressions of the country. The excerpts

and translations of English authors confirm what was already
known of his predilection for Dryden, Pope, and Addison. In the
notebooks Voltaire is seen in characteristic attitudes as he observes every aspect of English life—commenting on commerce,
religion, politics, and personalities. His taste is revealed more
clearly than ever as he copies or translates philosophical passages from Dryden, elegant rococo satire from the *Rape of the
Lock,* or a bawdy jingle of Rochester. Jokes and anecdotes preserve in Voltaire's lively English prose the aroma of the coffee-
house. Finally the notebooks offer a rare occasion of viewing the
artist at work as he transforms rough literary and personal impressions into finished creations.

The Alienated Hero
in *Le Rouge et le Noir*
and *The Princess Casamassima*

by
John Roland Dove

"ALIENATION IS A fact," writes Professor F. H. Heinemann in his discussion of the modern situation. "There exists a feeling of estrangement in modern man which has considerably increased during the last hundred years."[1] Few students of contemporary literature would find cause to quarrel with this statement. Again and again in the fiction and drama of our times, one encounters the alienated hero, the man who has lost his faith in human society and in any principle that transcends society. One meets him in the works of Franz Kafka, Jean-Paul Sartre, Albert Camus, Jean Genêt, Samuel Beckett, and in many other representative writers. His characteristic gesture is one of rejection. "Dehors!" exclaims the *declassé* hero of Sartre's *Le Diable et le Bon Dieu* (II, iv), "Refuse ce monde qui ne veut pas de toi! Fais le Mal: tu verras comme on se sent léger."[2] It is to the predicament of the alienated man that Rainer Maria Rilke refers in memorable fashion in the seventh elegy of the *Duineser Elegien:* "Jede dumpfe Umkehr der Welt hat solche Enterbte,/ denen das Frühere nicht und noch nicht das Nächste gehört."[3]

Yet the alienated hero is not without an ancestry. If he comes into his own in the twentieth century, he is not absent from the literature of the nineteenth: Camus's *L'Étranger* would have been impossible without Dostoevski's "underground man," and Goethe's Werther is a still earlier hero whose *Weltschmerz* relates him to the tradition. In works as diverse as *Moby Dick,*

The Brothers Karamazov, and *Jude the Obscure* we are confronted with characters whose relation to society and the universe is problematic in the extreme, whereas an almost clinical interest in alienated states inspired works such as *Madame Bovary* and *Hedda Gabler.* Alienation, however, is rarely regarded as an inexorable fate by the nineteenth-century writer, nor is the alienated man usually considered the normative or representative man as he is in the writings of Sartre or Genêt. In the novels of Dostoevski, for example, an unremitting struggle is in progress against the negativism implicit in alienation. Thus, in *The Brothers Karamazov,* Ivan, the radically alienated man, is offset by Alyosha, the exponent of Christian love and faith; and it is Alyosha, rather than Ivan, who is presented to us as the real hero of the novel. A similar struggle against negation is to be detected in Melville. As Dostoevski dismisses Ivan, so Melville dismisses Captain Ahab, and Ishmael the searcher, the man who believes that answers can be found to the problems that harassed Ahab, emerges as the real hero of *Moby Dick.*

There are, nevertheless, two nineteenth-century writers who confront the problem of alienation without in any way trying to alleviate it: Stendhal in *Le Rouge et le Noir* (1830), and James in *The Princess Casamassima* (1885). These two books, widely separated as they are in points of time, were written by men of completely different backgrounds and temperaments, and there is not a shred of evidence to suggest that the later novel was in any way indebted to the earlier one. In both of these novels, however, we can discover a prototype of the alienated hero as we meet him in contemporary literature. The relationship between the protagonists and society is problematic from beginning to end. They are both poverty-stricken young men of humble background who struggle to transcend the barriers of class and win social recognition. Yet their efforts to identify themselves with the community finally prove abortive, not because the class problem is insurmountable, but because they both suffer from a spiritual alienation that is deeper than class alienation. In both cases the psychological need for social involvement in counteracted by a growing sense of moral detachment from the community. They find themselves in a position of absolute isolation from the group, whose ways are not their ways and whose governing principles they find morally repugnant, and in the last resort it is no longer society that is hostile to them but they who are hostile to society; it is no longer they who are alien, but society that is alien to them. For both of them, the only solution to this impasse is repudiation. In *Le Rouge et le Noir,* a suicidal motif is latent; in *The Princess Casamassima* is it explicit. Stendhal's hero, Julien Sorel, neither protests against a death sentence that is obviously unjust nor makes any concerted effort to get it mitigated, and he impresses us at the end of the novel as a man who would rather die than accept society on its own terms; James's hero, Hyacinth Robinson, shoots himself.

The negative attitude towards humanity that unites these two heroes is all the more arresting in view of their marked divergence in social orientation. Their original presuppositions about society are entirely at variance and, indeed, reflect the particular *Zeitgeist* that prevailed when the novels were written. Stendhal wrote *Le Rouge et le Noir* at a time when the idealistic and imperialistic impulses of the Revolutionary era and the First Empire had exhausted themselves, and when utopian and nationalistic fervors had given way to the bourgeois ideals of the countinghouse. The tone of society was materialistic and reactionary, and in his worldliness and his opportunism Julien reveals himself as a typical product of his period. He courts success and tries to push his way to the top because success is the only value that society respects. He never seriously envisions the possibility that society might be transformed through political action or that he might overcome his social alienation by associating himself with a political cause and working for the good of humanity. He thinks of society as a static and unchanging entity governed by uniform laws of self-interest. Hence the only possible *modus operandi* is to adapt oneself to the laws of the jungle, and this is what Julien does. Yet he is the perpetual critic of the role he plays and the society that forces him to play it. Through most of the novel, Stendhal presents him to us as a man with a suppressed longing for moral values which he can satisfy only by deploring their absence. At the close of the novel, however, his indictment of society becomes articulate and un-ambiguous, and we are confronted with the paradoxical spectacle of one of the most self-centered of literary heroes crying out against the selfishness and greed of humanity in the name of a personal moral idealism that has never found any adequate social outlet.

The later novel, on the other hand, was written at a time when the *status quo* was threatened and when it was once again possible to believe in the possibility of radical historical change. International revolutionary movements under the leadership of men like Bakunin were fermenting behind the ordered façade of European society, and these offered to victims of the existing social order a means of common political action. James's hero passionately responds to the ideal of an ultimate redress of social injustice through revolutionary subversion, and he pledges him-self to a subterranean society of radical anarchists that has cells all over the European continent. Thus in contrast to Julien Sorel, Hyacinth hopes to identify himself with the community by means of self-dedication and self-commitment, and his initial approach to humanity is entirely idealistic. Not only does he entertain the highest ideals of community action, but he also entertains the highest ideals of friendship and love. While Julien Sorel's approach to personal relationships is as exploitative as his approach to society at large, Hyacinth Robinson shows him-self as willing to commit himself absolutely to the people he loves as he is willing to commit himself absolutely to the cause of political reform; and, as we shall see, it is almost impossible to separate Hyacinth's love life from his political life, for in this novel, as in *Le Rouge et le Noir,* the closest relationship is es-tablished between the hero's public life and his personal life. In the long run, however, both Hyacinth's social ideals and his personal ideals are completely betrayed; and, like Julien Sorel, he is eventually forced to recognize that the ideals to which he subscribes have no relevance whatever in the larger community. We should thus consider Julien Sorel and Hyacinth Robinson as characters that complement one another rather than as charac-ters that basically contrast. Although they travel along different routes, both routes eventually lead to the same destination.

II

Stendhal's hero is presented as a young man who is prepared to go to any lengths to achieve social status, an attitude which immediately places him at the widest possible remove from the Byronic hero who prides himself on his superiority to the group and dramatizes his own isolation. The alienated state holds no charms for him: on the contrary, he makes every effort to win a place for himself in the community. Ostracized by his own class because of his intelligence and his sensibility, he addresses himself to the problem of rising in a hierarchical society with all the unscrupulousness of a dedicated careerist. He idolizes Napoleon as an archetype of the self-made man and learns from his memoirs the importance of a strategic approach to success. He has a natural capacity for Machiavellian intrigue, and dissimulation proves to be his strongest weapon. He deceives his confessor, his employers, his mistresses. He simulates piety to Father Chélan; he plays the part of a loyal servant to M. de Rênal while engaged in seducing his wife; he ingratiates himself with the Marquis de La Mole while campaigning to marry his daughter; he conquers Mathilde by pretending to be in love with another woman. These tactics, as such tactics frequently do, pay high dividends. This sawyer's son passes from class to class. He becomes the secretary and confidant of one of France's greatest noblemen; he has every prospect of high ecclesiastical preferment. Yet even this does not exhaust the measure of his success. However reluctantly, the Marquis de La Mole finally decides to countenance Julien's marriage to his daughter and in order to preserve appearances creates him a lieutenant of the hussars. In Julien's case, then, the problem of class does not prove to be insurmountable; and it is worth pointing out that if Mme de Rênal had not exposed him to the Marquis at so inopportune a moment, Julien would have ended up as the son-in-law of the Marquis de La Mole. No wonder, then, that with the impulsive fury of a frustrated *arriviste* Julien should have attempted to kill his former mistress.

If we could think of Julien Sorel as a conniving opportunist whose plans fell through at the last moment, he would present no problem to us. He is, however, far from being so simple. Stendhal, as F. C. Green points out, disapproved of Shakespeare's Hamlet, referring contemptuously to him as an "étudiant allemand,"[4] but there is nevertheless something of Hamlet in Julien Sorel. He is, like Hamlet, self-conscious and detached: he is the perpetual critic, the judge, the observer; and, like Hamlet, he is never able to involve himself completely in action. As a man of action he is as greedy for prestige as the Rênals and Valenods, notwithstanding his nostalgia for the First Empire, and he is capable of abandoning himself to fits of blind fury when he is thwarted; unlike them, however, he is also capable of looking at himself and at society in a spirit of critical objectivity. "En verité, l'homme a deux êtres en lui" (p. 486),[5] reflects Julien while he is in prison, and this could not be more true so far as his own character is concerned. There are indeed two Juliens, and it is this rather than his humble birth that makes his relationship with society so problematic. There is, on the one hand, Julien the social climber who courts society; and there is, on the other hand, the Julien who assesses the society he courts and becomes increasingly critical of its moral limitations. The first Julien, ambitious intriguer though he certainly is, often deludes himself about upper-class life, and, like many underprivileged people, tends to romanticize what lies beyond his own social horizon. Consider, for example, how greatly he is impressed by the young Bishop of Agde. He sees this glittering figure as the symbol of everything desirable, and he almost swoons when the bishop prays aloud in a side chapel of the abbey of Bray-le-Haut. "Ce spectacle fit perdre à notre héros ce qui lui restait de raison. En cet instant il se fût battu pour l'inquisition, et de bonne foi" (p. 108). The second Julien, however, has no patience with romantic illusions. He is a realist who becomes increasingly aware that there is not the slightest relationship between high social rank and true personal worth. The higher he rises in society, the more he realizes that morally speaking all classes are interchangeable.

Thus Julien is a divided being whose social triumphs turn to ashes in the mouth because of his progressive disillusionment with society. In no respect is this the result of the refutation of a high ideal of human nature; it is the result, paradoxically enough, of the confirmation that he finds on every level of French society of his underlying premise that all men are motivated by self-interest. For Julien the most oppressive fact about the human situation is that all men are basically the same, and at least one cause of his spiritual malaise is the monotony involved in encountering in provincial society, in ecclesiastical society, and in aristocratic society, the same drab spectacle of unalleviated human selfishness.

His first extensive contact with society takes place at Verrières, the town of his birth. Here at the beginning of the novel Stendhal introduces us to provincial life with some comments that anticipate what Ibsen has to say about the "divine majority" in *An Enemy of the People*. "La tyrannie de l'opinion, et quelle opinion! est aussi *bête* dans les petites villes de France qu'aux États-Unis d'Amérique" (p. 6). Public opinion, moreover, respects nothing more than money. *"Rapporter du revenu* est la raison qui décide de tout dans cette petite ville qui vous semblait si jolie" (p. 8). This unequivocal indictment is amply confirmed by Julien's experiences with all strata of provincial society. His father, the incarnation of peasant greed and avarice, hates him because he considers him a financial liability, and Julien has nothing but contempt for him. He has equal contempt for M. de Rênal, the mayor of the town, who employs him as a tutor for his son, and who, as a member of the minor nobility, is far above his father in rank. Petty, coarse, grasping, and consumed with desire for social prestige, he is the essence of small scale ambition and dingy egotism. He is, unfortunately, a thoroughly representative figure. His rival, M. Valenod, the superintendent of the poorhouse, is a man of the same cast. Although Julien realizes that the goodwill of such men is necessary if he wants to succeed, he finds it difficult to conceal his disgust and almost indulges himself in a tirade of denunciation when M. Valenod talks about the necessity of honesty and square dealing at the home of M. de Rênal. He gives vent to his feelings of outrage in the privacy of the garden. "Quels éloges de la probité! s'écria-t-il; on dirait que c'est la seule vertu; et cependant quelle considération, quel respect bas pour un homme qui évidemment a doublé et triplé sa fortune, depuis qu'il administre le bien des pauvres!" (p. 34).

Julien's bitterness is more than the bitterness of the intelligent outsider who realizes that the world is controlled by fools. He is genuinely disturbed at the total absence of moral standards, and nowhere is this more evident than in his reactions to the Valenod household. As the dinner guests gorge the expensive food, they are disturbed by the singing of one of the exploited inmates in the adjoining poorhouse. M. Valenod glances at one of his servants, and in a moment the singing stops. For Julien this incident sums up the callousness of provincial life. "Il avait les manières, mais non pas encore le cœur de son état. Malgré toute son hypocrisie si souvent exercée, il sentait une grosse larme couler le long de sa joue. Il essaya de la cacher avec le verre vert, mais il lui fut absolument impossible de faire honneur au vin du Rhin. *L'empêcher de chanter!* se disait-il a lui-même, o mon Dieu! et tu le souffres!" (p. 140).

What is true of secular life is equally true of life in the seminary. All of Stendhal's considerable satirical gifts are concentrated on Julien's fourteen months as a theological student. There are one or two talented students, but "le reste des trois cent vingt et un séminaristes ne se composait que d'êtres grossiers qui n'étaient pas bien sûrs de comprendre les mots latins qu'ils répétaient tout le long de la journée. Presque tous étaient des fils de paysans, et ils aimaient mieux gagner leur pain en récitant quelques mots latins qu'en piochant la terre" (p. 176). For most of them the Church is simply a means to an end. This is, of course, just as true of Julien, but unlike the others Julien has the intelligence to recognize his own motives for what they are. Intelligence, however, is regarded with extreme suspicion by the reactionary authorities. Always on the alert for signs of radicalism or free-thinking, they prefer bovine stupidity to brilliance, and Julien falls out of favor. "A leurs yeux, il était convaincu de ce vice énorme, *il pensait, il jugeait par lui-même,* au lieu de suivre aveuglément l'autorité et l'exemple" (p. 179). In vain he attempts to regain the confidence of the authorities by playing the role of a pious illiterate: such hypocrisy is beyond even his capabilities. Yet he recovers his lost prestige when the bishop of the diocese, impressed by his knowledge of the classics, presents him with a set of Tacitus. "De ce moment, il n'y eut plus d'envie; on lui fit la cour bassement: l'abbé Castenède, qui, la veille en-

core, était de la dernière insolence envers lui, vint le prendre
par le bras et l'invita à déjeuner" (p. 208). This incident teaches
Julien that in the Church as in the world political considerations
are paramount. Those who, like Father Chélan, cultivate a "fugitive and cloistered virtue" are passed over with a sneer. Julien
leaves the seminary with a Voltairean contempt for the Church
as an institution.

From the seminary Julien passes into the patrician world of
the Marquis de La Mole, only to discover that the bright façade
of Parisian life conceals a boredom as profound as that which
existed in the provinces. Obsessed with their ancient lineage
and preoccupied with the problem of how to regain their lost
power, the nobility are as calculating and as self-promoting as
the provincial *bourgeoisie,* and Julien finds amongst them the
same reaction and the same hostility to liberal ideas that he had
found in the seminary. Conformity is the price one has to pay for
existence: "Pourvu qu'on ne plaisantât ni de Dieu, ne des prê-
tres, ni du roi, ni des gens en places, ni des artistes protégés par
la cour, ni de tout ce qui est établi; pourvu qu'on ne dît du bien
de Béranger, ni des journaux de l'opposition, ni de Voltaire, ni
de Rousseau, ni de tout ce qui se permet un peu de franc-parler;
pourvu surtout qu'on ne parlât jamais politique, on pouvait
raisonner de tout" (p. 251).

It is not surprising that Julien should consider this society
"un désert brûlant de la médiocrité" (p. 322), and that the privilege of living in this rarified sphere should turn out to be a mixed
blessing. While making every effort to win the esteem of his
superiors, he feels a growing contempt for the ossified conventions and prejudices that confront him at every turn, and he
complains to Father Castenède that he can scarcely endure the
insufferable monotony of dining every day at the table of the
Marquis de La Mole. The Marquis is himself fully aware of this
contempt that Julien feels for Parisian society. He finds it, however, rather amusing and original. "Les autres provinciaux qui
arrivent à Paris admirent tout, pensait le marquis; celui-ci hait
tout. Ils ont trop d'affectation, lui n'en a pas assez, et les sots le
prennent pour un sot" (p. 273).

Julien's longing to identify himself with the community is

thus frustrated by a moral alienation that isolates him from it. Yet since so much of this novel is concerned with Julien's love affairs, we must ask whether he is any more successful in transcending his isolation within the smaller community constituted by intimate personal relationships. In view of the passionate reconciliation between Julien and Mme de Rênal at the end of the novel, it might be argued that love provides Julien with an ultimate solution of his problems. "Sache que je t'ai toujours aimée, que je n'ai aimé que toi" (p. 491), Julien cries out in rapture when Mme de Rênal first visits him in prison, and as they weep in each other's arms, he feels that he is experiencing one of the greatest moments of his life. "À aucune époque de sa vie, Julien n'avait trouvé un moment pareil" (p. 491). Thereafter she visits him repeatedly, and the last days of his life are enlivened by mutual ecstasies and passionate avowals. Nothing would make him more happy, he tells her, than to live with her forever. It is, however, highly significant that Julien makes no effort to ensure the realization of this romantic aspiration by fighting against his sentence.

Stendhal's whole approach to the question of love in this novel should caution us against taking this last-minute revival of the affair between Julien and Mme de Rênal too seriously. Here, as in his celebrated study *De l'amour,* his attitude to love is entirely unidealistic, and his highly analytical and detailed treatment of Julien's relations with Mme de Rênal and Mathilde de La Mole presupposes the view that egotism and competitiveness are as paramount in the relations between the sexes as they are in society as a whole. Julien's approach to love is conditioned by his study of Napoleon's memoirs. In emulation of his hero he associates love with ambition and conceives of woman as a natural ally in his struggle for social recognition. His interest in both Mme de Rênal and Mathlide is primarily as exploitative one, for he is attracted to both of them because they are in a position to forward his career. Sexual conquest he regards as a form of social conquest, his original campaign against the virtue of Mme de Rênal being inspired solely by social ambition and devoid of the slightest trace of erotic passion. Indeed, no passage in Stendhal is so rich in ironic implication as his famous account of Julien's first visit to Mme de Rênal's bedroom. From first to last, the experience is a painful ordeal. Julien feels that he owes it to himself to seduce her, but he would give anything to be spared. He is bitterly disappointed when he finds that she is sleeping alone. If she had been sleeping with her husband, he would have had an excuse to retreat! Prompted by the ideal of "duty," however—of duty, that is, to his own career—he rises manfully to the occasion. It is a disillusioning night. "Mon Dieu! être heureux, être aimé, n'est-ce que ça? Telle fut la première pensée de Julien, en rentrant dans sa chambre" (p. 87).

If Julien is using these women, they in their own way are using him. While he regards them as a way to conquer society, they regard him as a way to escape it. Both of them are victims of ennui. Mme de Rênal, an earlier version of Mme Bovary, is a passionate woman married to a bore. She accepts the humdrum monotony of her starved provincial life without protest until she meets Julien. Young, sensitive, and attractive, he is the antithesis of her husband in every way. Her religious scruples are no match for her growing infatuation with him. She sees in him the man she might have married had circumstances been different. Adultery for her is essentially a form of protest against her fate. Julien is a symbol of freedom. The same psychological considerations underlie Mathilde's infatuation. Bored with the young men of her own class, she pines for the unconventional, the dramatic, and the unexpected, and her heroine is Marguerite of Navarre who outraged society by asking for her lover's head. Julien, a man of the humblest possible origins, presents Mathilde with an opportunity of her own to outrage society by throwing class distinctions to the winds in the name of love, and she submits to him primarily in order to assert her independence of established conventions.

Stendhal's conception of love anticipates both what Freud has to say about the intimate relation between love and hate, and what Sartre has to say about the appropriative element in human relationships. As Stendhal sees it, both parties in a love affair regard one another as means rather than as ends and as symbols rather than as persons; and affection, mutual understanding, and sincerity are *ex hypothesi* ruled out of court. The word "love" is, indeed, a misnomer, since lovers so-called are basically antagonists who want to mould one another in accordance with their separate illusions. Neither wants to reckon with the authentic personality of the other, since in such a relationship authenticity is always obtrusive. Julien realizes this when he makes the mistake of expressing his admiration for Napoleon in front of Mme de Rênal. For once the real Julien is speaking, but his mistress has no use for Julien as he really is. "Il vit tout à coup Mme. de Rênal froncer le sourcil, elle prit un air froid et dédaigneux; cette façon de penser lui semblait convenir à un domestique" (p. 93). He never errs in the direction of sincerity again.

Stendhal is, of course, aware that love has its consolations. If there is no true self-realization in love, there is at least self-oblivion in the intoxication of mutual passion. Erotic passion is, however, unpredictable and accidental. When Julien leaves for the seminary, he forgets Mme de Rênal completely. In Paris he is entirely preoccupied with Mathilde. Yet in prison he finds Mathilde's visits unutterably boring, and when Mme de Rênal reappears Mathilde is dismissed and forgotten. Surely the tables would have been turned once again had Julien not been guillotined. Mathilde's star would have risen, Mme de Rênal's star would have waned. As Julien tells Mathilde: "Il faut convenir, chère amie, que les passions sont un accident dans la vie, mais cet accident ne se rencontre que chez les âmes supérieures" (p. 472).

In love, then, as in society, Julien fails to overcome the problem of alienation. All his efforts to identify himself with the community prove abortive; at the end, as at the beginning, he is the isolated man, *l'étranger*, the man flung back on himself. There is, however, this difference. From the time of his arrest until his death he confronts his situation and accepts it. Retreating into his own personal world of reflection and soliloquy, he makes no effort to protest his sentence and return to the world of men. "Il n'avait plus d'ambition" (p. 456), writes Stendhal. He refuses to co-operate with his lawyers; he outrages the jurors by airing his views on the problem of class; he adopts an attitude of blithe indifference to the efforts that are made by his friends to obtain his release. Although he is not guilty of murder, he insists that he deserves death. It is not without reason that his confessor warns him that unless he wishes to fall into the frightful sin of suicide, he must do everything possible to win a pardon.

As Julien sums up his experiences of life in his cell, we realize that his indifference to his own future is merely a symptom of the profound disgust that the spectacle of human life evokes in him. He sees no redeeming features in civilization. All men, even the great Napoleon, are fundamentally dishonest and corrupt. "Partout hypocrisie, ou du moins charlatanisme, même chez les plus grands; et ses lèvres prirent l' expression du dégoût . . . . Non, l'homme ne peut pas se fier à l'homme" (p. 499). Avarice is the predominant factor in life; his own father, he reflects bitterly, will welcome his execution if he is left two or three hundred louis. "Un dimanche après dîner, il montrera son or à tous ses envieux de Verrières. A ce prix, leur dira son regard, lequel d'entre vous ne serait pas charmé d'avoir un fils guillotiné" (p. 499). There are no absolute principles or natural laws: life is governed by necessity and the rule of self-preservation. "Il n'y a point de *droit naturel* . . . . Avant la loi, il n'y a de *naturel* que la force du lion, ou le besoin de l'être qui a faim, qui a froid, le *besoin* en un mot . . ." (p. 498). Nor has Julien the slightest confidence in any transcendent religious principle. He hates the God of the Christians. "Je n'ai même jamais voulu croire qu'on l'aimât sincèrement" (p. 485). Like Voltaire, he loathes conventional religion. He asks himself how it is possible to believe in the great name of God after the terrible abuse the priests make of it. Nevertheless, he has a certain nostalgia for the divine. He wishes a true priest existed who could speak of the true God. "Ce bon prêtre nous parlerait de Dieu. Mais, quel Dieu? Non celui de la Bible, petit despote cruel et plein de la soif de se venger . . . mais le Dieu de Voltaire, juste, bon, infini . . ." (p. 500). Unfortunately, such a priest does not exist, and even Voltaire's God is insusceptible of proof. "Qui sait ce que l'on trouve dans l'autre vie?" he asks Mme de Rênal. "Peut-être des tourments, peut-être rien du tout" (p. 492).

In such a meaningless and valueless world, the struggle to survive seems futile. As Stendhal says with great aptness: "Cette philosophie pouvait être vraie, mais elle était de nature à faire désirer la mort" (p. 499). It is, however, possible to behave with integrity by refusing to comply with conditions that one deplores. This is precisely what Julien finally does. His indifference to the world gives him the courage to defy it. Weary of dishonesty and dissimulation, he counters dishonesty with honesty. He denounces the class prejudices of the jurors unequivocally, although he realizes that such candor must ensure his conviction. When his confessor tells him that if he wants his sentence to be rescinded, he should announce his religious conversion, he dismisses the suggestion with scorn. "Et que me restera-t-il," Julien replied coldly, "si je me méprise moi-même?" (p. 505).

There is a certain nobility about Julien during his last days. His frankness excites our admiration. According to Green, Stendhal intended to emphasize "the stoic courage of this man who goes fearlessly to his death, with no hope of future reward, upheld only by the calm assurance that he has never been false to his private ideals."[6] This is true as far as it goes; but there is an undercurrent of irony in these last chapters to which Green fails to respond. One has to place Julien's loyalty to his "private ideals" in the context of a world in which ideals are meaningless. There is something completely gratuitous, if not a little fatuous, about nobility in an ignoble universe. From one point of view it would be legitimate to say that Julien saves his own soul by preferring truth to falsity. From another point of view this decision on behalf of truth is an excellent illustration of what Camus refers to as the absurd. It has no social significance whatsoever. It is not in harmony with society, since society is based on lies; it is not in harmony with natural law, since there is no natural law; it is not in harmony with God, since there is no God—or if there is, His nature has not been disclosed to us. In the last resort, Julien's decision for truth may be described most appropriately as an act of empty defiance against all existing conditions.

III

Hyacinth Robinson, the hero of *The Princess Casamassima*, is, like Julien Sorel, a man without a class whose energies are

directed towards finding a social identity. Hyacinth's relation to
the problem of class is, however, more complicated than Julien's.
Julien was a misfit in his own class; Hyacinth Robinson is tormented by the sense of not having any unambiguous social roots.
He is the unclaimed and unrecognized bastard son of an English
nobleman and a French girl of the working class. His birth is
tainted not only by illegitimacy but also by murder, since his
father died by his mother's hand. As James put it vividly, he is
"the bastard son of a murderess, spawned in a gutter out of which
he had been picked by a poor sewing girl" (p. 378).[7]

These disparate social and, indeed, national strains in his
family background affect Hyacinth throughout his life. Julien
Sorel criticized fate for consigning him to the bottom of society
when he really belonged at the top; Hyacinth's problem is that
he never knows where he belongs. At times he thinks of himself
as a man of the people like his maternal forebears; at other times
he feels that he belongs to the aristocratic race of his father.
"There was no peace for him between the two currents that
flowed in his nature, the blood of his passionate, plebeian mother
and that of his long-descended, super-civilized sire. They continued to toss him from one side to the other; they arrayed him
in intolerable revenges and defiances against himself" (p. 407).
Brought up in all the squalor of the London slums by a penuri-
ous seamstress and apprenticed at an early age in a bookbindery,
he considers himself, on the one hand, a member of the working
class, and identifies himself with the workers to the extent of
pledging his life to revolutionary movement that will, he believes, ensure the triumph of the masses. On the other hand,
Hyacinth scorns the mass mind from the standpoint of an engrained aristocratic fastidiousness. He is drawn to the private,
the exclusive, and the elegant; the happiest moments of his life
are spent in the company of the Princess Cassamassima, for him
the symbol, the essence, of a patrician mode of life, discussing
literature, music, and painting in the ordered seclusion of her
country home.

At odds with society and psychologically at war with himself,
Hyacinth's problem, like Julien's, is to overcome his isolation
and merge himself with the community. This he attempts to do

on two separate levels, a political one and a personal one. Although they continually dovetail into one another—his eagerness to be admitted into the inner revolutionary circle is, for example, at the same time a bid for the friendship of his hero, Paul Muniment—in the interests of clarity we shall consider them separately.

As has been pointed out, Hyacinth's approach to society is, in contrast to Julien's, an idealistic one, and in the first part of the novel James traces his hero's growing infatuation with the ideals of a subterranean socialist society. Everything predisposes him in favor of the movement. As a child he is conditioned to think ill of the *status quo* by his friend Mr. Vetch, a seedy violinist who constantly harps on the theme of social injustice. He starts his work at the bindery under the auspices of Eugene Poupin, a socialist *émigré* of the most radical persuasion, and the young chemist, Paul Muniment, whom he admires to the point of adoration, is in close contact with Hoffendahl, the international leader of the movement. Moreover, as a victim of a hypocritical and caste-structured society himself and as an intelligent observer of the misery and degradation around him, he understands only too well the exploitative nature of the established order. Revolutionary socialism, on the other hand, has the enormous moral persuasiveness of a program which announces the end of the exploitation of the many by the few.

On the one hand, then, we have a disinherited young man on the fringes of society; on the other, a political cause that speaks for justice and political equality, while it contrasts the decadent, unhappy society of the present with an ideal society of the future in which all class distinctions will be abolished and all problems of social maladjustment relegated to the wicked past. It is a cause that provides Hyacinth with an opportunity for working in the closest association with the men he admires, and it offers him the encouraging prospect of a future community in which he will no longer be a stranger. Fired with utopian enthusiasm, he assiduously attends secret meetings at a public house in the slums. He is not content, however, with the role of a sympathetic witness. He resents the fact that he is on the periphery of the movement; he wants to commit himself absolutely and without reservations. He is convinced that there is an inner revolutionary circle operating behind the scenes, and he aspires to be accepted by it. His opportunity comes. At the close of a smoke-filled meeting at the "Sun and Moon," he jumps up on the table and declares his readiness to risk everything, even life itself, for the cause. "I'm ready to do anything that will do any good; anything, anything—I don't care a damned rap. In such a cause I should like the idea of danger. I don't consider my bones precious in the least, compared with some other things" (p. 244). His offer is accepted. He is introduced to Hoffendahl immediately after the meeting, and he pledges himself to murder some reactionary as yet unknown when the summons comes. It means nothing to Hyacinth at this point that this will possibly involve his own death. Even if he never lives to take his place in the society of the future, he will have had the privilege of having worked for its advent.

Yet almost immediately after Hyacinth has committed himself to this social ideal, he begins to lose faith in it. His change of heart is the direct result of a prolonged visit at the elegant country home of the Princess Casamassima, followed by a short but momentous vacation on the Continent. The Princess introduces her bemused young friend to the amenities and civilities of a life of leisured wealth; in Paris and Florence he implements this lesson by studying at first hand the monuments, buildings, and *objets d'art* that patrician societies have produced. The result is a growing insight into what one might refer to as the moral ambiguity of the historical situation. Hyacinth is compelled to recognize that the old social order, corrupt and exploitative as it certainly was, gave birth to certain definite spiritual values—the values implicit in courtesy, *gentillesse*, and good form, and, more especially, the values implicit in great works of art. Alternatively, he is compelled to recognize that the democratic society of the future, emerging already in the form of revolutionary socialism, will inevitably trample on these primarily private and individualistic values because it will be dominated by the mass mind. He is confronted, then, with the fundamental paradox that a series of basic values, values that need to be preserved, may flourish in an unjust society and decline in a just one. He expresses this vividly in a letter to the Princess: "The monuments and treasures of art, the great palaces and properties, the conquests of learning and taste, the general fabric of civilisation, as we know it, based if you will upon all the despotisms, the cruelties, the exclusions, the monopolies and the rapacities of the past, but thanks to which, all the same, the world is less of a 'bloody sell' and life more of a lark—our friend Hoffendahl seems to me to hold them too cheap and wish to substitute for them something in which I can't believe as I do in things with which the years and tears of generations have been mixed" (p. 344).

Does this put Hyacinth in the ironic position of a revolutionary who has committed himself up to the hilt only to discover too late that he is really a reactionary? On the contrary, Hyacinth's insight into the moral ambiguity of history does not reconcile him to the old social order. He is as aware as he was before that the existing social order is unjust and exploitative and as convinced as he was before that a new social order is inevitable and from the standpoint of social justice much to be desired. He does not switch from one camp to another: he detaches himself from both camps. Admittedly he is attached to the cause of revolution by virtue of his pledge to Hoffendahl, but it is merely a formal attachment. "Isn't it enough to give my life to the beastly cause," he asks the Princess, "without giving my sympathy?" (p. 282).

The final outcome of Hyacinth's excursion into politics is to aggravate rather than to allay his sense of exile, since he realizes that he would be just as misplaced in the society of the future as he is misplaced in the society of the present. He takes it for granted that "the flood of democracy was rising over the world; that it would sweep all the traditions of the past before it; that, whatever it might fail to bring, it would at least carry in its bosom a magnificent energy; and that it might be trusted to look after its own." But he does not feel that he himself could be part of "democracy's own." Although he is deeply sensitive to the plight of the masses, he is repelled by "their brutal insensibility, a grossness proof against the taste of better things and against any desire for them," and he sees in their coming triumph a threat to the concept of individuality—"he is afraid the democracy wouldn't care for better bindings or the finer sorts of conversation" (pp. 406-7). He recognizes that an egalitarian society will be by its very nature uniformitarian and hostile to exclusively personal values, and in such a society he has as little wish to live as Julien Sorel wished to live in the uniformitarian society of the Restoration.

Hyacinth's abortive efforts to transcend isolation through politics are paralleled by his equally abortive efforts in the dimension of personal relationships. His approach to friendship and love is characteristic of most of the protagonists in James's major novels and is in strong contrast to that of Julien Sorel. As opposed to Stendhal, James conceives of love as an existential attempt at self-completion whose erotic aspects are always secondary.[8] The Jamesian protagonist appeals to the beloved to rescue him from a personal life that has become too complex and problematic, and he expects to escape from his own individuality by dedicating himself to the other and identifying himself with him completely. This presupposes an idealistic and exalted attitude towards the other who is, indeed, regarded in a redemptive light. In the Jamesian dialectic of the personal, this attitude invariably turns out to be unfounded, the protagonist is betrayed, and his appeal is denied.

Hyacinth Robinson loves three people, each of whom repudiates him—the Princess Casamassima, the young chemist Paul Muniment, and the cockney shopgirl Millicent Henning. It is the Princess, however, who excites his greatest affection, and his attitude toward her is one of inexpressible gratitude and undeviating devotion. She is a woman of exquisite taste, sensibility, and manner who displays on all occasions a sublime disregard for conventions, and in Hyacinth's admiring eyes she is a matchless representative of the aristocratic. He regards her not without justice as the most civilizing influence in his life, and his stay with her at Medley turns him away forever from the ideal of a society dominated by the masses. The whole house is permeated with her personality, her refinement, and her charm, and Hyacinth surrenders himself entirely to her spell. "The cup of an exquisite experience—a week in that enchanted palace, a week of such immunity from Lomax Place and Old Crook as he had never dreamed of—was at his lips; it was purple with the wine of romance, of reality, of civilisation, and he couldn't push it aside without drinking. He might go home ashamed, but he would have for evermore the taste of nectar" (p. 271). This highly romantic conception of the particular ambience of the Princess, Hyacinth never surrenders, and on one level she always remains for him a splendid being living in an atmosphere of regal splendor. Even when she rents a squalid little house in London in order to satisfy her caprice of living among the people, Hyacinth still admires the way her inherent superiority places her above her environment. "Her beauty," he reflects, "always appeared in truth to have the setting that best became it; her fairness made the element in which she lived and, among the meanest accessories, constituted a kind of splendour" (p. 409).

It is not the romantic remoteness of the Princess that prompts Hyacinth to devote himself to her with such unwearying persistence—writing to her, introducing her to his friends, and visiting her as frequently as she permits him. He is inspired, on the contrary, by the hope that in his own way he may become an indispensable part of her world, and he longs to be accepted by her as an equal, a friend, and a lover. In view of his background these aspirations are, he realizes, presumptuous, but the Princess herself has encouraged them. She acknowledges that extreme social barriers exist between them, but she insists that they can be bridged. "I recognize perfectly the obstacles in practice as you call them; but though I'm not by nature persevering, and am really very easily put off, I don't consider they'll prove insurmountable. They exist on my side as well, and if you'll help me overcome mine, I'll do the same for you with yours" (p. 206). She persuades him that the sordid conditions of his upbringing have not obscured the marks of the true aristocrat—"You haven't a common gesture," she tells him, "you never make a mistake" (p. 283). She treats him as a confidant, telling him all about her early struggles, her unhappy marriage, and her political views; he, on his side, pours into her sympathetic ear the story of the miseries and torments of his youth. "Haven't you kept anything?" he asks her after she has sold her property and moved into a London suburb. "I've kept you," she answers significantly, and passes her hand into his arm (p. 352).

Yet in the last resort all Hyacinth's hopes are doomed to failure.

She is essentially a bored and capricious woman, like Mathilde; and, as Hyacinth sadly realizes, her interest in him, like her interest in the problems of the proletariat, was prompted mainly by ennui and the desire for novelty. A new distraction is provided when she meets Paul Muniment, and how characteristically Jamesian it is that Hyacinth should lose the woman he admires most in the world to the man he admires beyond all others. One of the most moving passages in the novel is that in which Hyacinth stands in the street with Prince Casamassima and watches the Princess disappear with Paul Muniment into her house. Like Shakespeare's Cleopatra, the Princess is "no more but e'en a woman," and as such she eventually reveals herself to be far more interested in the passionate sensuality of Paul than in Hyacinth's idealistic devotion.

The last confrontation between them takes place after Hyacinth has received word from Hoffendahl that the time is now ripe for the assassination. Repelled at the whole idea of the murder, he is in a state of the gravest emotional disturbance, and more than at any time of his life he needs her love. He knows that she has turned away from him, but he harbors the irrational hope that she may turn to him again, save him from himself, and provide him with a reason for living. He makes no attempt to evoke any false sympathy by telling her of his plight, but simply presents himself to her again as her most reliable friend. Yet it is hopeless. From the beginning he knows that his cause is lost, and his ideal of a relationship with her that will heal the wounds of circumstance and lift him above the tensions of his personal life collapses never to be renewed. He still loves her—"there's no one else in the world and has never been any one in the world like you," he tells her, his eyes full of tears (p. 495)—but he no longer expects anything of her.

Similarly, he abandons his expectations of any fundamental relationship with Paul Muniment, whom he had approached in the light of what James calls "an ideal of friendship." Characterized by his sturdy common sense, inner independence, and strong sense of political direction, Paul had attracted Hyacinth as the living antithesis of himself, and throughout the novel he turns to him for approval and advice and attempts to model himself after him. His interest in the revolutionary movement is colored by the fact that Paul is one of the underground leaders. He continually strives to impress him by his revolutionary zeal and hopes to break through his reserve and win a place in his heart by pledging his life to the cause. Surely, Hyacinth feels, the imminent possibility of his death will draw Paul closer to him. Unfortunately, this does not prove to be the case. Paul is the archetype of the revolutionary who has no room for personal feelings. From his point of view Hyacinth is a mere pawn in the political game. He refuses to take him seriously as a person, since personal involvement is incompatible with complete dedication to the cause. His nearest approach to personal involvement is not with Hyacinth: it is with the woman Hyacinth loves.

Millicent Henning, that ebullient child of the gutter, takes her part also in this drama of personal exclusion. Millicent is never a romantic figure for Hyacinth: he has known her too long and too well. She is the tried friend, the old reliable, dependable in a crisis. Cheerful, raucous, and sentimental, she personifies for Hyacinth the whole struggling, vivacious cockney world. He makes no claims on her: he is fully aware that she lavishes her affections with a certain lack of discrimination. Her promiscuity is, however, ultimately irreconcilable with the monopolistic personal attention that he craves and needs. This is brought home to him just before his death. After visiting the Princess, he goes to call on Millicent, who is now his last hope. Once again he has to reconcile himself to the fact that he is not wanted. She is previously engaged—her attentions are claimed by another visitor, Captain Sholto. Once again Hyacinth is forced to acknowledge that the kind of friendship he has to offer cannot compete with a relationship whose binding force is an erotic interest.

The novel closes with Hyacinth's suicide. Rather than co-operate with Hoffendahl, he prefers to kill himself. The necessity of extricating himself from the consequences of an impulsive vow is not, however, the primary reason for his death. Suicide was far from being the only solution to his problem. He could have extricated himself from his obligations much less drastically, or at the very least he could have made an attempt to do so, as Julien could have made an attempt to win a reprieve. But in Hyacinth's case, as in Julien's, the will to live has become atrophied; and his death, like Julien's, symbolizes his total alienation.

Like Julien Sorel, Hyacinth reaches a point where the human situation seems to offer him nothing that he can believe in and nothing that he can endorse. He who has followed the path of commitment finds at the end that commitment is no longer possible. Admittedly Hyacinth differs from Julien in conceding that certain moral values are present in society. The democratic society of the future will, he believes, put an end to social oppression and in this respect will confer positive benefits on humanity. However, Hyacinth's assent to what is positive in the new social order is qualified by his conviction that the coming society will be as oppressive in its own way as the existent one. In certain moods, moreover, Hyacinth feels that the limited amelioration promised by the future is of no consequence whatsoever in view of the engrained baseness of human nature.

> There were nights when every one he met appeared to reek with gin and filth and he found himself elbowed by figures as foul as lepers. Some of the women and girls in particular were appalling—saturated with alcohol and vice, brutal, bedraggled, obscene. "What remedy but another deluge, what alchemy but annihilation?" he asked himself as went his way; and he wondered what fate there could be in the great scheme of things for a planet overgrown with such vermin, what redemption but to be hurled against a ball of consuming fire. If it was the fault of the rich, as Paul Muniment held, the selfish congested rich who allowed such abominations to flourish, that made no difference, and only shifted the shame; since the terrestrial globe, a visible failure, produced the cause as well as the effect (p. 410).

The spectacle of human depravity arouses in Hyacinth, as in Julien, feelings of moral nausea and spiritual disgust. Unlike Julien, however, Hyacinth is prepared to grant that humanity occasionally rises above itself in the dimension of art. Yet art never offers Hyacinth an existential alternative: he never thinks of art as a means of personal redemption; he never considers that aestheticism might be a possible way of life. As a bookbinder he is, of course, himself a kind of artist—the craft of bookbinding is symbolic of his ambivalent origin and motivation—but he never thinks of his craftmanship as an end in itself. On the contrary, all his artistic work is inspired by the most personal motives. He thinks of himself as a craftsman in the service of the Princess, and all his skill is dedicated to pleasing her and winning her esteem. From this standpoint all his laborious efforts represent so much misapplied labor, since they ultimately fall short of their purpose. Bitter experience teaches him that the work of art is incapable of bridging the gap that separates one human being from another.

At the end of *The Princess Casamassima* Hyacinth Robinson finds himself confronting a world analogous in all basic respects to the world that confronted Julien Sorel. In the last eventuality the three individuals whom Hyacinth loved and idealized turn out to be as self-centered, as disloyal, and as coarse spiritually as the people to whom Stendhal introduces us in *Le Rouge et le Noir,* and Hyacinth finds himself forced to adopt a view of humanity as disillusioned as that of Julien Sorel. Social inequity is as omnipresent in Hyacinth's society as in Julien's; and Hyacinth finally takes Julien's view that, inequity and injustice being endemic to the human situation, it is hopeless to look for any radical improvement. No more than Julien is he able to find any consolation in the idea of a benevolent God or a divinely planned universe. Like Julien he is stranded in a predicament for which there is no final explanation—the predicament of a man who prefers to invoke oblivion and nothingness rather than reconcile himself to the sterility of existence.

IV

Today the negativism that characterizes the attitudes of Julien Sorel and Hyacinth Robinson is familiar to the point of triteness: it is part of the contemporary *Weltanschauung.* In the last century, however—the century, after all, of Comte, Darwin, Marx, Huxley, and Spencer—alienation was not regarded as an inescapable predicament, and it is primarily in those works that we tend to label "modern"—works, that is, anticipating the issues of our times—that the problem receives consideration. From this standpoint, *Le Rouge et le Noir* and *The Princess Casamassima* are particularly modern in feeling and tone, and it is significant that they have both received increasing critical acclaim in recent years.

The conflict between the individual and society is central throughout literature, but the alienated hero who emerges in these novels belongs to an entirely new type in modern fiction. He is as distinct from the tragic hero as from the romantic hero. While the tragic hero frequently criticizes society, he criticizes it in the name of universal values. These values may have lost their force in society at large, as in Hamlet's Denmark, but the hero can always count on a select minority who still acknowledge their validity. Thus Hamlet can turn to Horatio and Fortinbras, while King Lear can turn to Cordelia, Edgar, and Kent. The tragic hero is always a member of a community, even if it is a community in exile; and he is never radically isolated. Julien and Hyacinth, in contrast, belong to no community, neither a community of the past, the present, nor the future. They judge society according to criteria that are peculiar to themselves. In both of them the human condition evokes a sense of malaise or spiritual dismay that is private and incommunicable. The result is a feeling of absolute isolation which leaves them no alternative but renunciation and death. Unlike the isolation of the romantic hero, their isolation is never a source of pride. On the contrary, it frustrates their urgent longing to belong to the community. The alienated hero is the defeated hero. Yet if we are prepared to accept the somewhat terrifying picture of the human situation as we find it in these novels, the hero's refusal to accept life on its own terms may not unjustifiably be regarded as an assertion of human dignity, however futile such an assertion may be.

Longfellow's Lyrics
"From the German"
by
Carl Hammer, Jr.

"THE GERMANS HAVE so much poetry in their natures and in
their lives!"[1] In these words, penned apropos of a friend's account of a German wedding at Cambridgeport, Longfellow expresses a sentiment fully consonant with his varied role as a
cultural mediator between Germany and America. We see him
fulfilling that function as a Harvard professor of languages and
literature; as a belletristic critic and interpreter of many German
writers in his widely-circulated novel *Hyperion*, as well as in various journals; as editor of an epoch-making anthology of which
a fourth is devoted to German verse;[2] as an original poet often
inspired by Teutonic sources to produce works extensively translated into German; as a promoter of interest in Germany's music
—inseparable from her poetry; as a man of innumerable personal
contacts with the German-speaking world, which he understood
and loved; and, finally and most unequivocally, as a translator
of German lyrics and ballads. To evaluate Longfellow's accomplishment in the last-named capacity is the endeavor of this
study, which, owing to limitations of space, must essay to be
suggestive rather than exhaustive.

Much praise has been accorded, early and late, to his translations of German poems; only a few instances need be given
here. Ferdinand Freiligrath, who turned a number of Longfellow's works (including *Hiawatha*) into German, considered the
renditions which his "transatlantischer Freund" made from Johann Ludwig Uhland and other poets to be among the most

155

successful ever attempted in English.[3] Oscar Thiergen cites three
of them as examples to show "wie vollständig treu Longfellow
diese Gedichte wiedergab," adding that they also prove the
fundamentally Germanic character of the English tongue.[4] The
close kinship of the translations and the contemporaneous original poetry is signaled by Fred Lewis Pattee, who attributes Longfellow's immediate popularity in America and England to the
German romantic element in his work.[5] Mark Van Doren included eight German poems Englished by Longfellow in his
well-known collection.[6] James Taft Hatfield, who comprehen-
sively investigated German inspirational forces affecting the
poet's own production, lauds the perfection of form and spirit
in the translated lyrics and asserts that they played an important
part in winning the American people over to poetry.[7] According
to J. W. Thomas, the significance of Longfellow's criticisms and
translations can hardly be overestimated in any consideration
of German influences on American letters; at the same time, he
received the most valuable stimulation for his original works,
which thereby acquired a greater depth of content and a freer
impulse, while some of his poetic renditions became a part of
America's literary heritage.[8] Lastly, Edward Wagenknecht, who
likewise pays tribute to the excellence of Longfellow as a translator, states that, aside from Dante's masterpiece, the literature
of Germany became more important for him than that of any
other nation on the Continent.[9]

It was Longfellow's ideal, at a time when he was likewise
ably interpreting poetry of other languages, especially Romance and Scandinavian,[10] to help achieve in American literature
a synthesis of the thoughts and feelings of the various nations.
As Mr. Churchill in *Kavanagh* expresses it: "We shall draw from
the Germans, tenderness; from the Spaniards, passion; from the
French, vivacity,—to mingle more and more with our English
solid sense. And this will give us universality, so much to be
desired."[11] In that spirit Longfellow undertook the editing of
The Poets and Poetry of Europe, in which he assembled a vast
body of translations for the purpose of bringing continental
writers into the ken of his compatriots. He included many of
his own—fifteen poems from the German.[12] This extensive trans-

lating and editing was done at a time when, as Wagenknecht remarks, Longfellow was not yet entirely committed to composing original poetry.[13]

For that period, before he ventured upon his most ambitious literary endeavors, *Christus: A Mystery* and his translation of Dante's *Divina Commedia*, Longfellow's conception of the translator's task was largely that which he expresses in the preface to his English version of the *Coplas de Don Jorge Manrique* (1833), as follows: "The great art of translating well lies in the power of rendering literally the words of a foreign author while at the same time we preserve the spirit of the original." Yet he considered it an open question as to how far it is permissible, in the case of "the less flexible material" of another tongue, to make use of "slight and judicious embellishments." He admits having resorted to this device of employing "an additional epithet or a more forceful turn of expression" whenever he could not render the words of the original without doing violence to their spirit.[14] It is a standpoint which must be borne in mind while one considers the majority of his renditions of German poetry. Yet how different is the attitude of the mature Longfellow! His "Prelude to the Translations" (1870) voices the elusiveness of songs turned into another language. Comparing them to "treasures . . . deep buried in sea-sands," he asks whether it would not be better to let them remain "locked in their iron chest," and concludes with the lines:

> I have but marked the place,
> But half the secret told,
> That following this slight trace,
> Others may find the gold.[15]

The early *Outre-Mer* (1833), an account of Longfellow's first "pilgrimage beyond the sea," with chief emphasis on France, Spain, and Italy, contains eight lines from Bürger's *Lenore* as its longest quotation from German poetry.[16] It is *Hyperion*, the literary precipitate of his second and chiefly formative sojourn in Germany, which deals most fully with her writers, and with such enthusiasm that even Mrs. Longfellow once called that country her husband's native land.[17] This loosely-constructed novel, in the line of descent from *Wilhelm Meister,* attained a comparative popularity not readily conceivable today. James Morgan Hart says that for Americans of the 1840's and 1850's, *Hyperion* represented German literature.[18] Some twenty-five authors are discussed, or at least mentioned, and there are translations of seven poems (beside a number of fragmentary passages). Of these, several were reprinted in the volume *Voices of the Night* (1839) and later in *The Poets and Poetry of Europe* (1845), which likewise includes those which appeared that same year in *The Belfry of Bruges and Other Poems.* Still others were written expressly for the anthology.

Most of Longfellow's translating from German sources was therefore done within the decade 1835-45; after the latter date only rare instances occur. His entire published output consists of twenty-nine complete poems along with twelve epigrams by Logau and numerous fragments of a few lines each. The ten years in question embrace not only his second and third visits to Germany (1835-36 and 1842), but also the initiation of his carefully prepared Harvard lectures on German literature, especially Goethe's *Faust.*[19] At the beginning of that period German poetry brought him solace after the death of his first wife; later it was his companion during his difficult though eventually successful wooing of Frances Appleton (the "Mary Ashburton" of *Hyperion*). When, in 1835-36, efforts to bury himself in concentrated study at Heidelberg failed, the German poets came to his aid, with a resultant change of emphasis in his life: in keeping with his natural endowments, Longfellow turned from any previously intended emulation of Ticknor's scholarship to lyric expression of emotion and sentiment.[20] From then on, his poetry became, in the words of Willis A. Chamberlin, "suffused with feeling," indicating a broadening of his human sympathies born of profound inward experiences of his own; then only did he attain truly creative inspiration and make his vocation as a poet secure.[21] Longfellow's ultimate progression to Goethe and an active existence of work led gradually through the nocturnal dreamworld of Romanticism, where he temporarily took refuge and began the new phase of his poetic career.[22]

The lyrics inspired by that preoccupation with the German
Romanticists are the original poems and translations collected
under the title of *Voices of the Night*, itself suggestive of Novalis,
whose *Heinrich von Ofterdingen* Longfellow read in Heidelberg
with Clara Crowninshield.[23] In the second poem, called "Hymn
to the Night," there is a noteworthy similarity to the third of
the *Hymnen an die Nacht*. Here we are in what Pattee styles
"the full current of Romanticism"; in the same category is "Footsteps of Angels," where the life of the night becomes the only
reality, and the day an unreal existence.[24] That Novalis at once
stimulated independent production, perhaps explains his omis-
sion from Longfellow's published translations, among which
various lesser figures of elegiac bent are included.[25]

As a translator of German poety Longfellow mainly concerned
himself with the period from the sixteenth to the nineteenth
centuries. Notwithstanding his repeated praise of the Minne-
singers, above all Walther von der Vogelweide, no renditions of
their songs appear in the *Works*; his interest in the German
Middle Ages (particularly evidenced by *The Golden Legend*)
is almost solely reflected in original verse.[26] The sixteenth century is represented by two translations: an early one of *Hüt du
dich* ("Beware!") and one of his latest, *Ein' feste Burg* ("Our
God, a Tower of Strength Is He"), in some respects the most
forceful English version thus far composed.[27] For purposes of
comparison with the German, a stanza of each is given below,
the first being the opening lines of the folksong:

Ich weiss mir ein Maidlein	I know a maiden fair to see,
hübsch und fein,	
Hüt du dich!	Take care!
Sie kann wohl falsch und	She can both false and
freundlich sein,	friendly be,
Hüt du dich! Hüt du dich!	Beware! Beware!
Vertrau ihr nicht,	Trust her not,
Sie narret dich!	She is fooling thee!

Here the bantering air and the lightness of the *Volkslied* are
retained with a certain facile carelessness and no special concern

about metrical exactness. By contrast, the second example (the last stanza of the hymn) manifests the determined effort of a mature craftsman to deal with the challenging power of Luther's utterance:

Das Wort sie sollen lassen stahn	The Word they shall perforce let stand,
Und kein Dank dazu haben!	And little thanks they merit!
Er ist bei uns wohl auf dem Plan	For he is with us in the land,
Mit seinem Geist und Gaben.	With gifts of His own Spirit.
Nehmen sie den Leib,	Though they take our life,
Gut, Ehr, Kind und Weib;	Goods, honors, child and wife,
Lass fahren dahin!	Let these pass away,
Sie haben's kein Gewinn;	Little gain have they;
Das Reich muss uns doch bleiben.	The Kingdom still remaineth!

Longfellow's selections from Wilhelm Müller's anthology of seventeenth-century poets, which attracted his attention to that era, are for the most part disappointing.[28] We find Opitz, Dach, and Logau, but not even Paul Flem[m]ing, who lends his name to the hero of *Hyperion*. Such greater lyric talents as Gryphius and Gerhardt, to both of whom the Müller collection gives much space, are conspicuously lacking. The following will illustrate the rather free treatment of Opitz's *Die Sterne* ("The Stars"), a conventional—typically Opitzian—poem to the eyes of his beloved:

Schöne glänzt der Mondenschein	Shines the moonlight clear and cold.
Und die gülden Sternelein;	Shine the little stars of gold,
Froh ist alles weit und breit,	Glad are all things far and wide;—
Ich nur bin in Traurigkeit.	I alone in grief abide.

Of a higher order and better known is *Anke van Tharaw*,

translated by Longfellow as "Annie of Tharaw," of which the second and third couplets read:

Anke van Tharaw heft wedder eer Hart	Annie of Tharaw, her heart once again
Op my geröchtet ön Löw' on ön Schmart.	To me has surrendered in joy and in pain.
Anke van Tharaw, mihn Rihkdom, mihn Goet,	Annie of Tharaw, my riches, my good
Du mihne Seele, mihn Fleesch on mihn Bloet.	Thou, O my soul, my flesh and my blood.[29]

While these lines, replete with cognates, show great fidelity to the original (except "surrendered" for *geröchtet*), Dach's ode, *O wie selig seid ihr doch, ihr Frommen*, was virtually paraphrased by Longfellow, under the title "Blessed are the Dead."

The series of "Poetic Aphorisms," from Logau's *Sinngedichte*, begins with *Geld* ("Money"):

Wozu ist Geld doch gut?	Whereunto is money good?
Wer's nicht hat, hat nicht Mut;	Who has it not wants hardihood,
Wer's hat, hat Sorglichkeit;	Who has it has much trouble and care,
Wer's hat gehabt, hat Leid.	Who once has had it has despair.

Another, *Göttliche Rache*, translated as "Retribution," is said to have become, in Longfellow's wording, one of the most hackneyed quotations in the English language:[30]

Gottes Mühlen mahlen langsam, mahlen aber trefflich klein;	Though the mills of God grind slowly, yet they grind exceeding small;
Ob aus Langmut er sich säumet, bringt mit Schärf' er alles ein.	Though with patience he stands waiting, with exactness grinds he all.

Among translations by Longfellow of poems concerning death, perhaps the most outstanding instance, aside from the three Uhland ballads, is what Paul Flemming in *Hyperion* calls "a sweet and mournful poem from the Swiss Salis-Seewis," namely, *Das stille Land*, rendered as "The Song of the Silent Land."[31] The first of the three stanzas will serve to illustrate Longfellow's technique:

Ins stille Land!	Into the Silent Land!
Wer leitet uns hinüber?	Ah! who shall lead us thither?
Schon wölkt sich uns der Abendhimmel trüber,	Clouds in the evening sky more darkly gather,
Und immer trümmervoller wird der Strand.	And shattered wrecks lie thicker on the strand.
Wer leitet uns mit sanfter Hand	Who leads us with a gentle hand
Hinüber, ach! hinüber Ins stille Land?	Thither, oh, thither, Into the Silent Land?

If the lines quoted achieve a generally favorable impression, they do so through the total effect and in spite of characteristic weaknesses or discrepancies. "Into the Silent Land," differing in meter and stress, does not coincide with the simple brevity of *Ins stille Land*. The second line, burdened by "Ah," lacks the directness of Salis. In contrast to *hinüber-trüber*, "thither" and "gather" can scarcely be said to rhyme. The fourth line of the original expresses, through *immer trümmervoller wird*, a sense of motion not fully conveyed in the translated version, just as *hinüber* is stronger in meaning than "thither." Nevertheless, the spirit and atmosphere of Salis's poem are preserved to a remarkable extent.

The "Elergy Written in the Ruin of an Old Castle," i.e., Matthisson's *Elegie in der Ruine eines alten Bergschlosses geschrieben*, reminiscent of Gray in substance as well as title, is apparently the longest metrical translation from the German made by Longfellow—196 lines.[32] It begins:

Schweigend, in der Abenddäm-
merung Schleier,
  Ruht die Flur, das Lied
  der Haine stirbt,
Nur dass hier, im alternden
Gemäuer,
  Melancholisch noch ein
  Heimchen zirpt.
Stille sinkt aus unbewölkten
Lüften,
Langsam zieh'n die Herden von
den Triften,
  Und der müde. Landmann
  eilt der Ruh'
  Seiner väterlichen Hütte
  zu.

Silent in the veil of evening
twilight,
  Rests the plain; the wood-
  land song is still,
Save that here, amid these
mouldering ruins
  Chirps a cricket, mourn-
  fully and shrill.
Silence sinks from skies without
a shadow,
Slowly wind the herds from
field and meadow,
  And the weary hind to the
  repose
  Of his father's lowly
  cottage goes.

One sees how congenial the elegiac form and mood are to the American translator, who adheres more closely than usual to the meaning and rhythmic structure. "Hind," of course, bears a connotation not found in the more current German term *Landmann*. The adjectives "shrill" and "lowly" are but too instances of many where epithets have been added by Longfellow in the process of translating German poetry.

Still another poem in the mournful category is "The Dead," based on Stockmann's *Wie sie so sanft ruhn*. Further contemporaneous pieces of a minor sort are "The Wave" (*Die Welle*) by Tiedge and "Song of the Bell" (Schreiber's *An die Glocke*). One of the most often reprinted translations is "Allah" by Mahlmann. Its pleasing lilt has been rendered yet more popular by Chadwick's musical setting.[33] As one of Longfellow's last poetic interpretations, it reproduces its model with a greater faithfulness than is evident in some of his earlier renditions. The third (and final) stanza runs:

Fröhlich zu Allahs Wohnung
  Werd' ich hinüber gehn,

Gladly to Allah's dwelling
  Yonder would I take flight;

| Dort wird die Nacht verschwinden, | There will the darkness vanish, |
| Dort wird mein Auge sehn! | There will my eyes have sight! |

The only great lyrics from the classical period contained in the *Works* are the two "Wanderer's Night-Songs" from Goethe. Although Longfellow's version of the second *Wanderers Nachtlied* has been frequently praised, Walter Silz has recently pointed out various instances where the translator understandably fell short of the artless simplicity which characterizes the original.[34] Also, E. H. Zeydel stresses the desirability of a nearer approach to Goethe's meaning.[35] In spite of occasional padding (like "descending") or other imperfections, the first of these poems is unquestionably the more happily rendered:

Der du von dem Himmel bist,	Thou that from the heavens art,
Alles Leid und Schmerzen stillest,	Every pain and sorrow stillest,
Den, der doppelt elend ist,	And the doubly wretched heart
Doppelt mit Erquickung füllest,	Doubly with refreshment fillest,
Ach, ich bin des Treibens müde!	I am weary of contending!
Was soll all der Schmerz und Lust?	Why this rapture and unrest?
Süsser Friede,	Peace descending,
Komm, ach komm in meine Brust!	Come, ah, come into my breast![36]

Translations from Goethe not published by Longfellow are "Wanderer's Song in a Storm" (approximately a third of *Wanderers Sturmlied*), Faust's monologue in the scene *Wald und Höhle,* and the brief tenth number of *Venezianische Epigramme;* of these, the soliloquy is the most effective, with its unusual accuracy of meaning and skillful retention of the iambic pentameter.[37] Another poem left in manuscript is Schiller's *Kolumbus,* which Longfellow put into English for Charles Sumner (presumably in 1859). Of the various short fragments from Goethe, probably none is more competently rendered than the first stanza of *Harfenspieler* II, used as a motto for *Kavanagh*:

Wer nie sein Brot mit Tränen ass,	Who ne'er his bread in sorrow ate,
Wer nie die kummervollen Nächte	Who ne'er the mournful midnight hours
Auf seinem Bette weinend sass,	Weeping upon his bed has sate,
Der kennt euch nicht, ihr himmlischen Mächte!	He knows you not, ye Heavenly Powers![38]

Best represented is the Romantic era, or the early nineteenth century, with several of Longfellow's admirable translations of outstanding poems, which offset a number of mediocre pieces. Among the lyrics most often reprinted we find "The Sea Hath Its Pearls," namely the first three stanzas of *Nachts in der Kajüte*, by Heine, beginning:

Das Meer hat seine Perlen,	The sea hath its pearls,
Der Himmel hat seine Sterne,	The heaven hath its stars;
Aber mein Herz, mein Herz,	But my heart, my heart,
Mein Herz hat sein Liebe.	My heart hath its love.

Not one of Heine's masterpieces, it typifies in some degree the triviality and lack of earnestness which Longfellow deplored in its author, while admiring his talent.[39] Absence of end-rhyme in the original (there is, of course, assonance) manifestly facilitated a completely literal version, although the larger number of monosyllables in the English causes metrical variation and shorter lines throughout.

"The Hemlock Tree" (*Der Tannenbaum*) early attained popularity as a Christmas song; it is still sung by school children. Longfellow's fondness for German student ditties is reflected in his translating the *Fuchslied*, or *Was kommt dort von der Höh'?* (rendered as "What Comes There from the Hill?"), which occurs in *Hyperion*, in all its interminable length of twenty stanzas.[40] The originals of "The Happiest Land," "Song of the

Rhine," and "Forsaken"[41] are of anonymous authorship; "Silent Love," printed as a separate poem, is actually a stanza from the folksong *Gute Lehre*. Others from that period to be mentioned before we turn to the more salient examples, are: Müller's "The Bird and the Ship" (*Schiff und Vogel*) ; "Two Locks of Hair" (Pfizer's *Der Junggeselle*), one of the most appealing specimens of poetry dealing with sadness and death; and two, of a religious or contemplative nature, by Julius Mosen, "The Statue over the Cathedral Door" (*Das Standbild am Dome*) and "The Legend of the Crossbill" (*Der Kreuzschnabel*, No. 3) . This story of the humble creature's attempt to release the dying Saviour ends thus:

Kreuzesschnabel heisst das Vöglein:	And that bird is called the crossbill;
Ganz bedeckt von Blut so klar,	Covered all with blood so clear,
Singt es tief im Fichtenwalde	In the groves of pine it singeth
Märchenhaft und wunderbar.	Songs, like legends, strange to hear.

Thomas Moody Campbell ranks Uhland third among German authors of greatest significance for Longfellow, placing only Goethe and Jean Paul ahead of him.[42] Indeed, parallels between Uhland and Longfellow—with regard to their external lives as well as their poetry and scholarship—have been drawn repeatedly.[43] In the opinion of Pattee, the American poet's original ballads "might be translations from Uhland."[44] With what skill he reproduced *Das Glück von Edenhall*, as "The Luck of Edenhall," is evident from these lines (just after the fateful breaking of the goblet) :

Einstürmt der Feind mit Brand und Mord,	In storms the foe with fire and sword,
Der in der Nacht erstieg den Wall;	He in the night had scaled the wall,
Vom Schwerte fällt der junge Lord,	Slain by the sword lies the youthful Lord,
Hält in der Hand noch den Kristall,	But holds in his hand the crystal tall,
Das zersprungene Glück von Edenhall.	The shattered Luck of Edenhall.

Am Morgen irrt der Schenk allein,	On the morrow the butler gropes alone,
Der Greis in der zerstörten Hall';	The greybeard in the desert hall,
Er sucht des Herrn gebrannt Gebein,	He seeks his Lord's burnt skeleton,
Er sucht im grausen Trümmer- fall	He seeks in the dismal ruin's fall
Die Scherben des Glücks von Edenhall.	The shards of the Luck of Edenhall.

One may regret the use of "sword" twice in the first of the two stanzas quoted, and the number of feet varies in some lines, in a few of which there is a change from the stress of the original. The general metric pattern, however, is retained, while the unusual wealth of cognates and the consistent preservation of masculine rhymes contribute toward making it one of Longfellow's ablest feats as a translator. On the whole, he shows himself uniquely successful in conveying the spirit and atmosphere of the German ballad. Even "the crystal tall" is a phrasing justified by more than the exigency of rhyming with "Edenhall," for the ninth line of Uhland's poem reads: *Das hohe Trinkglas von Kristall*, which Longfellow renders as "The drinking-glass of crystal tall." This translation, dating from 1841, exhibits considerable progress beyond the two other renditions from Uhland, both inserted in *Hyperion*.

First, "The Black Knight," after Uhland's *Der schwarze Ritter* (a poem of singular appeal to Longfellow), shows less dexterity of form and phraseology.[45] Content is for the most part closely followed, but the effect is somewhat offset by an excess of masculine rhymes, while the German text has a preponderance of the feminine, as will be apparent from the passage recounting the banquet scene:

Und zur reichen Tafel kamen	To the sumptuous banquet came
Alle Ritter, alle Damen.	Every Knight and every Dame;
Zwischen Sohn und Tochter innen	'Twixt son and daughter all distraught,

Mit bangem Mute	With mournful mind
Der alte König ruhte,	The ancient King reclined,
Sah sie an mit stillem	Gazed at them in silent
Sinnen.	thought.
Bleich die Kinder beide	Pale the children both did look,
schienen;	
Bot der Gast den Becher	But the guest a beaker took:
ihnen:	
"Goldner Wein macht euch	"Golden wine will make you
genesen."	whole!"
Die Kinder tranken,	The children drank,
Sie täten höflich danken:	Gave many a courteous thank:
"Kühl ist dieser Trunk	"Oh, that draught was very
gewesen!"	cool!"

In certain lines, obviously, Longfellow has not quite attained the simple directness of the original, as in "to the sumptuous banquet" for *zur reichen Tafel*; or "the ancient King reclined" for *der alte König ruhte*. The "Oh!" at the end of the second stanza is another case of unlucky padding. "With mournful mind" retains alliteration but strays from the sense of *mit bangem Mute*, although a suggestion of the latter may be found in "distraught"—otherwise an extraneous element. Still, these and further possible strictures do not prevent Longfellow's version from being a good ballad per se, and one which to a great extent recreates the medieval setting and character of its model.

"The Castle by the Sea" could almost be called an adaptation of *Das Schloss am Meere*, in the light of the "embellishments" which Longfellow substituted for the direct language of Uhland. Some of the principal merits and defects of the former's ornate tendency are demonstrated by the following stanzas:

"Es möchte sich niederneigen	"And fain it would stoop downward
In die spiegelklare Flut,	To the mirrored wave below;
Es möchte streben und steigen	And fain it would soar upward
In der Abendwolkenglut!"	In the evening's crimson glow."

"Wohl hab' ich es gesehen,
Das hohe Schloss am Meer,
Und den Mond darüber stehen

Und Nebel weit umher."

"Der Wind und des Meeres
    Wallen,
Gaben sie frischen Klang?
Vernahmst du aus hohen
    Hallen
Saiten und Festgesang?"

"Die Winde, die Wogen alle

Lagen in tiefer Ruh',
Einem Klagelied aus der Halle

Hört' ich mit Tränen zu."

"Well have I seen that castle,
That Castle by the Sea,
And the moon above it
    standing,
And the mist rise solemnly."

"The wind and the waves of
    ocean,
Had they a merry chime?
Didst thou hear, from those
    lofty chambers,
The harp and the minstrel's
    rhyme?"

"The winds and the waves of
    ocean,
They rested quietly,
But I heard on the gale
    a sound of wail,
And tears came to mine eye."

Of the four stanzas above, the third is probably the most successfully rendered; the first, for all its fine imagery, suffers from
a double use of initial "and," not found in the original. "Solemnly," in the next stanza, is a further instance of a "more
forceful epithet" or of padding, depending on one's viewpoint.
Wallen, interpreted as "waves," is a verb used substantively to
describe the undulating motion which produces the *Wellen*
themselves. The chief examples of Longfellow's "embellishing"
are: "on the gale a sound of wail," for *einem Klagelied aus der
Halle*, and (in the last strophe of the poem) "They were moving
slow in weeds of woe," for *In schwarzem Trauerkleide*. Such
freedom with the wording inevitably entails metrical variations.
Yet, once again, in spite of the translator's liberties, he has given
us a ballad which, in its total impression, essentially and beautifully imparts the mood created by Uhland.

Among his translations of songs in the tone of the *Volkslied*, Longfellow has best recaptured the freshness and verve of the German utterance in "Whither?" (Wilhelm Müller's *Wohin?*). "I am persuaded," he makes Flemming in *Hyperion* say, "that in order fully to understand and feel the popular poetry of Germany, one must be familiar with the German landscape."[46] Thereupon, in connection with their discussion of Müller's lyric cycle "Die schöne Müllerin," the Baron recites its second poem, the one mentioned above. How well the author of *Hyperion* himself was qualified for poetic interpretation relating to the German scene, is evident from the three stanzas (out of six) which follow:

Ich hört' ein Bächlein rauschen	I heard a brooklet gushing
Wohl aus dem Felsenquell,	From its rocky fountain near,
Hinab zum Tale rauschen	Down into the valley rushing,
So frisch und wunderhell.	So fresh and wondrous clear.

Ist das denn meine Strasse?	Is this the way I was going?
O Bächlein, sprich, wohin?	Whither, o brooklet, say?
Du hast mit deinem Rauschen	Thou hast, with thy soft murmur,
Mir ganz berauscht den Sinn.	Murmured my senses away.

Lass singen, Gesell, lass rauschen	Let them sing, my friend, let them murmur,
Und wandre fröhlich nach!	And wander merrily near;
Es gehn ja Mühlenräder	The wheels of a mill are going
In jedem klaren Bach.	In every brooklet clear.

If here, too, Longfellow has varied the meter and occasionally added an epithet, and if, for example (in another stanza), " 'Tis the water-nymphs that are singing / Their roundelays under me" does not seem entirely adequate for *Es singen wohl die Nixen /*

Dort unten ihren Reihn, nevertheless, the poem in its entirety shows animation and sprightly motion almost rivaling the original. Longfellow introduced Müller to the English-speaking world primarily ,through this song, hardly equaled for spontaneity among the earlier translations.[47]

Literalness and adherence to form became increasingly important ,to Longfellow in his later years. Probably nowhere has he realized greater fidelity to a German original (outside of unrhymed verse) than with "Remorse," as he entitled his rendering of Platen's *Wie rafft' ich mich auf* (1870) for the second edition of *The Poets and Poetry of Europe,* published in 1871. Stanzas two and three are particularly deserving of attention:

Der Mühlbach rauschte durch felsigen Schacht,	The mill-brook rushed from the rocky height,
Ich lehnte mich über die Brücke,	I leaned o'er the bridge in my yearning
Tief unter mir nahm ich der Wogen in acht,	Deep under me watched I the waves in their flight,
Die wallten so sacht	As they glided so light
In der Nacht, in der Nacht,	In the night, in the night,
Doch wallte nicht eine zurücke.	Yet backward not one was returning.
Es drehte sich oben, unzählig entfacht,	O'erhead were revolving, so countless and bright,
Melodischer Wandel der Sterne,	The stars in melodious existence;
Mit ihnen der Mond in beruhigter Pracht,	And with them the moon, more serenely bedight;
Sie funkelten sacht,	They sparkled so light
In der Nacht, in der Nacht,	In the night, in the night,
Durch täuschend entlegene Ferne.	Through the magical, measureless distance.

Here the challenge of rhythmic structure and poetic diction by a supreme master of metrics is at least skillfully met, albeit not perfectly. Above all, the effect of the vowel *a,* as in *Nacht* and *sacht*, could not be achieved by the *i*-sound of "night" and "light." In view of the extraordinary difficulties encountered, it seems unlikely that this version will be surpassed. The three poems, "Remorse," "Whither," and "The Luck of Edenhall," represent, in my estimation, the height of Longfellow's art as a translator of German poetry.

Longfellow's poetic translations from the German, although spanning four decades, belong mainly to the years 1836-45, before he became almost completely occupied with the composition of his own longer works and the monumental task of turning Dante into English verse. One can observe a gradual evolution in the direction of greater exactness of content and metrical form. For instance, the lyrics interspersed throughout *Hyperion*, despite their impression of youthful vigor and inspiration, are technically less carefully wrought than the late renditions from Luther and Platen. Already in the 1840's, however, there are indications of an advance in his versification toward the ideal of close adherence to the original which the mature Longfellow cherished.

Whether they fully justify Hatfield's all but unconditional praise or not, the best of these translated versions evince a high order of proficiency in reproducing the substance and spirit of the German poems concerned. Longfellow cannot be dissociated from his time. If he was less conscientious than some twentieth-century translators regarding the number of feet in a given line or the strict retention of the rhythmic scheme, he usually compensated for such inaccuracies with a touch of genius sufficient to make the foremost examples of his talent a part of the American poetic tradition. It is only necessary to compare his accomplishments with those of his contemporaries (except Bayard Taylor, noted for an unsurpassed rendering of *Faust*), to appreciate Longfellow's unique merit as an interpreter of the German lyric. While one may take exception to individual translations, his aptitude in general and his astonishing versatility remain beyond all doubt.

Marinetti's *Le Futurisme* and Apollinaire's *Les Peintres Cubistes*

by
Richard M. Payne

THE INCREASING ATTENTION currently being devoted to Cubism and its French origins and the recognition of its importance have aroused an interest in Futurism, a similar and contemporaneous Italian movement in modern art. Guy Habasque has recently explained: "There is no question that, for all its shortcomings, Futurism made a very real contribution to the art of the period; its sincere, if too vociferous, advocacy of an omnipresent 'dynamism' could not fail to have profound repercussions and to arouse an interest all the greater for answering to the aspirations of other painters."[1]

Futurism embraced all the arts—from architecture to music—and practitioners of those arts were formal members of the movement, issuing manifestoes and participating in programs. The impact of Futurism on the art world, however, has never been equal to that of Cubism, for several reasons. In the first place, Futurism did not attract the talent generally considered comparable to that enlisted in the French movement. Though painters such as Boccioni, Carrà, Russolo, Balla, Severini, and writers such as Marinetti, Soffici, and Papini were Futurists at one time, they have never attained the international renown of Léger, Delaunay, Gris, Braque, Picasso, or of Apollinaire, Jacob, Réverdy, Cendrars, and Salmon.

Another reason for the preponderance of critical attention paid to the French movement, especially to its painters, is the ability of the French to promote their intellectual *démarches* on an international scale. Their critical and organizational genius has made them the impresarios of the art world. By comparison, the Italians have never been effective, since the Renaissance, in making an art program felt on the international scene. There is perhaps an historical explanation: artistic efforts are scattered throughout the peninsula; there is no focus in one city, a result of the political and linguistic anarchy of a people united in comparatively recent times.

The third apparent reason which may be suggested for Futurism's failure to compete with Cubism is the comic character of the Futurists' activities, which were often dismissed laughingly and frequently applauded with rotten vegetables. The Cubists—who never went to such extremes—were accorded a serious hearing. (Only the Dada movement of 1916 was a target of similar ridicule.)

The different tenor of the two movements can be ascribed in part to the unique personalities of their spokesmen, Filippo Tommaso Marinetti and Guillaume Apollinaire. The careers of these two men up to the time of the important manifestoes of their movements—Marinetti's *Le Futurisme* (1909) and Apollinaire's *Les Peintres cubistes* (1913)—show a parallel of literary talent and interest. Marinetti was the older, born in 1876 in Alexandria where his father was practicing law. When he was twelve, his parents put him into a *collège* there conducted by French Jesuits. This educational experience was cut short when he was expelled for introducing Zola novels into the school and publishing a literary periodical. His father then decided on Paris as a place for his son's education, and young Marinetti spent the next two years —from 1893 to 1894—in Paris. This sojourn ended when his father called him to Milan, where the family had settled. Though Signor Marinetti wanted his son to become a lawyer, the literary world had already captivated him. For some time he had been submitting poems in French to the *Anthologie Revue*, a Franco-Italian publication; and in 1898, he won first prize in a contest sponsored by a poetry-reading association organized by Catulle Mendès and Gustave Kahn. Hurrying to Paris, the young poet heard his poems read by Sara Bernhardt at one of the association's *Samedis populaires*. The publicity from the prize brought Marinetti invitations from literary periodicals, and his career in letters began. In the early part of the century, some of his poems were published in book form under the titles of *La Conquête des étoiles* and *Destruction*.[2] The poems were in free verse and in French. *La Conquête des étoiles* is conventional—and over-written—in its treatment of the sea as a symbol of man's struggle with the Absolute. The poetry of *Destruction*, however, contains the germ of Futurism with its demands for complete, anarchical freedom.

Marinetti's leadership in the literary world was evidenced when, in 1904, he founded a literary magazine in Milan, entitled simply *Poesia*, and was able to attract contributors of renown. The temerity of his leadership was demonstrated the next year by his vigorous defense of his friend Alberto Notari, who had been charged with publishing pornography. Marinetti's friendship was extended to politicians as well, and this alliance inspired his play *Roi Bombance*, which appeared in book form in 1905 and shortly afterward in an Italian translation.[3] This play, a sort of political allegory, dramatizes a struggle between the "haves" and "have-nots" in which the ruling class's main concern is food. It is an outrageous burlesque and seemed much more coarse and vulgar at the time of publication than it does today. The large number of impassioned critiques it evoked is evidence of its impact, and Marinetti sensed what force lay in such an attack on the taste of the time.

The Futurist program came to him, he wrote later, in October of 1908, and the first manifesto was drafted in the next few months; but it was not published until February 20, 1909, in *Le Figaro*. The manifesto, especially the Italian version which appeared in Volumes I and II of *Poesia* in the same year, doubtless caused excitement in artistic circles, as did *Roi Bombance* when it was produced that same year at the Théatre de l'Oeuvre —an event which has been considered by later critics as the beginning of Futurism.[4] Thus, Futurism was inaugurated, and manifestoes for the movement became almost a commonplace: political manifestoes; manifestoes by painters, by sculptors, by musicians, by architects, by feminists; manifestoes damning Venice, Montmartre, and all monuments of the past; in sum, manifestoes indicating the Futurists' attitude toward every phase of life including, finally, cooking.

World War I, which the Futurists acclaimed, ironically enough ended the movement for all practical purposes. But in spite of the changes in every sphere of art brought about by the war, Marinetti was relentless in his campaign for Futurism, continuing to issue manifestoes and other writings until the outbreak of World War II. He welcomed that war as he did all others and participated in it as long as he was physically capable. He died December 2, 1944, in Bellagio on Lake Como.

If Apollinaire did not equal Marinetti in longevity, there were yet many similarities between their lives. They had, for instance, Italian blood in common, for, if Marcel Adéma is right,[5] Apollinaire's father was Italian. His liaison with a Polish girl of twenty-two resulted in Apollinaire's birth in the Trastevere section of Rome in 1880, four years after Marinetti's birth. When he was a child of five, his mother took him and his brother to Monaco where Apollinaire attended a private Catholic school. During these schoolboy years on the Riviera, he started a literary periodical and began his poetical career. In 1900—after a brief stay in Belgium—Apollinaire reached Paris, where at first he was obliged to earn his living as a ghostwriter and pornographer. Leaving Paris in 1901, he acted as a tutor of French and in that capacity travelled around Germany. He returned to Paris in 1902 and henceforth considered it his home.

Apollinaire had been writing poetry since his youth. In 1903, he and André Salmon started the literary magazine, *Le Festin d'Ésope.* It did not last long but was followed by others; by 1907, Apollinaire had become something of a figure, one of sufficient stature to act as host for literary gatherings at his apartment. Surrounded by artists and writers, he began to assume leadership of the directions in paintings, all the while increasing his literary output. Henry Kahnweiler, the Paris art dealer, published his *L'Enchanteur pourissant* in 1909; the *Mercure de France* published his *La Chanson du Mal-Aimé* in the issue of May 1, 1909; and P. V. Stock in 1910 published his novel *L'Hérésiarque et cie.,* which almost won him the Prix Goncourt for that year. This publicity brought him a regular post with the *Mercure de France* and, later, with *L'Intransigeant*. The ebullience he felt from such good fortune was not long lasting, however, for the next year he was implicated in the theft of Leonardo's *Gioconda* from the Louvre and unjustly imprisoned for several days. But after a period of despondency, he rallied and returned to his literary activity with renewed energy, with Salmon and René Dalize founding another literary magazine, *Soirées de Paris*. He was also active in the art world arranging Cubist exhibitions, and he played a decisive part in the important Cubist exhibition at the *Salon des Indépendants* of 1911. In 1913, using and expanding material that had appeared previously as separate articles, he published his *Les Peintres cubistes*. This work was subtitled *meditations esthétiques*. Although other studies—*Du Cubisme* by Albert Gleizes and Jean Metzinger, also published by E. Figuiére in 1912, and *La Jeune Peinture française* by André Salmon, published by E. Messein in 1912—had been issued earlier, none evoked so much interest as *Les Peintres cubistes*. In 1913, too, Apollinaire's manifesto *L'Antitradition futuriste* was published both in Italian and French.[6]

At the outbreak of the war, Apollinaire enlisted in the army and eventually received a commission. He was seriously wounded at the front in March, 1916, and after undergoing a trepanation was returned to Paris for convalescence. During that period he published two collections of his writings, a play, and engaged in some journalistic work. But he never fully recovered from the wound, dying on November 9, 1918, in the influenza epidemic that was ravaging Europe.

Parallels abound in the careers of Marinetti and Apollinaire. Both, in the first place, were the products of a Catholic-Franco-Italian culture—by virtue of birth and education. They demonstrated literary interests at an early age and were part of the intellectual world of Paris during "La Belle Époque." Travelled cosmopolites, both defended the latest developments in the arts, intensely concerned with pushing the frontiers of art in a new direction. Apollinaire's childhood, however, was certainly more irregular than Marinetti's, for he was left largely in the trust of a nurse while his mother and father were on lengthy trips. Nor did his mother's long and tumultuous liaison with Jules Weil, a banker several years her junior, add to the boy's confidence. Marinetti's early years were not nearly so traumatic, for he was showered with affection by his parents. In fact, the greatest shock of his youth came when his mother's death occurred shortly after that of his brother.

Apollinaire, in spite of a childhood lacking in stability, was much warmer by nature than Marinetti. This difference is reflected in their poetry, for Apollinaire's is amorous and nostalgic while Marinetti's is aggressive and impersonal. Moreover, innovations abound in Apollinaire's poetry in contrast to the rather traditional style and manner of the Italian. Marinetti, on the other hand, displayed his originality in dramatic form, in *Roi Bombance*. Its special quality resides in its vulgarities, which are of an order found only in Alfred Jarry's *Père Ubu*. Offensive language and bad taste confront the reader at every turn as Marinetti mocks man's political institutions and his weaknesses. When the play was produced at the Théatre de l'Oeuvre in Paris in 1909, it incited a riot and received some strong condemnations from literary critics—one from the young Léon Blum. The same violence and unrestrained satire are characteristic of his manifesto on Futurism. While Apollinaire sets forth startlingly new ideas, he refrained from this militant tone.

The fact that Marinetti and Apollinaire knew each other undoubtedly resulted in amicable exchanges of theory in the early years. Marinetti met Apollinaire about the time of the publication of the Futurist manifesto when the Italian was in Paris and frequented a café popular with the Cubists, La Closerie de Lilas. Marinetti brought some of his Futurist cohorts to Paris in 1911 at Severini's insistence, and when their first exhibition was held there in 1912, their work became known to the Cubists. Up to the time of the publication of *Les Peintres cubistes* and for a short time thereafter, a warm relationship existed between the two schools. Apollinaire wrote his *L'Antitradition futuriste*, and an Italian translation was published in *Lacerba* on September 15, 1913. Soon, however, strained relations set in, apparently first caused by Apollinaire's discussion of "cubisme orphique,"[7] to which some Futurists took exception. By 1914, Marinetti was disclaiming Apollinaire's Futurist manifesto as not being in keep-

ing with true Futurist thought.[8] And in 1918, Apollinaire wrote
of the "désordre des italiens" in an article which appeared post-
humously in the *Mercure de France*.[9] Although the rupture
which developed was keenly felt, the movements obviously influenced one another to a large degree; for instance, a Futurist influence is discernible in the paintings of Cubists such as Marcel
Duchamp and Jacques Villon, and a Cubist influence is discernible in the Futurist Gino Severini.

Many of the differences and similarities between the two movements are to be found in the original manifestoes, which vary
considerably in length. Marinetti's consists of a relatively brief
introduction, eleven numbered points, and a conclusion. Apollinaire's is longer, filling seventy-five small (12mo) pages and
is divided into two sections, the first a general discussion of
contemporary art—most important for this study—and a second
part, entitled "Peintres nouveaux," analyzing the work of individuals.

The first paragraph of the Futurist manifesto sets the stage
for the melodrama of its creation, in an atmosphere of midnight
conspiracy and discovery: "Nous avions veillé toute la nuit, mes
amis et moi, sous les lampes de mosquée dont les cupoles de
cuivre aussi ajourées que notre âme avaient pourtant un coeur
électrique. Et tout en piétinant notre native paresse sur d'opu-
lents tapis persans, nous avions discuté aux frontières extrêmes
de la logique et griffé le papier de démentes écritures."[10] The
reaction to their unspecified dilemma (really Marinetti's, for the
friends were non-existent) is inspired by the rousing noise of
the double-decker trolley and passing automobiles; it consists of
Marinetti's call to action: "Allons, dis-je, mes amis! Partons!
Enfin, la Mythologie et l'Idéal mystique sont surpassées. Nous
allons assister à la naissance du Centaure et nous verrons bientôt
voler les première anges!" He rushes to his car and speeds through
the sleeping city into the country, toying with Death. This furious
drive, in a powerful automobile, is more than just a gesture; it
has other implications: "Sortons de la sagesse comme d'une
gangue hideuse et entrons comme des fruits pimentés d'orgueil
dans la bouche immense et torse du vent! . . . Donnons-nous à
manger a l'Inconnu, non par désespoir, mais simplement pour

enrichir les insondables résévoirs de l'Absurde." Immediately after uttering these words, his car plunged into a ditch. This misfortune apparently catalyzed Marinetti's thoughts for, on emerging from the ditch, he dictated the principles of Futurism. These eleven principles exhort man to violent, aggressive action (including war, "seule hygiène du monde") and expound a scorn for the past. Beauty is found only in conflict, and Art only in force. In an epilogue, he elaborates on these principles and adds the requirement of youthfulness for a Futurist, a requirement apparently distinctive in contemporary Italian movements.[11] Throughout the document, emphasis is placed on the vision of these young men, one that will last until they reach forty. Then, Marinetti predicts, they in turn will be destroyed by a younger generation. But for the moment, he feels that mankind is on the edge of a new, promising world in which theoretical changes of scientific theory (such as Einstein's) are taking place: "Nous sommes dur le promontoire extrême des siècles! . . . A quoi bon regarder dernière nous au moment qu'il nous faut défoncer les vantaux mystérieux de l'Impossible! Le Temps et l'Espace sont morts heir. Nous vivons déjà dans l'Absolu, puisque nous avons déjà crée l'éternelle vitesse omniprésente."

Although Walter Vaccari reports that the manifesto did not elicit much comment,[12] its position on the front page of *Le Figaro* gave it an air of authority and prestige. The Italian translation which followed shortly in Marinetti's magazine *Poesia* reinforced the French version and brought adherents to the movement. The date of Futurism's creation was fixed, a landmark in the artistic revolutions of our time.

Apollinaire's *Les Peintres cubistes* was a series of portraits of Cubist painters including, as the subtitle "Méditations esthétiques" indicates, the author's cogitations on Art and an exposition of artistic motives. As a point of departure, Apollinaire declares, on the first page of text: "Ce monstre de la beauté n'est pas éternel."[13] The idea of impermanence and change in art, obviously allied to Marinetti's insistence on motion, is essential to the understanding of Cubism. In a similar vein, he proclaims that Truth—which Art is to reveal—is not discoverable without a constant change of perspective: "La verité sera toujours renouvelée."[14] And he—like Marinetti—decries Pastism as an obstacle to clear vision: "On ne peut pas transporter partout avec soi le cadavre de son père. On l'abandonne en compagnie des autre morts. Et, l'on s'en souvient, on le regrette, on en parle avec admiration. Et, si l'on deveint père, il ne faut pas s'attendre à ce qu'un de nos enfants veuille se doubler pour la vie de notre cadavre."[15] Another related tenet is that man must no longer be a slave to Nature, for "Il est temps d'être maître."[16] He must discard it as a model for painting: "La vraisemblance n'a aucune importance, car tout est sacrifié par l'artiste aux verités, aux nécessités d'une nature supérieur qu'il suppose dans la découvrir. Le sujet ne compte plus ou s'il compte c'est à peine."[17]

Throughout the book, as indeed throughout his life, Apollinaire furthers the notion that the arts are entering a new phase, an era of discovery, either by direct statement as when he declares, "[La peinture pure] est un art plastique entièrement nouveau,"[18] or by using the word "nouveau" or a derivative.

It is well known that the manifestoes of Marinetti and Apollinaire have been extremely influential in present-day art. The points on which they speak in agreement defined some of the bases of the new direction in art. These similarities between them can be grouped into two categories, positive and negative. Both Marinetti and Apollinaire deprecated the past and its glories, although their tones are quite different. Marinetti urged an immediate and complete destruction of the museums and libraries (in the Italian version he added academies), and Apollinaire used the image, in the passage cited above, "cadavre de son père" to dramatize his censure. Another negative feature of the manifestoes is the disdain shown toward nature. Apollinaire was specific in eliminating nature as a source of inspiration, albeit he modified this view in later writings; and Marinetti, though not explicit, implies as much by a cataloguing of mechanical objects as sources of beauty. For both, nature was a sterile void undeserving of the artist's attention.

Both writers are positive on the subject of the artist's source of inspiration, and both their recommendations involve action. Apollinaire—and other Cubists—felt that portraying a given object or person in diverse ways was an essential function: "Les grands poètes et les grands artistes ont pour fonction sociale de renouveler sans cesse l'apparence que revêt la nature aux yeux des hommes."[19] Marinetti considered action as an end in itself, the effect of which was not as important as its quality. In aggressive and energetic action alone resided beauty: "Nous déclarons que la splendeur du monde s'est enrichie d'une beauté nouvelle: la beauté de la vitesse. Une automobile de course avec son coffre orné de gros tuyaux, tels des serpents à l'haleine explosive . . . une automobile rugissante qui a l'air de courir sur de la mitraille est plus belle que la *Victoire de Samothrace*." Although they viewed the relation of action to art differently, the importance both men gave it endowed the works of the Cubists and Futurists with a special vital quality. A final positive point of similarity is the exhilarating claim of discovery. Both writers were intense about the purposes of the movements they sponsored and excited about their prospects, and these emotions are conveyed to the reader. Marinetti believed that his movement involved much more than art and would affect the destiny of the nation; hence the diversity of Futurist manifestoes which followed his. Apollinaire had no such grandiose or inclusive pretensions, for only in the essay *L'Esprit nouveau et les poètes* does he hint at some of the broader implications of Cubist esthetics.

Many of the differences in the documents are explained by the different roles Marinetti and Apollinaire played in their respective movements, for they were quite diverse. Apollinaire never attempted to direct the course artists should take, relying on the general tendency in their work to define a movement, for the foundations of Cubism had already been laid in the painting of Picasso and Braque. As a matter of fact, Apollinaire did not even name the Cubist movement, although he used the name with an approbation and gave it a glamor never intended by its originator Henri Matisse, who used the word "cubes" in a description of a Braque canvas. In contrast to Apollinaire's relationship with Cubism, Marinetti spent his life organizing Futurism, issuing manifestoes in its behalf, and ordering the program. The name itself was his own invention, a name reached after discarding others such as Electricism and Dynamism. In short, Apollinaire's contribution was analytic, Marinetti's directive. This does not mean that Marinetti singlehandedly blazed the way for a new direction in Italian art; other less visible signs of a poetic revolt had appeared. But Marinetti conducted such a campaign and fought so untiringly that his position as leader of the movement was never disputed. Although his autocracy eventually resulted in criticism and defection by some members of the group, among them Giovanni Papini, his forceful leadership served to maintain a united front in the early years. This was not true of Cubism, for striking differences existed among the artists from the beginning, differences noted by Apollinaire and substantiated by Picasso, who has said: "When we invented Cubism we had no intention whatever of inventing cubism. We wanted to express simply what was in us. Not one of us drew up a plan of campaign, and our friends the poets followed our efforts attentively, but they never dictated to us."[20] Since Marinetti saw himself as a crusader, the tone of his manifestoes is at once evangelistic and vindictive. He urged adherence to his program and heaped scorn on past traditions. Apollinaire was violent only once—and then at Marinetti's instigation—when he wrote the manifesto *L'Antitradition futuriste,* and even then he qualified its insults with praise and mitigated its force with subsequent explanations.

An essential difference in the manifestoes may be attributed to variant talents of Marinetti and Apollinaire. First of all, Apollinaire was a poet. He is remembered chiefly for his poems and the poetical innovations he introduced, rather than as an art critic—although his name invaribly figures in bibliographies of modern art. He seemed little concerned with politics; even the war, so disturbing to most writers, was a colorful spectacle to him, annoying only because it interferred with love-making. His prose is poetical and, therefore, much less direct than Marinetti's. Even the Futurist manifesto prepared for *Lacerba* has an insouciant grace and charm, in spite of the inclusion of a coarse word. Marinetti had the astuteness to admire this sophistication.

Marinetti's special quality and achievement should also be recognized. For he is a poet of stature but—most important—he adapted to the modern temper a widespread literary genre which evokes art theorists as diverse as Du Bellay and Wordsworth: the manifesto. One critic has emphasized this point: "Spesso i manifesti di Marinetti, a parte il valore pratico che il lettore potrà attribuire alle teorie in essi bandite, son null'altro che poesia. In essi il Futurismo è liberato in forma. È possibile che un manifesto sia per gli spiriti mediocri un contenuto grezzo che s'impone per diventare forma: in Marinetti è arte; negli altri può essere materia pratica: in lui è lirica; negli altri può essere cultura: in lui è sentimento; negli altri scuola: in lui vita."[21] There was ample opportunity to exercise this talent, and Marinetti wrote countless manifestoes (he himself did not know how many) on a variety of subjects. In these pronouncements the charm and subtlety of Apollinaire are lacking; instead, there is a direct and ringing cry to action. Like so many of his fellow countrymen, Marinetti displays emotion—in contrast to Apollinaire's thoughtfulness. Marinetti was at the forefront of an extreme group, exhorting greater extremes; Apollinaire remained in a position where his analysis of the battle would prove more effective and influential.

His aggressive emotionalism is the basis of Marinetti's misguided glorification of war and of his frenetic exploitation of the mechanical world, never utilized to such a degree by Apollinaire. The intensity of Marinetti's feelings may account for his diatribes against reverence for the past and its monuments. In spite of the gross word directed against past institutions and creations in his manifesto *L'Antitradition futuriste*, Apollinaire viewed the past with appreciation and even explained that word in a letter: "Le merde en musique de mon manifeste ne s'appliquait pas à l'oeuvre des anciens, mais à leur nom opposé comme barrière aux nouvelles générations."[22]

The most significant distinction between Cubism and Futurism lies in their views of motion in relation to art. The Futurists held that forceful, energetic—"dynamic" is the word they used—motion was essential to art; and they placed the artist at the vortex of that motion, seeking expression in radiating, swirling lines. Thus the artist's orientation toward action is conceived of as an interior one, contrary to the Cubists who believed that, instead of being caught up in a force, the artist should systematically use motion or action to explore all aspects of a subject. "The right of the painter to move freely around his subject," as John Golding puts it,[23] was at variance with the concept of the Futurists, particularly of Marinetti. Apollinaire is not specific in requiring motion, since Cubism is to some extent concerned with static conditions, but it is implied by his remarks concerning the renewing of appearances, where a shift in viewpoint must be presupposed. From these two opposing approaches to motion— fundamental in understanding Futurism and Cubism—comes the real distinction between the two schools. Both views represent a fresh departure in the arts, a break with academic pedantry and a dividing line in the history of creative activity. This was in itself an important contribution.

Marinetti and Apollinaire fixed the movements by their mani- festoes, *Le Futurisme* of 1909 and *Les Peintres cubistes* of 1913, and these documents may be regarded as foundations of the two movements. It would be inaccurate to say that Marinetti and Apollinaire were responsible for Futurism and Cubism. They did, however, have the keenness of vision to capture the creative spirit of the time and give it form: they were augurs of a new epoch in the arts.

T. S. Eliot, Rémy de Gourmont, and Dissociation of Sensibility

by

T. R. Rees

A SINGLE PHRASE of T. S. Eliot's has set off one of the most heated controversies in twentieth-century literary criticism. Critics and scholars have argued for more than a generation over this phrase, heaping a prodigious mass of erudition and literary squabbling on either side of the argument. Indeed, as one scholar facetiously remarked, the quarrel of the Ancients and the Moderns in Swift's *Battle of the Books* seems rather tame in comparison with the present battle of sensibilities and critical temperaments over Eliot's term, "dissociation of sensibility."

Paradoxically enough, few if any of the disputants have bothered to investigate fully Eliot's Continental sources in this matter, chief of whom is Rémy de Gourmont, the leader of the French Symbolist movement at the turn of the century. The present paper will attempt, therefore, to illuminate Eliot's doctrine by the light of comparative Anglo-French studies.

One of Eliot's most formidable antagonists in this controversy is F. W. Bateson, who actually traces his use of the terms *dissociation* and *sensibility* to the prose writings of de Gourmont.[1] Had he pursued his investigation further, the critic might have contributed a good deal toward the full explication of these terms. But his investigation stops short; it degenerates into a mere quibble with Eliot and an attack on de Gourmont. Let us first assess the tenability of Bateson's position, and then consider Eliot's doctrine in reference to de Gourmont's aesthetic philosophy.

Bateson correctly remarks that Eliot first employed the term "sensibility" in an essay entitled "The Metaphysical Poets" in

1921. In that essay he stated that the metaphysical poets were possessed of unified sensibility, in which both thought and feeling were merged into one act of thinking; he perceived in Chapman a "sensuous apprehension of thought" and commended Jonson and Chapman because they "incorporated their erudition into their *sensibility*: their mode of feeling was . . . altered by their reading and thought." But in the second half of the seventeenth century, writers began to think and feel "by fits"—they thought in prose and felt in poetry. Eliot calls this a "dissociation of sensibility."[2]

Since all clear thinking proceeds from logical definitions, Bateson first attempts to define sensibility in terms of Eliot's use of the word. He wisely concludes at the outset that Eliot was not referring to the ability to feel "the Misery of others with inward Pain," which is one of the eighteenth century senses of the term.[3] He states that Eliot referred both thought and emotion to the faculty of sensibility and that a "unification of sensibility" implied a harmonious relationship between one's thoughts and one's emotions and feelings. But what particularly seems to puzzle Bateson is the suspicion that the *New English Dictionary* does not recognize Eliot's use of the term. He seems to believe that sensibility is nothing more than "the faculty which registers sensations"—and yet the *New English Dictionary* lists "mental perception" as one of the alternate definitions.[4] If thought is not a species of mental perception, then our whole system of lexicography applicable to psychology will have to be revised.

Hereupon Bateson conjectures that Eliot must have grafted the term as a French loan-word: but in French, as "susceptibility of impression," it refers to both thought and emotion, for impressions may be sensuous, emotional, or intellectual; and although parts of the definition refer *specifically* to sensation, other parts refer *generically* to thought, emotion, and sensation.[5] The real villain, according to Bateson, is the French critic Rémy de Gourmont, from whom Eliot is accused of borrowing the term. Sensibility in the works of de Gourmont "does and does not include the element of thought." Yet, like Eliot's use of the term in English, de Gourmont's double use of the word proceeds from the authority of French dictionaries, and his employment of the term is not at variance with other French writers who wrote from the 1880's to the present day. Since French is almost universally conceded to be a rather precise language, it is not likely that the term *sensibilité* could remain in active circulation among scholars, critics, and philosophers without any serious semantic disputes, unless it preserved its purity as a definitive and logical aesthetic term.

As if anticipating his failure to prove Eliot wrong in including both thought and emotion in his conception of "sensibility," Bateson next searches for inconsistencies in Eliot's employment of the term. He discovers what he calls a "paradox." In certain places Eliot has employed "sensibility" as a synthesis of our capacity to think and to feel; but in one place he appears to have restricted the sense of the term to feeling or sensation: "The feeling, the sensibility, expressed in the 'Country Churchyard' is . . . cruder than that in the 'Coy Mistress.'" Exception is taken to this because "the word 'sensibility' is obviously being used here to define the word 'feeling.'" But does this particular grammatical or syntactical structure necessarily imply definition?

The second word might also be used to expand the meaning of "feeling"—since feeling itself has a wide and variable range of definition. It might be restricted to the tactile sense—to *feel* a hot stove. Or it could apply to the perception of metaphysical truths—e.g., to *feel* the truth of the existence of God. If it is true, for example, that Brahms had a "feeling" for Beethoven's methods of composition, or that the pianist Walter Gieseking had a "correct feeling" for executing the piano compositions of Debussy, we may definitely infer an intellectual grasp of these composers' works resulting from long hours of repeated practice, study, and exposure to the influence of these masters. It used to be said that the late Maestro Toscanini conducted "with authority." This authority proceeded from a "correct feeling," and this correct feeling in turn proceeded from an intimate familiarity with the composers' scores; his musician's intelligence, furthermore, enabled him to view synchronously several parts moving at once. Feeling, then, is often a *technical* matter, involving both intellectual and emotional elements, as in music.

Even if the word "sensibility" were used in Eliot's sentence to define "feeling," it merely transposes feeling into its generic key—that is, into a sense including both intellectual and emotional elements. Therefore, while recognizing the usefulness of Bateson's efforts as a contributor to our dictionary of critical terms, we must reject the notion of paradox in Eliot's employment of the term in question, in which emotion and thought turn out to be the synthesized elements of a unified sensibility.

The critic now arrives at the conclusion that Rémy de Gourmont, whose psychology he describes as a "ramshackle affair," has been a bad influence on Eliot, and he traces Eliot's use of "dissociation" and "sensibility" to him. Even Eliot must have sensed de Gourmont's inadequacies as a critic, Bateson goes on to say, because Eliot's own ideas and intuitions are "incomparably profounder and more original than Gourmont's." This denigration of Rémy de Gourmont does him no credit. It would be strange if a member of the French Academy, well-trained in philosophy; a careful student of French literature, whose reading, judging from the vast range and quality of his critical studies, was extensive and profound; a skilled amateur in the study of physiology; and the leading critic and exponent for the Symbolist poets as well as one of the main promoters of Nietzsche's high reputation in France—strange indeed if such a man should evolve a theory of psychology which turned out to be a "ramshackle affair."

One of the chief tasks of any aesthetic critic is to evaluate the artistic qualities of living geniuses in terms of universal principles which apply equally for all civilized ages within a given system of culture. De Gourmont's translator, William Aspenwall Bradley, considers this French critic to be "perhaps the most corrosive intellectual agent of our time, after Nietzsche," and the student of literature will probably find "no intellectual poison more subtly stimulating."[6] His *Problème du style* is described by Martin Turnell as "one of the finest works of general criticism that has appeared during the past fifty years"; and it should be "almost as valuable to the English as to the French specialist."[7] His observation that " 'style is a specialization of sensibility' is a landmark in the history of criticism."[8] Turnell believes, further-more, that de Gourmont is "more stimulating, more of a critic than Saint-Beuve."[9]

Let us now examine Bateson's proposition that Eliot derived his theories of sensibility chiefly from the French critic. It would seem more likely that Eliot syncretized his own theory from multiple sources, which of course included de Gourmont, but which did not exclude all others. Eliot wrote in 1923 that F. H. Bradley, Sir James Frazer, and Henry James were the "three major influences affecting his work."[10] From Bradley, on whom he wrote a doctoral dissertation at Harvard, he gained the notion that the life of the mind " 'exists in the union of intellect and emotion.' "[11] And within the Hegel-Bradley frame of reference, each sensation has a "thought side" as well as a "felt side." If, for example, we feel a twitch of pain, we might exclaim, "What is this?" "This" refers to the *pure sensation* of pain (Lockean) ; the "what" refers to the *thought* of it, or its relativity to other pains.[12] A unified sensibility, therefore, would comprehend both sides of a particular feeling.

But let us dispense at once with the ambiguous terms "thought" and "feeling," inasmuch as each term overlaps extensively into the other's field of definition. If we were to say, for example, "We *thought* we heard a noise," and "We *feel* the interior correctness of Einstein's theories of atomic fission"—then the first sentence would imply an almost purely auditory sensation, and the second sentence would clearly imply intellectual comprehension.

Cognizant of the ambiguity of such terms, let us designate the three coexistent and coinvolgent faculties of the human mind by the more scientific terms of philosophical psychology: (1) sensory, (2) affective or emotional, and (3) cerebral or intellectual. While we are distinguishing these three different but inseparable faculties, we must bear in mind, with Coleridge, that "distinction is not division." But in order "to obtain adequate notions of any truth, we must intellectually separate its distinguishable parts."[13]

A single thought or sensation involves all three of these faculties working together, but the *relative proportion* of sensory, affective, and intellectual elements varies both with individuals

and with any given moments of time within the scope of an individual's existence. Also, the degree of co-ordination between
these three faculties varies with different individuals at different
moments of time. A unified sensibility implies a high degree of
co-ordination; whereas a *dissociated* one, one that thinks and
feels, let us say, "by fits," would be necessarily unco-ordinated
to a high degree. And, of course, we discover graduated stages
of co-ordination between these three general faculties of the
human mind. In neither case, however, could we consider these
terms in the *absolute* sense (i.e., in terms of pure intellect or
pure sensation), inasmuch as there are no absolutely perfect or
absolutely imperfect human creatures—this we hold to be axiomatic.

Now we must explore the "ramshackle" psychological observations of Rémy de Gourmont in order to discover the nature of
the cerebration as it exists in what the academic world regards
as geniuses of the highest order: the type of thinking, in short,
which is the product of a unified sensibility.

In an essay entitled "Subconscious Creation," which is an original contribution to the field of philosophical psychology, Rémy
de Gourmont strikes close to the very roots of the creative thinking process. And it is here, I suggest, that T. S. Eliot discovers
the scaffolding for his notions of the "unified sensibility." The
relationship between the unified sensibility and the subconscious
reasoning process, incidentally, is ignored in Bateson's essay.

De Gourmont tells us, for example, that through repeated
training and systematic exposure to the facts of life, science and
art, the normal human mind not only accumulates a "deep reser-
voir of verbal memory"[14] but also develops *subconscious* powers
of *inductive reasoning* which are superior to ordinary deductive
logic; and that conscious deductive reasoning, proceeding from
the analytic faculty, often interferes with this subconscious cerebral state, which has the power to syncretize and synthesize diverse elements of thought. In short, we frequently disturb unconscious "mental assimilation" by "premature logic";[15] we
"break the series of association in order to create in the mind the
first link of a new volitional idea."[16] As examples of men in whom
this type of thinking may be observed, de Gourmont cites the

cases of Goethe, Mozart, and von Humboldt, all of whom specifically subordinate the role of conscious deductive reasoning to the higher and more synthetic faculty of subconscious creation. This mode of cerebration does not exclude scientists and philosophers: "Imaginative intellectual creation is inseparable from the frequency of the subconscious state, and in this category of creations must be included the discovery of the scientist and the ideological construction of the philosopher."[17]

This essay constitutes merely the fruition and consolidation of previous materials on the same subject, but it nevertheless survives as one of the most comprehensive theories of subconscious creation to date. The germs of this theory, however, seem to originate with Sir Joshua Reynolds; and although de Gourmont was evidently unfamiliar with this particular discourse of Reynolds, the similarity of their ideas on the subject of reasoning is surprisingly close.

Recognizing that all arts "address themselves only to two faculties of the mind, its imagination and its sensibility,"[18] Reynolds thereupon extends his logic into the very nature of reasoning itself: "There is in the commerce of life, as in art, a sagacity which is far from being contradictory to right reason, and is superior to any occasional exercise of that faculty; which supersedes it; and does not wait for the slow progress of deduction, but goes at once, by what appears a kind of intuition, to the conclusion."[19] Indeed, with this type of reasoning there is such a rapid induction of particulars that the thinker "cannot recollect and bring before him all the materials which gave birth to his opinion."[20]

But are we to conclude from this that man's most correct observations are merely the result of haphazard opinions, which in turn are products of chance variation? By no means. In fact, "the right impression still remains fixed in his mind" as the "result of the accumulated experience" of his "whole life"; and furthermore "this mass of collective information . . . ought to prevail over that reason, which . . . will probably comprehend but a partial view of the subject; and our conduct in life as well as in the arts is, or ought to be, generally, governed by this habitual reason. . . ."[21] Therefore, man's thoughts "proceed, not perhaps from caprice," but from the "fulness of his mind"; and they suffuse his mind "without any conscious effort."[22] For example, a scholar who had dedicated his life to the study of Poe or Flaubert would not be apt to utter haphazard opinions in regard to these authors; his opinions, or rather judgments, would be the product of a lifetime of studious observation and collection of facts and hence would often be logical conclusions arrived at inductively through the intense natural study of particulars. His remarks would be conditioned and weighted by his experience in these fields of scholarship.

Nor is this type of thinking restricted to sensory perception or the affective states of mind. It is "not addressed to the gross senses, but to the desires of the mind."[23] And, by parity of reasoning, the proper sensibility would not be confined to the lower faculties but would involve the harmonious operation of all faculties of the human mind—sensory, affective, and intellectual.

Wordsworth tells us that the true thinker, if he has "more than usual organic sensibility" or capacity to receive mental perceptions, and if he repeats his thoughts on the same subject often enough—this man will be able to communicate with his reader and enlighten him, "for our continued influxes of feeling are modified and directed by our thoughts, which are indeed the representatives of our past feelings."[24] Here Wordsworth is alluding to a special co-ordination between our thoughts and feelings, a quality of truly meditative minds: this is not unlike the views of T. S. Eliot on the unified sensibility.

Shelley recognizes that conscious volition and deductive reasoning are at variance with the processes of poetic composition: "Poetry is not like reasoning, a power to be exerted according to the determination of the will. A man cannot say, 'I will compose poetry.' "[25] Indeed, poetic composition is "experienced principally by those of the most delicate sensibility and most enlarged imagination." Conclusions are arrived at with such rapidity and force that the mind cannot account for "the origin, the gradations, or the media of the process"; as an example of one in whom this process operated, Shelley elicits Milton, who conceived the *Paradise Lost* as a whole "before he executed it in portions."[26]

Sir Herbert Grierson refers to this same phenomenon, which he calls "intuitional reasoning." This is "reason working on more subtle and complex data than the thinker can hope to define clearly"; it lies in a region which is "half conscious, half unconscious," and "the premises are so subtle, so delicate, so numerous that it is almost impossible but that some of them will escape us." He recognizes this type of thinker in Pascal's *"l'esprit de finesse,"* as opposed to *"l'esprit de géometrie,"* the latter being a deductive type of thinker.[27] He also recognizes the biblical prophets, Milton, and the metaphysical poets as being representatives of the intuitional reasoning process; these are men who experience intense moments of emotional strain, in which thoughts occur with "compelling force" and struggle for expression.[28]

Unfortunately, Shelley and Grierson, by restricting this process chiefly to poetical composition or religious revelation, have neither penetrated the problem as deeply as Reynolds nor comprehended it as philosophically and as completely as de Gourmont. They seem to regard subconscious reasoning as some mysterious, half-religious and half-superstitious force which transforms the thinker into a visionary or mystic, into an agent of some supernatural exterior influence. The loose term "intuition" cannot explain this process in scientific terms. It would be better to call it subconscious inductive reasoning, since it refers to the automatic processes of cerebration as they really existed in such highly organized minds as Mozart or Poincaré, the French mathematician—processes which are common to both artist and scientist.

This is not to say that deductive reasoning is altogether useless, but rather that it is complementary though subordinate to the subconscious inductive reasoning process. In fact, the main points in the "Discourses" of Sir Joshua Reynolds, written in praise of inductive methods, are perhaps arrived at by reasoning processes chiefly *deductive*. The office of philosophical inquiry is mainly to discern analogical operations and abstract principles of consistency from them; to analyze and then to synthesize the diverse phenomena of nature into organic patterns of truth—and for this, both modes of reasoning are necessary. Nevertheless, conscious reasoning merely " 'combines, modifies and directs' " what has already been conceived; " 'it cannot create, because the vital principle is not in it.' "[29] It is pertinent to observe that after Coleridge and Arnold launched into analytical criticism, they no longer created poetry. An intelligence possessed of a unified sensibility, therefore, would be better equipped to perform the technical functions of philosophy than an intelligence whose sensibility has been partially dissociated into its sensory, affective, and intellectual components, for the force of the whole mind must be brought to bear on the subject, whether it be a philosophical inquiry or an artistic composition.

The properly conditioned sensibility, therefore, is trained and nurtured by masses of heterogeneous facts, theories, works of art, and other exterior cultural influences, all of which form the subject-matter from which reasonable judgments are inferred. A person trained in deductive logic alone, whose sensibility to higher cultural influences is relatively uncultivated, is apt to err in matters of high judgment. As T. S. Eliot has remarked: "On the contrary, the true generalization is not something superimposed upon an accumulation of perceptions; the perceptions do not, in a really appreciative mind, accumulate as a mass, but from themselves as a structure; and criticism is the statement in language of this structure; it is a development of sensibility."[30]

I have cited the use of the term "sensibility" by Reynolds, Shelley, and Wordsworth, and with each we discover an inclusion of intellectual elements. Let us see whether other writers restrict sensibility merely to the faculty of sensory impression or sensation, as Bateson would have it in his criticism of Eliot's usage.

In Chapter XIV of his *Biographia Literaria*, Coleridge informs us that Wordsworth's admirers were found chiefly "among young men of strong sensibility and meditative minds."[31] By sensibility Coleridge here means susceptibility to aesthetic influences, these influences being both intellectual and emotional in character. Speaking in Chapter XVII about the capacity "for the human soul to prosper in rustic life," he warns that "education, or original sensibility, or both, must pre-exist, if the changes, forms and incidents of nature are to prove sufficient stimulant. And where these are not sufficient, the mind contracts and hardens by want of stimulants: and the man becomes selfish, gross, and hard-hearted."[32] Since this passage refers to the development of the mind, does the term "sensibility" not imply a susceptibility to *mental* influences? Here Coleridge has related one's capacity to think to his original sensibility: so that faulty perception might impair one's powers of conception.

E. D. H. Johnson's use of the term comprehends a high proportion of intellectual elements. He notes that in Matthew Arnold's time there was no longer any communication between individuals on the "level of the deeper sensibilities."[33] Is he alluding here to the level of mere sensory impression? Does he mean that the educated members, the intelligentsia of Victorian society, despite the presence of Gilbert and Sullivan, were no longer able to transmit and receive sensory impulses among themselves? I think not. Browning felt that a great work of art would always communicate "so long as the sensibilities of its audience had not been deadened by tradition or materialized by social pressures."[34] Surely our capacity to appreciate great art is not simply a matter of sensation. Johnson speaks also of the true "aesthetic sensibilities" of artists. If the term *aesthetic* implies both affective and intellectual elements, how could this type of sensibility exclude its intellectual component? And "aesthetic sensibility" seems to be a rather common term among literary critics.

In referring to Matthew Arnold, Alba H. Warren strongly implies that the term "impressionable sensibility" is nearly synonymous with "poetic temperament."[35] Here he appears to be stressing the sensory and emotional elements of sensibility, but this does not necessarily rule out the intellectual.

Edgar Allan Poe, a precise user of terms, appears to conceive of sensibility as a sort of sensitive filter for aesthetic-sensory impressions; as a faculty which not only *perceives* exterior influences with a certain adroitness but also *executes* "exalted" works of art: "I was aware, however, that his very ancient family had been noted, time out of mind, for a peculiar sensibility of temperament, displaying itself, through long ages, in many works of exalted art . . ."[36] As a result of this strange "sensibility of temperament," Roderick Usher "suffered much from a morbid acuteness of the senses; the most insipid food was alone endurable; he could wear only garments of certain texture; the odours of all flowers were oppressive; his eyes were tortured by even a faint light; and there were but peculiar sounds, and these from stringed instruments, which did not inspire him with horror."[37] What does this mean? It means simply that his acute faculty of perceiving sensory impressions manifested itself in the creation of works of art, including music and literature, two highly complex art-forms not devoid of intellectual ingredients. The successive members of the ancient house of Usher, therefore, were possessed of "unified sensibilities" inasmuch as they, like Eliot's metaphysical poets, could translate sensations into thoughts. It is thus that we arrive at the conclusion that the "formal, intellectual and emotional aspects of the image or symbol" are really "inseparable," and "its indissociability is its prime quality."[38]

And yet, despite the fact that many well-known authors and critics include either intellectual or affective elements, or both, in their aggregate conception of the term "sensibility," Bateson asks that we restrict its application to the faculty of mere *sensation*. This seems hardly possible or plausible in the light of almost universally accepted usage.

To recapitulate, then, let us say that Eliot includes intellectual, emotional, and sensory elements in his comprehension of the term "sensibility," insofar as a man's sensibility is the product of his nature, his training, and his exposure to exterior influences. All other things being equal, a man's mind is conditioned and developed by his experience, and this will in turn develop his sensibilities or his faculty of perceiving as well as executing diverse effects in the real world.

That which is *purely* intellectual exists only in the realm of abstractions; similarly for things considered as *purely* sensuous. Nothing exists in pure state, *in vacuo*, except that which we wish to distinguish arbitrarily for intellectual purposes. The correlevance of all mental faculties in the execution of complex thoughts is a fact well recognized by contemporary psychologists. For these reasons it would be impossible to restrict the term "sensibility" to mere sensory phenomena if we are to add a real living term to our critical vocabulary—i.e., a term which encompasses real phenomena. The philosophical psychologist considers the divorce of one mental faculty from another unsound and unreal. From studies of the physiological chemistry of the brain, we discover that Rémy de Gourmont did not err when he stated that thought was merely the "flowering" (*la floraison*) of a physiological process: his observations concerning the subconscious inductive reasoning process bear this out fully.

In conclusion, it can be said that the term *sensibility*, by which is meant "susceptibility of impression," is a valid aesthetic term within the framework of the subconscious inductive reasoning process. Without such a term and the aesthetic philosophy behind it, literature and the arts would be markedly poorer. For this reason a comparative Anglo-French reading of such terms as "sensibility" and "dissociation" will ultimately enhance the exactness of our critical terminology. Since the first of these has reappeared as a French loan-word, let us incorporate it into our own critical vocabulary and use it as the French and T. S. Eliot have used it, thereby increasing the precision of our language as an instrument of thought.

Marc Connelly's *The Green Pastures* and Goethe's *Faust*

by
John T. Krumpelmann

THE LITERATURE OF Western Europe presents diverse masterly treatments of the biblical theme of the fall and subsequent redemption of man. In Dante's medieval, Catholic version emphasis is placed on the "Inferno," the "Purgatorio," and the "Paradiso," that is, on the submundane and supermundane phases of the theme, but even there earth is not lost sight of. As C. H. Grandgent points out: "His [Dante's, man's] only way lies through the earth from side to side, traversing the whole of Hell, after which he is to ascend the mountain of Purgatory. . . . Thence he is to be lifted up to Heaven."[1] In the northern Europe of Puritanical England Milton's muse sings in *Paradise Lost:*

> Of Man's First Disobedience, and the Fruit
> Of that Forbidd'n Tree, whose mortal taste
> Brought Death into the World, and all our woe.
>
> (I,1-3)

In his less successful *Paradise Regained* the redemption of the human race is the theme. In Germany Goethe in his youth surreptitiously read Klopstock's popular Milton-inspired epic of the redemption, the *Messiah.*

In the Germanic epics the protagonist, subordinate to God and Satan, is "man" in the generic sense, whereas Goethe, the individualist, writing in a century of individualism, more in the

199

manner of Dante makes *"a* man," Faust, the hero of his great
work, which is no longer, as were its predecessors, an epic poem,
but a drama presenting on the stage action which leads *Vom
Himmel durch die Welt zur Hölle* (242), and introduces on the
stage as a character in the drama *der Herr,* God, the Father. This
innovation was considered by many of Goethe's contemporaries,
and is still considered by the British public in general, as sacri-
legious.[2]

Goethe, the last man of the Renaissance, chooses as his protagonist a sixteenth-century Renaissance individual, who would
take as his province not only all knowledge but also all experience. In the present century, when the emphasis has been shifted
from individualism to the group, "racism," as, for example in
Gerhart Hauptmann's dialect drama *Die Weber* (*Da Waber,*
1892) and Ernst Toller's *Masse-Mensch,* (1919), Marc Connelly
in *The Green Pastures* depicts the fall and redemption, not as
typified by the vicissitudes of a titanic personality, but as the
story of the fall and redemption of the human race as set forth
in the experiences of the naïve, childlike ("Unless you become
as one of these you shall not enter the kingdom of Heaven")
colored race, our southern (Louisiana) Negro-folk. Not the individual, as in the classical Greek drama, in the Elizabethan plays
and in Goethe's *Faust,* but the group, the race, is here the tragic
character.

In spite of the difference in treatment of a common theme by
the nineteenth-century German and the twentieth-century American, the points of similarity existing between the two dramas are
so numerous and striking as to demand attention.

Each drama is based on an earlier prose narrative taken from
its own national lore—Goethe's, on that of the legendary magician
Faust found in the old German *Faustbuch,* Connelly's on the
quasi-folk tales of Roark Bradford's *Ol' Man Adam an' His Chillun.*

Even as the biblical narration is divided into the Old and the
New Testament, and Milton's account into *Paradise Lost* and
Paradise Regained, in like manner both *Faust* and *The Green
Pastures* are divided into Part One and Part Two. Goethe's Part
One is not subdivided into acts, but is a series of some twenty-

five scenes. Nor is there any subdivision into acts in Connelly's play. Two series of scenes, ten and eight respectively, constitute the two parts of this drama. Whereas the bipartition of the German drama is functionally justified inasmuch as Part I, the Gretchen Tragedy, represents the "Fall" of Faust and Part II represents his "Redemption," the partition of the American play is based on the ante-diluvian and post-diluvian history of the race. It should be further noted that Goethe also accents the dualism of his hero:

> Two souls, alas! reside within my breast,
> And each withdraws from, and repels, its brother.
> One with tenacious organs holds in love
> And clinging lust the world in its embraces;
> The other strongly sweeps, the dust above,
> Into the high ancestral spaces.[3]

In the American drama we observe not only the dualism of the human race (*halb Gott, halb Kot*) but also a dualism of the Deity who throughout most of the play is "de God of wrath and vengeance,"[4] the God of the Old Testament, but who, toward the end, shows a transfiguration. The "God of Hosea" "ain't a fearsome God no mo'" but "de God of mercy," "through sufferin'," the God of the New Testament, the God of Love, the God of Goethe's *Faust*.

There is another feature common to the divided parts. In the first part of *Faust* the hero is presented to us only in his "microcosm," his small, individual world, whereas in Part II he is presented in a "macrocosm," the larger, socio-political world.

In Part I we encounter the scholar Faust in his ivory tower and follow him on his ramble before the city gate where he mingles only with bourgeois and peasant strollers (scene ii). His next departure from his study takes him to Auerbach's cellar, an ordinary assembly place for ribâld carousers, then to the Witch's Kitchen (scene vi), with its primitive occupants. On the street he accosts an obscure maiden who tells him her social position is below that of *Fräulein* (scene viii). This Margarete (Gretchen) has lived as cloistered as a pearl in an oyster. The next scene finds Faust in Gretchen's room, then in the garden of Gretchen's neighbor, Frau Martha, "ein Weib wie auserlesen zum Kuppler und Zigeunerwesen" (3,029 f.) . In a brawl before Gretchen's door Faust murders her brother Valentin, an enlisted soldier. He flees to the mountains and participates in a wild Halloween-like revel (*Walpurgisnacht*) with witches and other unsavory characters. Finally he stealthily visits the demented Gretchen, who is incarcerated awaiting her execution on the morrow.

Part I of *The Green Pastures*, after the "Fish Fry" scene in Heaven, presents God with the newly created Adam and Eve in Eden. Next Cain kills Abel. Then the banished Cain meets "Cain's Gal" at the "Nod Parish County Line." We next meet Zeba singing the blues and accompanying the song on her ukulele on the Sabbath morn. This scene also introduces "Cain the Sixth," a group of gamblers playing craps, and the degenerate Rucker family. Noah is a respectable country Preacher, but even he is very fond of "likker." In the following scene (ix) "Cain the Sixth" murders Flatfoot for flirting with Zeba. In the final scene the Ark is grounded and Noah is as "drunk as a fool."

So we note that in this part of *The Green Pastures* as in *Faust* Part I there are no human beings of high social rank or political station. Both dramatists devote Part I exclusively to the common folk.

In the second part of Goethe's drama Faust is no longer a man concerned exclusively with his personal affairs and associated with everyday, run-of-the-mill people. In Act I we behold him in the Hall of the Throne of the Imperial Palace of the Emperor of the Holy Roman Empire involved in affairs of state. Act II introduces a journey through the lands of Grecian antiquity with its sphinxes, griffons, nymphs, and sirens. The third act presents the "Helena" episode in which Faust has a liaison with the famous, or infamous, Helen whose face, or fame, "launched a thousand ships" and whose flame "burnt the topless towers of Ilium." In the fourth act Faust, by means of his magic arts, wins victory for the Emperor's Army and as a reward obtains an imperial grant which entitles him to the tidelands which he intends to reclaim from the sea. In the final act he dies in the midst of this great humanitarian work of reclamation and his spirit is carried to Heaven.

Similarly in the second part of *The Green Pastures* the commonplace interests of the "little man" are left behind and the action concerns itself with mighty persons and affairs of historical import. In the opening scene "de Lawd" summons Abraham, Isaac, and Jacob, and, after a conference, decides to bestow the Promised Land on their progeny. Moses, the future lawgiver, is sent by "de Lawd" to appear in the throne room of Pharaoh in Egypt. Here, by his magic arts, he forces the ruler to release his people from this land of bondage. Moses dies just before reaching the Jordan, after having instructed Joshua how to accomplish the destruction and capture of Jericho. Scene five representing the captivity in Babylon brings us into the presence of the "King of Babylon." Scene seven presents a "corner beside the walls of the temple in Jerusalem" where "ol' Herod" "say he's goin' to take de temple tomorrow" (p. 645).

It will further be noted that Part I of *Faust* begins with a "Prelude on the Stage," which serves humorously to prepare the audience for the sort of action it is to witness in the coming drama, which moves through the circle of creation and runs the gamut of sensations and passions from the celestial through the mundane to the diabolical and bestial.[5] Similarly in the opening scene of *The Green Pastures,* Mr. Deshee's Sunday School serves to introduce the play and to give a naïve suggestion of the material on which the work is based.

This scene is immediately followed by "A Fish Fry." The place is Heaven before the Creation of Earth and Man. *"Many voices are heard singing* 'Rise, Shine, Give God the Glory,' *A mixed company of angels."* There are an Archangel and Gabriel.[6] God ("de Lawd") himself appears, participates in the fish fry and chats very informally with the persons present. The "Prologue in Heaven," which immediately follows Goethe's "Prelude," presents: "The Lord. The Heavenly Hosts. *Afterwards* Mephistopheles." The Archangels Raphael, Gabriel, and Michael sing the chorus of the creation which begins:

> The sun-orb sings, in emulation,
> 'Mid brother-spheres his ancient round:

Mephistopheles salutes the Lord thus:

> Da du, O Herr, dich einmal wieder nahst
> Und fragst, wie alles sich bei uns befinde,
> Und du mich sonst gewöhnlich gerne sahst,
> So siehst du mich auch unter dem Gesinde.
>
> . . . .
>
> Mein Pathos brächte dich gewiss zum Lachen,
> Hätt'st du dir nicht das Lachen abgewöhnt.
> (ll. 271ff.)

The conversation seems as friendly as that of "de Lawd" with his black angels after Gabriel announces his approach with his informal: "Gangway! Gangway for de Lawd God Jehovah!"

At the end of the Prologue, Mephistopheles soliloquizes:

> Von Zeit zu Zeit seh' ich den Alten gern,
> Und hüte mich, mit ihm zu brechen.
> Es ist gar hübsch von einem grossen Herrn
> So *menschlich* mit dem *Teufel* selbst zu sprechen.[7]

We feel that this Lord is closely related to "de Lawd" who directs: "Let de fish fry proceed," accepts a "little b'iled custud" and a "ten cent seegar," "passes" a miracle so as to get "a bit mo' firmament" into the eggnog, and goes down to visit Adam, even as Mephistopheles has reported a visit from the "Herr" in *Faust*.

Of the final scene in *Faust* (V, vii) : "Mountain-Gorges, Forest, Rock, Desert" Bayard Taylor writes: "This closing scene, although it ends in the higher regions of Heaven, appears to begin on Earth."[8] In *The Green Pastures* the concluding scene is a return to the setting of the original "Fish Fry" of the opening scene. Thus in both dramas the circle is completed. To quote a phrase of Schiller descriptive of his procedure in his drama *Die Jungfrau von Orleans*, "so beiszt sich die Schlange in den Schwanz."[9] The action of both plays concludes where it had begun. However, the Heaven of the last scene in *Faust* is a Catholic

Heaven. Instead of the actors being God, the Father, and the Archangels, we witness the appearance of the "Mater Gloriosa,"

> Virgin, pure in brightest sheen,
> Mother sweet, supernal,—
> Unto us Elected Queen,
> Peer of God Eternal!
>
> (ll. 12,009 ff.)

to whom Gretchen's spirit prays:

> Incline, O Maiden,
> With Mercy laden,
> In light unfading,
> Thy *gracious* countenance upon my bliss!
> My loved, my lover,
> His *trials* over
> In yonder world, returns to me in this![10]

and whom the "Pater Marianus" addresses:

> Virgin Holy, Mother, Queen,
> Goddess, *gracious* be![11]

Consequently the final lines in the story of Faust's salvation and ascension into Heaven reveal that his redemption has been accomplished by "mercy" (love) after his struggling and suffering.

> The Woman-Soul leadeth us
> Upward and on!
>
> (12,100 f.)

Connelly's heaven in the final scene also represents a transition from "Dat ol' God of wrath and vengeance" to the God of Hosea (p. 646), the God of mercy, and postulates that man is to be saved by "Mercy through sufferin'" (p. 648).[12] "The Voice" that utters the final word in the American play (as does the "Chorus Mysticus" in *Faust*) announces a vision of the passion and suffering of Jesus and *"All the angels burst into 'Hallelujah, King Jesus'"* (p. 648), just as the choruses and characters in the finale to *Faust* have sung Hallelujah to Mary, the "Mother [of Jesus], Queen and Goddess."

So much for the general structural resemblances of the two compositions. It is natural that all Christian concepts of Heaven should have some aspects in common. Hence one might expect to find many similar creatures and events common to both Goethe's work and *Thē Green Pastures*. The following details, however, seem to merit consideration. Goethe's archangels sing of the Creation:

> The sun-orb sings, in emulation,
> 'Mid brother-spheres, his ancient round:
> His path predestined through Creation
> He ends with step of thunder-sound.
> > (ll. 243 ff.)

and continue:

> The lofty works, uncomprehended,
> Are bright as on the earliest day.

They conclude by assuring the Lord:

> And all Thy Works, sublime and splendid,
> Are bright as in Creation's hour.

From Connelly's Heaven "de Lawd" and Gabriel look down on the newly created Earth:

GABRIEL: Looks mighty nice, Lawd . . . Yes, suh. Dat'd make mighty nice farming country.
GOD: It's a good earth.
GOD: [to Gabriel] You know dat matter of dem two stars? Git dat fixed up! (p. 611)

Later, in scene six, Gabriel informs God: "De moon people say it's beginnin' to melt a little, on 'count caize de sun's so hot."

God replies: "It's goin' 'roun' 'cordin' to schedule, ain't it?" thus suggesting a slight deviation from the Creation presented in *Faust*, and at least once giving a verbal echo of Goethe's presentation ("his ancient round").

Near the end of the Fish Fry (scene ii) "de Lawd," wishing to improve the "b'iled custard" (p. 610), says: "I'll jest r'ar back an' pass a miracle . . . Let it be some firmament! . . . Let it be a whole mess of firmament!" *"The stage"* becomes *"misty until God and the heavenly company are obscured. As he finishes the speech there is a burst of thunder."* At the end of the *Mummenschanz* (Carnival Masquerade), *Faust* II, I, iii, 5,972 ff., Plutus speaks:

> Smite, thou hallowed wand, and make
> Earth beneath thee peal and quake!
> Thou, the spacious breadth of air,
> Cooling vapors breathe and bear!
> Hither speed, around us growing,
> Misty films and belts o'erflowing,
> And the fiery tumult tame!
> Trickle, whisper, clouds, be crisper,
> Roll in masses, softly drenching,
> Mantling everywhere, and quenching!
> Ye, the moist, the broadly bright'ning,
> Change to harmless summer lightning
> All this empty sport of flame!—
> When by spirits we're molested,
> Then be Magic manifested.[13]

On Connelly's stage there are murmurs: "My, dat is firmament!" "Look to me like he's created rain."

So Connelly "busts up de fish fry" (p. 611) just after having "de Lawd pass a miracle," saturating the scene with wetness, and the earth is created, even as Goethe puts a quick end to the *Flammengaukelspiel* (l. 5,987) by having Plutus resort to magic and thus impregnate the scene with moisture.

In both versions of the story the Creator is pleased with the creatures in the celestial realm. They join him in rejoicing in the glory of the planetary system. There is, however, an evident divergence between the attitudes of "The Lord" and "de Lawd" toward the devil and the human creation. As we have seen, Mephistopheles rejoices in his conversation with the Lord who even tells him: "Ich habe deinesgleichen nie gehasst. Von allen Geistern, die verneinen, ist mir der Schalk am wenigstens zur Last" (ll. 337 ff.). The Lord gives him *"die Erlaubnis"* to attempt to seduce Faust to his own diabolical way (l. 314). On the other hand, Connelly's "Stout Angel" says, "de Lawd he don' *'low* us 'sociatin' wid de devil any mo'," while the "Slender Angel" laments, "Po' ol' Satan."[14]

The Lord tells Mephistopheles face to face that the latter will lose his wager and concludes:

> Und steh' beschämt, wenn du bekennen musst:
> Ein' guter Mensch, in seinem dunklen Drange,
> Ist sich des rechten Weges wohl bewusst. (ll. 1,327 ff.)

"De Lawd," on the other hand, sends his message to Satan in the "Big Pit" through his messenger Gabriel: "Lean over de brink and tell Satan he's just a plain fool if he thinks he kin beat anybody as big as me."[15]

As for the human race, it seems that "de Lawd" is, in general, disappointed with his creatures. His opinion of "man" resembles that expressed by Mephistopheles rather than that of Goethe's *der Herr*. In fact many of "de Lawd's" statements can be matched by utterances of Goethe's devil.

When "de Lawd" says: "It's only de human bein's makes me downhearted" (p. 618) and "I wasn't any too pleased wid dat job" (p. 616), he displays his disgust with "man," and when he later asserts: "I was displeased wid de mankind I las' seen" (p. 616), and "All I gotta say, dis yere mankind I been peoplin' my earth wid sho' ain't much" (p. 620), we might think that Mephistopheles is speaking. One of "de Lawd's" office-workers reports: "Well, it jest so happens dat de Lawd is riled as kin be by dat measly little earth. Or I should say de scum dat's on it." And continues: "Mos' of de population down dere has made de debbil king an' dey wukkin' in three shifts fo' him," and another

worker queries, "Ain' dat a shame to *plague* de Lawd dat way?"
(Part II, scene i, p. 629), recalling Mephistopheles' report to
the Lord:

> Ich sehe nur wie sich die Menschen *plagen.*
> Der kleine Gott der Welt bleibt stets von
> gleichem Schlag,
> Und ist so wunderlich als wie am ersten Tag.
> Ein wenig besser würd' er leben,
> Hätt'st du ihm nicht den Schein des
> Himmelslichts gegeben;
> Er nennt's Vernunft und braucht's allein,
> Nur tierischer als jedes Tier zu sein.
> Er scheint mir, mit Verlaub von Euer Gnaden,
> Wie eine der langbeinigen Cikaden,
> Die immer fliegt und fliegend springt
> Und gleich im Gras ihr altes Liedchen singt;
> Und läg' er nur noch immer in dem Grase!
> In jeden Quark begräbt er seine Nase.

Mephistopheles reports further of the earth:

> Ich find' es dort, wie immer, herzlich schlecht.
> Die Menschen dauern mich in ihren Jammertagen,
> Ich mag sogar die Armen selbst nicht *plagen.*[16]

Nevertheless, "de Lawd" is interested in this one of his handi-
works and is unwilling to despair of the potential worth of man;
nor, as we have seen, is he willing to let Satan "beat" him. In
this side of his nature we note that he assumes the role that
Goethe's Lord has taken in his argument with Mephistophles,
to whom this Lord never betrays the least indication of suc-
cumbing. "De Lawd" states: "Man is a kind of pet of mine and it
ain't right fo' me to give up tryin' to do somthin' wid him. Doggone, mankin' *mus'* be all right at de core or else why did I ever
bother wid him in de first place?" (Part II, scene i, p. 630).
When Mephistopheles challenges the Lord, the latter cites
Faust whom he calls, not his "pet," but *mein Knecht* (servant),

who "now serves" Him "still confusedly but whom" He "will lead into clarity." He concludes by telling the devil that "man" will err as long as he strives (or struggles); that a good man in his dark groping is ever concious of the "one true way" [Taylor]; and that the devil will not succeed in his attempt to win Faust's soul.

"De Lawd," seemingly in agreement with this philosophy, asks Gabriel: "Have you noticed dat every now and den, mankin' turns out some pretty good specimens?" (p. 630) and proceeds to state: "Why, doggone it, de good man is de man dat keeps busy. . . . I been goin' along on de principle dat he was something like you angels—dat you ought to be able to give him somethin' an' den jest let him sit back and enjoy it. Dat ain't so. . . . He ain't *built* jest to fool 'roun' an' not do nothin'." The same line of thought is expressed when "de Lawd" talks with Abraham and his sons (p. 631). "Seein' dat you human bein's cain't 'preciate anythin' lessens you fust wukk to git it and den keep strugglin' to hold it, why, I'm gonter turn over a very valuable piece of property to yo' fam'ly, an' den see what kin dey do with it."

Here are further echoes of Faustian philosophy. As examples of the *Tätigkeitsdrang* which permeates Goethe's drama, the following passages may be mentioned:

> Nur der verdient sich Freiheit wie das Leben,
> Der täglich sie erobern muss. (ll. 11,575 f.)

and:

> Wer immer strebend sich bemüht,
> Den können wir erlösen (ll. 11,936 f.)

and:

> Wie ich beharre, bin ich Knecht,
> Ob dein [Mephistopheles'],[17] was frag' ich, oder wessen.
> (ll. 1,710 f.)

and:

> Werd' ich beruhigt je mich auf ein Faulbett legen,
> So sei es gleich um mich getan! (ll. 1,692 f.)

Again, we may consider the much quoted words of the Lord concerning his reason for creating the devil:

> Des Menschen Tätigkeit kann allzu leicht erschlaffen,
> Er liebt sich bald die unbedingte Ruh;
> Drum geb' ich gern ihm den Gesellen zu,
> Der reizt und wirkt und muss als Teufel schaffen.
> Doch ihr, die echten Göttersöhne,
> Erfreut euch der lebendig reichen Schöne. (ll. 340 ff.) [18]

II

At the end of Part I of *The Green Pastures*, that is, after the Deluge has subsided, "de Lawd" announces, "Yes, suh, startin' all over again." So Part II opens with a scene in God's office in Heaven. After the close of Part I of *Faust*, that is, the end of the Gretchen tragedy, the second Part of Goethe's drama begins with "A Pleasant Landscape" in an Alpine region, whither Faust has withdrawn to forget the past and start a new life. Faust awakens from slumber:

> Des Lebens Pulse schlagen frisch lebendig,
> . . . .
> Du [Erde] regst und rührst ein kräftiges Beschliessen,
> Zum höchsten Dasein immerfort zu streben. (ll. 4,679 ff.)

Thus we may say that Faust too is starting all over again.

"De Lawd" has decided to give the Land of Canaan to the children of Abraham and to appoint Moses as their leader to bring them out of Egypt into the Promised Land. But Moses has killed a man in Egypt and is a fugitive from justice. So too has Faust killed Valentin, and he has also been responsible for the deaths of Gretchen's mother and of Gretchen and her infant. He too is a fugitive. Hence we have two fugitives who are to appear at the Court of a great ruler—Moses before the throne of Pharoah, and Faust in the throne room of the Emperor of the Holy Roman Empire. In each court a large number of high officials is present. In the German court are "Court Retainers of all kinds, splendidly dressed. The Emperor advances to the throne; the Astrologer on his right hand." At the Egyptian court "Pharoah is seated on the throne. . . . About the throne . . . are high officials, several of them with plumed hats, clothing that suggests military uniforms, and rather elaborate sword belts, swords and scabbards . . . one or two bearded ancients in brightly colored robes with the word 'Wizard' on their conical hats. . . . Sunday finery is noticeable everywhere. Most civilians have bright 'parade' ribbons and wear medals." Everything is elaborate and gaudy. Present also is a Candidate Magician "performing a sleight-of-hand trick" in front of Pharoah. Almost immediately enters a "Head Magician."

In the German play Mephistopheles,

> Gar köstlich. . . . . . . aufgeputzt,
> Doch fratzenhaft, dass jeder stutzt;[19]

enters immediately in the costume of the court jester, as substitute for the regular "Fool" who has "passed out."[20] He "stations himself on the Emperor's left hand." There arise "Murmurs of the Crowd" directed against the new fool. These murmurs occur five times during the scene, each time directed against Mephistopheles and/or the astrologer,[21] but only in the first instances are the words "of the assemblage" (*der Menge*) subjoined in the text.

In *The Green Pastures,* where the action is dominated first by the Magicians and then by the magic arts of Moses, early in the scene (p. 635) there are "murmurs of protest from the assemblage" directed against the "Head Magician." Also a "murmur" against Moses occurs twice more (pp. 636, 637). Amid these murmurs we find *"exclamations of the assemblage"* and *"exclamations"* (p. 637) evoked by the tricks of Moses and Aaron. It is remarkable that a majority of the "murmurs" of the crowd in both plays should occur in the respective scenes now under discussion and that, in each play, only to the initial occurrence have the words "of the assemblage" (*der Menge*) been added by the author.

In conclusion it might be noted that even as Moses has arrived

in Egypt to deliver his people from bondage, likewise the German
Emperor has just returned from Rome where he has

> . . . sich zu Nutz, euch zum Vergnügen,
> Die hohen Alpen überstiegen,
> Gewonnen sich ein heitres Reich.
>
> . . . .
> Nun sind wir alle neugeboren.
>   (ll. 5,069 ff.)

The Emperor has also brought back with him *das lustige
Karneval* which the court now proceeds to celebrate. In the
next scene the spacious hall and adjoining rooms, decorated
and adorned *zur Mummenschanz* ("Carnival Masquerade," Taylor), are the setting for more wizardry, Carnival jokes (*Masken-
spasz*, l. 5,728) and finally a *Flammengaukelspiel* ("jugglery of
flame," Taylor, l. 6,987).

Although there is no real parallel for this in *The Green Pastures*, carnival elements are present in the Pharoah scene (II, iii)
with its "Negro lodge room," "large parade banners of varying
sizes, colors and materials, bordered with gold fringe and tassels
on them" (p. 634). The inscriptions on these banners and the
scene in Pharaoh's court suggest the "Mardi Gras" spirit. If we
look further to scene five, representing the Babylon captivity,
"a room vaguely resembling a Negro night club in New Orleans,"
a table "Reserved for the King and guests," "flashy young men
and women . . . dancing in the foreground to the tune of a jazz
orchestra" and note that "the costumes are what would be worn
at a Negro masquerade to represent the debauchés of Babylon,"
we feel that these elements recall Goethe's *Mummenschanz* as a
possible source. Even though we realize that the American author must have been acquainted with the "Mummers' " annual
celebration introduced into his native Pennsylvania from
Goethe's native Frankfurt and its vicinity, and with the Mardi
Gras carnival of New Orleans which is the locus of Roark Bradford's stories on which *The Green Pastures* is based, we cannot
fail to recall in reading this scene the lines in Goethe's *Classische
Walpurgisnacht*

Ist eben hier ein Mummenschanz,
Wie überall ein Sinnentanz. (ll. 7,995 f.)

The deaths of Moses and Faust have much in common. When
Moses enters in the death scene (II, iv) "he is now an old man
. . . he totters toward the center of the stage." Goethe describes
Faust shortly before his death as *im höchsten Alter, wandelnd,
nachdenkend* (Act V, iii, 11,142). It is assumed that he has attained the age of one hundred years. Internal evidence in the
American play indicates that Moses is past eighty years.[22] Although he has been appointed by "de Lawd" to lead his liberated
people out of Egypt to the Land of Canaan, to be wrested from
the Philistines, it is ordained that he shall never enter the
Promised Land. Before his death he does say: "Little while back
I thought I *did* see a river ahead, and a pretty land on de other
side."

The land in which the aged Faust finds himself was bestowed
upon him, not by "de Lawd," but by the Emperor, to be reclaimed by him, not from the Philistines, but from the sea. This
is also a sort of "Promised Land" as is evident from the remarks
of a "Wanderer" who had known the tract before its reclamation
(ll. 11,043-11,050) and from Faust's anticipatory vision of it after
the reclamation shall have been completed.

Im Inneren hier ein paradiesisch Land (l. 11,569)

Shortly before his death Faust is stricken blind and says:

Die Nacht scheint tiefer tief hereinzudringen
Allein im Inneren leuchtet helles Licht (ll. 11,499 f.)

The dying Moses says: " 'Tis gettin' a little dark, ain't it?"
AARON: It ain't dark, Brother.
MOSES: No, it's my eyes . . . I jest can't seem to see.

So both Faust and Moses fail to attain their earthly paradise.
But "de Lawd" tells Moses that he is "gonter have a Promised
Land" even if he is not "gonter enter de country acrost de River."
Faust *im Vorgefühl von solchem hohen Glück* (the attainment

of his goal of reclaiming his tract of land from the sea) [23] *geniesst "den höchsten Augenblick"* (ll. 11,585) and sinks in death. Each departs this earth with his earthly goal within sight and is carried[24] to another Promised Land above the earth.

The first "Fish Fry" scene in *The Green Pastures* contains in the episode of the "Cherub on the Cloud" an intriguing suggestion of Euphorion in *Faust*. The "First Mammy Angel" says to the errant "Cherub": "Now, you heerd me. (The Cherub assumes several mocking poses, as she speaks.) You fly down yere. You wanter be put down in de sin book? . . . . Dat baby must got imp blood in him he so vexin' . . . . You want me to fly up dere an' slap you down? Now, I tol' you. (The Cherub starts to come down)'" (p. 608). Both these "flying" or "climbing" characters, Euphorion and the Cherub, are "babies." Each is a cherub or quasi-cherub. Goethe's Euphorion is portrayed thus:

A Boy is leaping from his mother's lap
(Schoss) to his father's.

. . . .

He, a Genius naked, wingless, like a Faun without
                          the beasthood,
Leaps upon the solid ground, yet the ground,
                          now reacting,
Sends him flying high in air.[25]

Of him Bayard Taylor says: "In his naked beauty, his pranks, and his sportive, wilful ways, he suggests . . . . the classic myths of Cupid and the child Hermes (Mercury)."[26] Of the latter we read in a paralipomenon to *Faust*: "Sie nennen ihn Euphorion: so hiess einmal sein Stiefbruder,"[27] referring to a mythical offspring of Helen and Achilles who did have wings. Of this earlier Euphorion Goethe writes:

Kräftig und zierlich aber zieht
Schon der Schalk die geschmeidigen,
Doch elastischen Glieder
Listig heraus, die purpurne,
Ängstlich drückende Schale

> Lassend ruhig an seiner Statt;
> Gleich dem fertigen Schmetterling,
>
> ....
>
> Flügel entfaltend behendig. . . .
>   (ll. 9,650 ff.)

The Euphorion in *Faust* first acquires "tassels from his shoulders swaying, fillets *(Binder)* flutter round his bosom" (l. 9,618). Finally Euphorion himself says:

> Yes! — and a pair of wings
> See me unfold!
> Thither! I must! — and thus!
> Grant me the flight!
>   (ll. 9,897 ff.)

He then falls like Icarus to his death.

Therefore we have two baby-cherubs who have taken flight to a height. One is a *Schalk,* the other has "imp blood in him." Both are not only volatile but mercurial. Each is reluctant to obey his mother.[28] The one "assumes several mocking poses," the other verbally mocks the entreaties of his parents:

> Let me be skipping,
> Let me be leaping!
> To soar and circle
> Through ether sweeping,
> Is now the passion
> That me hath won. (ll. 9,711 ff.)

With the words:

> Nur euch zu Willen
> Halt' ich mich an. (ll. 9,743 ff.)

Euphorion finally condescends to "moderate" his exuberance and join the Chorus in their dance (l. 9,744). But only shortly thereafter (ll. 9,785 f.) his parents lament:

Welch ein Mutwill! Welch ein Rasen!
Keine Mässigung ist zu hoffen.

The episode breaks off shortly in Connelly's work, but in Goethe's drama it ends with the death of the sprite after he had again mounted the heights.

There are several other points in *The Green Pastures* which may be reminiscent of *Faust,* but it is probable that any "Lawd" in any Heaven might so frequently have his attention drawn to such incidents that their occurrence here may be considered incidental rather than coincidental. Thus the remark "Nowadays Heaven's free of sin an' if a lady wants a little constitutional she kin' fly till she wing-weary widout gittin' insulted" (I, ii) might recall that Gretchen was insulted during her walk home from church by being accosted on the street in broad daylight by Faust, the confederate of the devil (ll. 2,605-2,608). Again, when "de Lawd" in Heaven says: "Listen to dat liar, dere. He don' intend to marry dat little gal. He don' even love her" (II, i), we might imagine that God is overhearing the deception being practiced by Faust on Gretchen in Martha's garden (ll. 3,073-3,216) shortly after Faust himself had called Mephistopheles *ein Lügner, ein Sophiste* (l. 3,050).

Scarcely worthy of notice but perhaps of some socio-literary significance, if not entirely accidental, is the fact that whenever a character in *The Green Pastures* bears a German name, he or she is a bad character. The small cherub who uses God's coattails as a trapeze, and whom the "Lawd" good-naturedly spanks, is named "Herman" (scene ii). The little boy, "de bes' crap shooter in town," who has "been chewin' tobacco, an' drinkin' sonny-kick-mammy wine" is named "Johnny Rucker" (I, vii, 619). "Mrs. Rucker" has "run away las' night wid a railroad man. She's *e*loped." Mr. Rucker "is flat under de table. He so drunk he cain't move."[29] The "case of dat young Willy Roback, a boy seventeen years old" who "*e*loped with his aunt" (I, viii, 62) completes the list of German nomenclature. There are no other names in the play that even suggest a German origin with the possible exception of "Nootzie Winebush," who is the "Third Girl Cherub" in Mr. Deshee's Sunday School, and the degenerate

"Jake," the "High Priest" of the Jews in Babylonian captivity.[30]

We are told that *The Green Pastures* has been called the "divine comedy of the modern theatre."[31] But surely this epithet cannot be intended to convey the same meaning as does the title of Dante's *Divine Comedy*.[32] Nor would we venture to call this composition Connelly's *Faust*, since it has no character who corresponds to Goethe's hero. We know that *The Green Pastures* is "an attempt to present" the story of the Old Testament up to the inception of the realization of the coming of the Redeemer as imagined by "untutored black Christians."[33] In assaying this subject the author treats many of those facets of man's earthly pilgrimage which Goethe had earlier presented in his story of *Faust*, just as Byron's *Manfred*, because of the similarity of theme, reveals many elements contained in Goethe's drama. Even as Goethe was of the opinion that he detected elements of his poem in Byron's drama,[34] so we may say that Marc Connelly has given us a drama which, in form, content, and some of its details, indicates that its author was, either directly or indirectly, consciously or unconsciously, a disciple of the author of the greatest poem in the literature of the Western world since the time of Shakespeare.

Malraux's Novels and the Arts

by
Rima Drell Reck

"THE TRAGIC POET expresses what fascinates him, not in order to free himself of it . . . but to change its nature: for, expressing it along with other elements, he makes it enter the relative universe of things conceived and dominated," wrote André Malraux in a preface to the French edition of Faulkner's *Sanctuary*.[1] Malraux's interest in the modern tragedy couched in novelistic form resulted in a scattered body of reviews, prefaces, essays, and lectures dating from the 1920's to the present. Certain critical terms and aesthetic predilections illuminating the fictional techniques of Malraux the novelist are discernible in these writings. Although at present Malraux appears to have abandoned the writing of novels for the interpretation of world art history, his influence has been felt by writers whose renown as novelists remains undiminished, Sartre and Camus. Malraux's *La Condition humaine (Man's Fate)*, which won the Prix Goncourt in 1933, remains a classic of our century, both in style and content. His *L'Espoir (Man's Hope)* is a storehouse of technical and poetic experimentation which has yet to be fully explored. An examination of Malraux's novels in the light of his critical pronouncements uncovers one of the most ambitious conceptions of the modern novel our age has produced.

I. An Art of Ellipse

"The dramatic conception of philosophy" which Malraux found in Keyserling's travel journal (1929) and which he recognized as a new form of philosophical expression, appeared to

219

point to a profound transformation of fiction.[2] Long before the advent of the so-called Existentialist novel, Malraux sensed the growing significance of literature as an instrument of metaphysical consciousness. His own novels are a revealing case in point. High adventure, philosophical discussions, poetic glimpses of cities and stars, torture, agony, death, lit up with reminiscences of paintings, music, and sculpture—these are the elements of novels whose style is alternately abrupt, spare, journalistic, and rhapsodic, strangely poetic. The unity of these novels is the unity of the author's private world, the strength of his obsession and his intensity.

Malraux's literary form is at first glance deceptively diffuse, his style obscurely telegraphic. His subject matter is chosen for the most part from the brutal realities of the twentieth century, war and revolution, with imagery which has elicited from Armand Hoog the comment that Malraux is "the only photographic genius of the French novel."[3] But the total effect of each novel is not that of a realistic account of some particular series of events. There are unsatisfying gaps in an otherwise realistic narration and also many gratuitous elements. Malraux's criticism provides the key to the difference between the nature of his subject matter and the treatment accorded it. He admired "the questioning of events by that which goes beyond events . . .,"[4] the eternal in what appears most ephemeral. Like many of his heroes, Malraux seeks the "quality" in man which gives him ascendency over events which tend to destroy him.

To express "the *poetic* connections between beings, between beings and things," the cinema and the novel are best adapted, Malraux pointed out in the *Psychologie du cinéma* (1946). He calls such an art an "art of ellipse," which brings together facts and allows their proximity to suggest their relationship. The crucial factor in a work so conceived "is in its white spaces," in what is omitted and seemingly unexplained. R. M. Albérès has called Malraux's literary style an art of *abridgement*. He explains it as the confrontation of the human act with its own metaphysical significance. Here, the author avoids "the 'buffer' formed, in psychological and social novels, by an analysis of motivations and of the act's repercussions on other characters." The end result, concludes Albérès, is an immediacy which plunges the reader into the hero's anguish with extraordinary force.[5] The *intentions* of this particular transformation of reality are central to an understanding of Malraux's vision of the novel.

Lucidity and poetry, according to Malraux, are the pillars of the modern novel. By lucidity he means the objective presentation of data. Poetry is born when the artist's will to dominate the world he records shapes the *récit*, when, as Malraux said in his preface to *Sanctuary*, the artist can transcend his horror and fascination before what is tragic in life by making it part of a special universe whose proportions he can control, whose elements exist only because *he* has *thought* them. In answer to critics who have thought Malraux confused, E. W. Knight has acutely pointed out that Malraux's elliptical turn of thought is a reflection not of his own confusion but of the ambiguity of existence. "Malraux's intelligence functions," he says, "not as a creator of systems, a finder of 'solutions,' but as *lucidity;* it tells more easily what is not than what is, because action is not something 'added' to life, it is life itself."[6] Ellipse is a mode of thought as well as a mode of art. The poetry of the modern novel testifies to a mystery. The war novel is, in Malraux's words, "a series of tableaus coordinated by a fatality."[7]

In an art of ellipse the narrative must take a special form, which Albérès calls the "telegraphic structure" and which Malraux himself has identified as *reportage*. One need only think of the first pages of *Les Conquérants,* sliced into parcels of scenery and action by a series of radio communiqués, to see what this technique looks like in fact. The organization of *La Condition humaine* by oddly-spaced date indications, the overwhelming division of *L'Espoir* into numerous scenes, indicate the lack of explicit narrative connectives, of "explanations" of the meaning and logic of his story by the author. *Ellipse* does not supply the logic of a well-made detective story; *reportage* does not give all the facts of a careful newspaper story. The meaning, the answers to the half-avowed questions posed by situations in a Malraux novel lie somewhere beyond the pale of rational discourse. The narrative is such that the author himself appears to be sensing the *questions* for the first time as he writes the scene. Malraux has defined the technique of *reportage* as "the intrusion of a character into a world which he reveals to us while discovering it himself."[8] The narrator of *Les Conquérants* sees Saigon in a series of disconnected observations, as one might quickly notice details in unfamiliar surroundings, without passion or judgment.

> Desolate, deserted, provincial city, with long avenues and straight boulevards where the grass grows under huge tropical trees. . . . My coolie is dripping with sweat: the ride is long. Finally we arrive in a Chinese quarter, full of gilded signs with fine black characters, little banks, bureaus of all kinds. In front of me, in the middle of a wide avenue covered with grass, wanders a little railroad. 37, 35, 33 . . . Stop! We stop in front of a house like all the others in this quarter: a "compartment." Some kind of agency. Around the door hang plaques of little known Cantonese business companies.[9]

Another form which *reportage* takes in Malraux is the connection of a face with a landscape, followed by a gaze which moves further into the distance, giving an impression of portent to what follows. When the observer's wandering glance is interrupted by the speaker, the presence of an ominous landscape or background grouping of objects remains, giving a special effect of intensification to the speeches.

> At first I have the impression that he doesn't want to answer me; no, he's thinking. Seen thus, his face is very fine. Evening is deepening. Above the noise of the car's motor, you hear nothing now but the rhythmic chirping of the grasshoppers. The rice fields pass endlessly along both sides of the road; on the horizon, a betal palm moves slowly,—"I don't think so," he continues . . . . (C, p. 16)

The passages cited strongly remind one of the techniques of the cinema, with varying angles of vision and "cutting" of scenes. However, as Albérès has pointed out, films had barely discovered the technique of cutting in 1928, when *Les Conquérants* was published. It is more germane to our understanding of Malraux's fictional technique to reflect on the human implications of his use of *reportage,* without reference to the camera eye of films.

(Film directors and novelists may very well discover similar modes of vision in the same era, without direct borrowing from each other.) What is seen is at all times visible from the point of view of the action or the actor of the novel's scene. We are never given a minute description of a landscape as a preparation, a full stage setting, for an action which will take place there at some future stage in the story. We see only what the characters see, and what they see is limited by a human perspective, a personal angle of vision. No God-like author hovers over the story providing the reader with more insight than any one of the characters. Nothing is explained, nothing is analyzed. Time becomes experience and has the shocks and the discontinuity of experience at moments of great stress. Experience can, of course, include immaterial insights, as we shall see a bit later. In any case, the connections to be made are intuitive, the insights poetic. The "dramatic concept of philosophy" gives birth to a novel whose movement *is* its meaning and whose characters are our only guides.

II. A Dramatic Conception of Psychology

Malraux's preference for a psychology of actions to one of subconscious analysis is apparent at every stage of his writings. His conviction that it is essentially impossible ever to *know* another being leads him to admire Dostoyevsky, not for the final clarity with which he dissects his personages, but for the *mystery* he is able to suggest in them. Psychological realism is unattainable and, in fact, undesirable. The novelist cannot supply *inner* knowledge of his heroes; rather, he must deal in "dramatic psychology," the secrets suggested by the actions and half-avowals of the character.

Malraux's theory of *la psychologie dramatique,* which is most clearly expressed in Part V of the *Psychologie du cinéma,* is amply illustrated by his own fictional heroes. The impression which characters conceived along these lines give to many readers is colorfully expressed by André Rousseaux: "From Garine to Vincent Berger, passing by Claude, Kyo, Alvéar, and the others, I can remember only silhouettes in dialogue, without human sub-

stance, all cut on the same model: a bomb in hand, and a metaphysical mind with which to meditate on the fate of man while
other men running in all directions fall under the machine-gun
fire."[10] Because the concerns of Malraux's heroes are so far beyond
the ordinary preoccupations of daily life, these heroes seem, at
a distance, to resemble one another. And yet Rousseaux's judgment does not take into account the diversity of this race of
would-be supermen, the fact that they have different faces and
different voices, that the *tone* of metaphysical inquiry which runs
through Malraux's fiction has many pitches and variations. Malraux readily admits a preference for the willful hero, "le per-
sonnage significatif." In his essay on Laclos, Malraux expresses
his extraordinary confidence in the power of a man's will and actions. Laclos had the genius, says Malraux, "to make fictional
characters act as a function of what they think."[11] Citing Faulkner, Dostoyevsky, Bernanos, and Balzac, Malraux insists that for
many authors, the greatest authors, the theme or idea of a scene
in fiction always preceded the conception of the characters. In
the light of his preference for will and ideas over psychological
dissection, it is all the more remarkable that Malraux is able
to bestow a great measure of individuality upon many of his
characters.

In general, Malraux describes his characters physically in two
ways, by a portrait in action or by a caricature. The first method,
which is a natural outgrowth of the *reportage* technique, gives us
one character as seen by another, with the qualities of *discovery*
and *movement* always present. As an example, the description
of Garine as seen by the narrator of *Les Conquérants:*

> He's barely aged, but, under the green lining of his helmet,
> each feature bears the mark of illness; the eyes have circles
> reaching to mid-cheek; the nose has grown still thinner; the
> two wrinkles connecting the nostrils with the corners of the
> mouth are no longer the deep, clear wrinkles of the past;
> they are wide wrinkles, almost folds; and all the muscles seem
> feverish, soft and so fatigued at once that when he becomes
> animated and they all stretch, the expression of his face
> changes completely. (C, p. 59)

Each line of the face is not fully drawn, but situated in terms of an active cause, in this case illness. We see the contours as they used to be and as they are now, all through the eyes of Garine's companion as they walk along a boulevard in the Oriental midday heat. The last portion of the description shows the effect of will and intelligence: Garine's inner strength is able to transform his very features, to give him the mask of action which expresses his psychological makeup. Claude sees a similar transformation on the face of Perken when the latter's essential self is imprinted upon the aging flesh: "The expression of the face: heavy, enveloping, with a singular firmness when, for an instant, an affirmation stretched the tired facial muscles."[12] Jean de Pontcharra has called this "hunt for the soul" in the living mobility of a man's face "psychological sculpture,"[13] emphasizing once again the fact that physical, visual reality in Malraux's fiction is never an end in itself. Description is a constant search and a discovery.

Malraux depicts by caricature when the same method of discovery is applied rapidly, so that what is conveyed is a quick impression, rather than a full portrait. We can see a halfway stage between the portrait in action and the caricature in this description of Borodine: "Now I see his face foreshortened, beneath the wavy, thick, back-combed hair which was all I could see when he first appeared to me, bent over his desk. He has the look of an intelligent wild animal because of the curved moustache, high cheek bones and narrow eyes. Forty years old, perhaps." With the designation of Gisors' face as "the mask of an ascetic abbé" (CH, p. 208), of Meunier's face as "the head of a facetious rabbit" (C, p. 32), we see the final abbreviation into distinct caricature. The baron Clappique is a fully rounded caricature, with a variety of "sketches" to describe his shifting personality, his lack of fixed psychological reality. Malraux is aware of using caricature, as in the following description of Chpilewski: "The curved, thin nose of Chpilewski, his bald forehead, gray hair in back, the high cheek bones, in spite of his very simple white clothes, always gave him the air of being disguised as an eagle. The monocle accentuates the caricature." (CH, p. 297)

Still other characters, living in *l'imprécis,* the half-shadow world of the background, contribute to the movement of the novels by sudden emergence from the shadows and fall back into obscurity when their function is fulfilled. These are the crowds, so frequent in those of Malraux's novels whose setting is the Orient. Crowds serve both a visual and psychological function, setting off the life of man in general from that of the heroes. The crowds exemplify man in his undifferentiated state, with little individuality and only a vague consciousness of the human condition. While Malraux's heroes claim to fight on behalf of these unselfconscious masses, they frequently confess a natural distaste for them. Malraux's own attitude is ambiguous, as can be seen in the following description of a crowd at a political meeting, seen through the eyes of the narrator of *Les Conquér-ants:*

> In this little room, there are four or five hundred men; near the office some female students with clipped hair. . . . Pressed one against the other or occasionally free, the audience: sol-diers, students, petty merchants, coolies, approve with one voice, with a forward movement of the neck like howling dogs, bodies motionless. No crossed arms, no elbows on knees, no chins in their hands; rigid, vertical, dead bodies, impassioned faces whose jaws move forward and always, by starts, these approbations, these barks. (C, p. 110)

There is will and passion in this crowd, but it is paralyzed by being fused into one mass, dehumanized, so that the sounds made are like the barking of dogs. There is an admirable quality of strength and conviction in the mass and also an execrable loss of beauty and individuality. It is not surprising that Garine says elsewhere in the novel, "I don't like men . . . the people, in short, those for whom I am going to fight. . . ." (C, p. 51) Crowds in motion fill the streets, die on the battlefields, and always by their very density and indistinctness seem the least likely objects of that virile fraternity and fraternal love which Malraux's novels invoke.

Crowds are described without cruelty and dehumanization only when they seem to suggest a pictorial processional, reminiscent of the sculpture of the middle ages or the pied crowds of Breughel, momentarily garbed in Oriental fashion.

> Since the end of the siesta, enthusiasm has succeeded gaiety. Dishevelled soldiers run through the decorated streets, everyone is outside his house; a dense crowd is going along the quai, slow, serious, tense with silent exaltation. With fifes, gongs and placards some cortèges are marching, followed by children. Troupes of students move forward, brandishing little white flags which wave, appear and disappear like sea foam above the white dresses and costumes close-ranked like an army. . . . The sky is white and low; in the heat, the procession advances as if toward a temple. . . . A distant sound of gongs, firecrackers, shouts and instruments rises from the ground along with the mingled noise of footsteps and the muffled clapping of myriad sandals. As high as a man, the dust dances, bitter, choking, and goes to lose itself in slow whirlwinds in the almost deserted narrow streets. (C, pp. 146-47)

Fused into a timeless image which blends movement, color and music against the sky, the crowd is in this instance apprehended as an artistic vision. Seen from the point of view of a character in the novel, the scene is described directly, almost journalistically. *Reportage* does not state or explain the significance of the scene, which remains a dramatic image whose meaning can only be sensed.

III. Dialogue

Malraux's novels provide no answers to the questions they pose. His heroes voice conflicting opinions, as if their dialogue were "the echo of an interior dialogue which haunts Malraux."[14] In his essay on Laclos, Malraux wrote that what is most striking about an author in his *tone*, that accent in his writing which conveys his personal obsession and informs the nature and meaning of his fiction. The novelist's heroes have a particular tone and the novelist's tone is the sum of all these voices, the "written voices" which flash from the inner consciousness like bursts of lightning. These flashes *suggest* more than they explain, in Malraux's characteristically elliptical style. This style has been described as the expression of an "art of possibility," one which attempts to suggest the hidden grandeur of man.[15] Malraux has referred to dialogue as the "third dimension" of fiction, the dimension which supplies the intellectual framework for the two-dimensional image. He predicts a renascence of "the tone of the moralist," which he finds in Laclos and other authors he admires. This tone of the moralist is conveyed in Malraux's novels by the dialogues.

Dialogue is a scenic device, supplying the most essential data for the continuity of a narrative which does not itself provide either time continuity, or psychological explanation. Dialogue is also a state of soul, the reverberation of an eternal questioning which finds expression in almost painfully abrupt formulations of thought, in sentences which are at once staccato and yet filled with an involuntary lyricism, "the very accent of the 'discourse on the passions' which is interrupted by a bitter complaint involuntarily uttered. . . ."[16] The speeches of Garine, Perken, Garcia, Gisors all have this tormented, questioning accent. The *dialogues,* however, are not dialogues in the true sense. They appear to be conducted by deaf men, who never hear what the other has to say, who speak their "truth" with a peremptory dogmatism which allows for no mediation. The over-all effect of such conversations is what Albert Camus acutely termed "passionate geometries." Malraux's criticism reveals that what he best remembers of the novels he most admires are symbolic scenes which confront man and the universe, such as the death of Prince Andre in *War and Peace* and dialogues like that of Raskolnikov and Svidrigailov in *Crime and Punishment.*

Contrary to a commonly expressed opinion, the characters of Malraux are not all alike. The cast of characters is so varied as to be, at times, confusing as in *L'Espoir.* But the *tone* of these characters is similar, the tone of accusation of human existence mingled with an irrepressible assertion of individual will. Each voice in a dialogue appears to be arguing with itself, confronting understanding of what is with desire for what ought to be—dialogues within dialogues. The very structure of a novel like *L'Espoir* is in the form of a dialogue, Victor Brombert has pointed out, dialogue between thought and passion, war scenes and intellectual discussions. Brombert distinguishes fifteen major conversations, each one separated from the others by scenes of action, each centering on a different topic and shuffling the participants.[17] This novel of the Spanish Civil War is, in Malraux's words, a "series of tableaus coordinated by a fatality"; its total structure is a dialogue on the meaning of human existence.

IV. Light and Shadow

The intellectual content of Malraux's novels is conveyed by a style which is, above all, auditory and visual. One can as easily recall the settings of Malraux's major dialogue as their substance, and the prose which lies between the dialogue scenes relies almost completely upon visual devices for its effect. Just as the individual characters are portrayed with an art akin to drawing and painting, so the masses of persons, the movement of active moments are set off by a careful use of light and shadow, like the paintings of Georges de la Tour, whom Malraux greatly admires.

The night in *Les Conquérants* is pregnant with violence, so that darkness is sensed as a physical threat. Soldiers running in the street are seen as silhouettes against the triangle of light cast by auto headlights, silhouettes striped with the black shadows of guns (C, p. 93). The theatrical lighting of *La Condition humaine*'s opening scene, in which Tchen commits his first murder, is achieved by artificial light from electricity outside the room. A roomful of revolutionaries is eerily lit and metamorphosed by a swinging lamp, so that faces appear and disappear, with changing expressions. "Passing above his head, the lamp strongly marked the downward slant of the corners of his mouth like a Japanese print; swinging away it displaced the shadows and this half-breed face seemed almost European. The swings of the lamp became shorter and shorter: the two faces of Kyo alternated, less and less different from one another." (CH, p. 187)

Almost all of Malraux's climactic scenes are set off with a nocturnal lighting effect which intensifies the features of his heroes, deepens the lines in their faces, gives their actions the relief of the plastic arts. The scenes are conceived as tableaus, isolated in time by the lack of explicit narrative connectives, isolated in space by the use of lighting. The frequent presentation of characters as silhouettes endows them with a symbolic presence, an immensity which detailed description could not achieve. Guernico wanders in the temporary headquarters of the secret police. Silhouetted against the staircase, he becomes the incarnation of the Christian knight.

> A thin, bent silhouette was climbing, alone in the center of the immense staircase. . . : On the ground floor, by now almost dark, were some suits of armor; and the Catholic writer, tall, blond and pale like so many of Velasquez's portraits, alone in the midst of these great historic stairs, seemed to have stepped from one of these historic armors, seemed destined to go back in with the dawn. (E, p. 690)

The crowds, so cruelly treated in the full light of day or under electricity, become symbolic of the will of a city as they build barricades in the Madrid fog, transformed into a "silent fantasmagoria." Other groups move over abandoned fortifications "in a tragic nocturnal ballet" (E, p. 694). These tableaus coordinated by a fatality are drawn up in sharp visual contrasts, with an art informed by graphic techniques and relying, for its expressiveness, on a confrontation characteristic of poetry and poetic tragedy.

V. The Symbolic Scene: An Accusation of Life

Destiny, fate, fraternity, eternity, millenary—these abstract words thread Malraux's fiction with an emotional intensity which is scarcely due to precise connotation. They are repeated often enough to lose completely any meaningful resonance with which the reader might endow them unaided by the author. Nevertheless these terms are essential to Malraux's vision and he restores to them the quality of mystery which is characteristic of all fundamental aspects of human experience, death, will, art. This revaluation is achieved by means of symbolic scenes, scenes which Malraux calls "accusations of life," which confront man with that which surpasses him and give incidents of human experience the quality of cosmic grandeur, the accent of metaphysical questions.

One of the novelist's most effective means of expression, he writes, is "to relate a crucial moment for his character to the atmosphere or the cosmos which surrounds him. Conrad uses it almost systematically and Tolstoy has drawn from this device one of the most beautiful novelistic scenes ever written, the night of wounded Prince André looking at the clouds after Austerlitz."[18]

Social and psychological explanations are in no way meant to illuminate the dilemmas of Malraux's heroes. Their drama is tragic because its implications go beyond the purely human. As in Pascal, man is compared to the universe, and his triumph consists in the fact of his lucidity. But Malraux carries his infinite-infinitesimal theme further, because he *must* carry it further. He is not willing to provide a religious solution to the almost physical *vertige* which characterizes his symbolic scenes. Instead he fashions triumph out of innate doom. Defeat falls like a transfiguration upon his heroes. The wounded aviators descend the mountain in *L'Espoir*'s most beautiful scene: "And this march of dark peasants, of women with their hair hidden under ageless kerchiefs, seemed less to be following wounded men than to be descending in an austere triumph" (E, p. 836). The fraternity of the aviators and the peasants is indeed part of this triumph, but not the heart of it. The essential victory lies in the author's ability to transform such a painful and essentially hopeless march into an *image* which redeems it, an image which is itself "as great as the mountains." This logic of the opposite, to use W. M. Frohock's term, affirms oracularly the opposite of what rational discourse affirms.[19] Malraux juxtaposes the facts with a picture, an image, a poetic symbol which raises the anguish of human experience above its innate futility to the level of a symbolic victory.

> This shattered leg with its pieces hanging by shreds, this limp arm, this mutilated face, this machine-gun on a coffin, all these risks accepted, sought; the solemn and primitive march of these stretchers, all this was as imperious as these pale meteorites which fell from the heavy sky, as the eternity of apples scattered on the ground. (E, p. 835)

The precise meaning of such scenes is not accountable in

words. It is impossible to say why the agonizing death of Perken seems to be a victory over death, why Tchen's ludicrous suicide has the accent of a heroic gesture. What is the cause of Manuel's sensation in the hospital, when he sees men with wounded arms moving in the next room?

> The wounded with arms in plaster were walking, arm wound in cloth held far from the body by the splint, like violinists, violins at their necks. These were the most troubling of all: the plastered arm like a gesture, and all these phantom violinists, carrying before them their immobilized and rounded arms, were advancing like statues being pushed, in the aquarium silence reinforced by the clandestine buzzing of the flies. (E, p. 514)

A careful reading of the two scenes quoted above reveals the techniques which inform them. In the descent from the mountain, Malraux imparts to the transient actions of men the quality of heroic gestures by placing them among the eternal aspects of nature. The hospital scene, on the other hand, vividly transforms the wounds of defeat into immobilized gestures which belong to the world of painting and sculpture; the gestures become timeless and painless, objective as works of art. In these two fictional devices we find the special idioms which distinguish Malraux's fiction. We also see the signs of a change in vocation which is more apparent than real. The distance between *L'Espoir* and *Les Voix du silence* is not very great; it is merely an intensification of interests present from Malraux's earliest significant work, *La Tentation de l'Occident*.

VI. Nature and the Personal Obsession

The novel is above all the expression of an author's particular obsession. It is "the least governed" of the arts, the art where the will of the artist finds the least play, where he speaks the unutterable because he cannot do otherwise.

How much *The Brothers Karamazov* and *Lost Illusions* dominate Dostoyevsky and Balzac, can be seen in reading these books after the beautiful paralyzed novels of Flaubert. . . . For their author, certain great novels were first of all the creation of the one thing which could overwhelm them. And, as Lawrence wraps himself in sexuality, Faulkner plunges himself into the irremediable. (Preface to . . . Faulkner, p. 745)

The eternal sentiments born of night, the seasons, death, blood, "the whole great cosmic and biological domain"[20] expressed in metaphors particular to each civilization, are called forth in Malraux's novels by the savage epic of our own age, by war and defeat and death. No detail of nature is merely decorative or realistic. A landscape or a sky is mentioned for the question it raises. The cosmos is a menacing presence, which seems to echo man's oppressive sense of *destin*, or it is a symbol of eternity which is suddenly equaled, in Malraux's special artistic logic, by the will of men. Malraux translates his personal obsession with death into universal myths.

Man's flesh is the substantial symbol of his mortality. Kyo discovers in prison the abasement to which torture of the flesh can constrain man, when he listens to the bestial howling of a man being beaten (CH, pp. 390-91). Tchen sees the man he is about to murder primarily as a foot, a snore, a body, living human flesh, and he is both fascinated and repelled. "Killing him was nothing: it was touching him which was impossible" (CH, p. 182). The body is described as a thing, a presence, which is in fact foreign to man's consciousness. Kyo does not recognize his own voice on a record; Perken looks at his hand, symbol of the flesh which is dragging him into death. Life has the sticky, swarming immensity which Claude discovers in the jungle; it is repulsive. Physical love has little sensuality; it is, for Malraux's heroes, "a mythology of the will."

And yet the flesh of man attains a grotesque and memorable grandeur in strikingly detailed descriptions of torture, of wounds, of blood which thread Malraux's narratives with images of human suffering. The bodies of Klein and his friends, stiffly upright, with their wounds gaping, are like a multiple crucifixion (C, pp. 133-36). Death and torture are glimpsed as part of an eternal cycle. Looking at the dead lying scattered on the ground, and seeming to shimmer in the brilliant sunlight, Garcia is moved by horror mixed with a passive acceptance of fate. "Garcia was still looking at the cemetery and was struck in the pit of the stomach by something troubled and eternal in these cypress trees and in these stones, was penetrated through and through by the endless odor of rotting flesh, as he watched the dazzling daylight mix the dead and the murdered in the same blaze" (E, p. 541). Death is timeless as the trees, linking man to the universe and making him part of and equal to that which appears to crush him.

Night is Malraux's favorite setting, not only for the dramatic contrasts of light it affords, but for its stars. The starry night is a constant presence in the novels, a *silence éternal* suddenly glimpsed during many of Malraux's most striking scenes. It serves a dual function: to underline man's finiteness and to suggest "man's hidden grandeur, of which he is unaware," that element in him which *is* at the level of the mountains and the stars. Only during moments of intense experience, when the will surmounts the flesh and its weaknesses, do instants of communication occur between man and the stars. For the murderer Tchen night is friendly, isolating and timeless: "world from which men had disappeared, eternal world . . ." (CH, p. 187). He begins to lose contact with the stars when re-entering the world of men. "The luminous sky. . . . Without knowing why, Tchen looked at it: how much closer to it he had been, just now, when he had discovered the stars! As his anguish weakened, as he rediscovered men, he went further away from it . . ." (CH, p. 186). Flying home from prison, Kassner senses "what is sacred in man," his will, his desire to tame the earth. But down in the street, re-immersed in the living presence of men, he is again aware of their blindness, "this crowd which was burying itself in life with its nocturnal smiles or tumbling into death with its wreaths and coffins, this heedlessly demented crowd which wasn't listening to that thing in itself which was answering death, lying in wait up there, in its steppes of stars. . . ."[21]

The artist must awaken men to their innate greatness, which remains buried except during privileged moments of courage, anguish, fraternity, will, Malraux wrote (TM, "Preface"). As prophet and shaper of this greatness, he must testify to it when it comes to light, he must create it when it is too far buried to be glimpsed. As a novelist, Malraux attempted to fulfill these functions by wresting from the wars and political turmoils of the twentieth century an image which was to be its transfigurative epic. In man's will and ability to act he found an expression of human self-transcendence which is memorably expressed in the figures of Garine, Perken, Tchen, Garcia, Hernandez, Manuel. But his heroes, while affirming the absolute value of man's will to act, were incapable of proving the efficacy of action itself. Man triumphed as an affirmation; he failed as an answer. And yet there were present many glimpses of an answer to man's dilemma, how to make eternal a gesture limited and shaped by the fact of death. These hints were voiced by Claude, Gisors, Alvéar, Lopez, the characters whose obsession with death had led them to an obsession with art—to transform human experience into an art form, in words, in stone, in paint, in sounds, to fashion something lasting out of man's ephemeral existence. When the artist can no longer testify to what is presently sublime in man, he must create that sublimity. The crowd Kassner sees in the streets is unaware of man's ability to answer death, to equal the immensity of the stars. But the novelist can confront the crowd with the stars in a phrase, a paragraph; he can affirm the existence of an answer, having created it. He can also transform the images of his literary art into those of painting, sculpture, music, if he finds in them a more satisfactory transmutation into a realm without time, without pain, where an object exists definitely, absolutely.

VII. Painting, Sculpture, Music

Sharp light and shadow, scenes conceived in pictorial terms, these are characteristic of Malraux's descriptive technique. He frequently points out the plastic inspiration of a scene, as in the description of Valéry's room full of the birds Ferral has loosed: "Now, on the furniture and on the curtains, in the corners of the ceiling, the island birds were fluttering, mat in the dim light like those of the Chinese frescoes" (CH, p. 344). Malraux uses a rich palette to describe the populace of Canton's houseboats, carefully setting off the sections of color with a brilliant sky.

> The youngest ones sleep, packets of black cloth hung on their mothers' backs. The blurring sunlight plays around the skeletons of the sampans and makes the blouses and trousers of the women, blue spots, and the children climbing on the roofs, yellow spots, stand out violently from their brown background. On the quai, the lacy profile of American houses and Chinese houses; above, the sky colorless from an excess of light; and everywhere, slight as a foam, on the sampans, on the houses, on the water, this light into which we penetrate as into an incandescent fog. (C, p. 56)

The pictures Malraux paints are magnified by the reader's memories of other pictures, perhaps in this case by Canaletto or the Impressionists. The painted processionals which crowds suggest appear to interest Malraux much more than their human elements. He is able to evoke the continuity of man by suggesting with images the continuity of man's art. The "people" who are so tenderly treated in *L'Espoir* are those of medieval sculpture, of Goya, of the stained-glass windows. Guernico is described as a figure from Velasquez, and Scali sees Alvéar for the first time as an El Greco whose curly hair makes him seem more like a baroque copy.

Women are often described by Malraux as art objects. In her sorrow May looks to Kyo like a funeral mask. Kassner thinks of his wife, and in his dark prison he imagines her face as beautiful and lifeless as a statue. As sexual partners women seem to assume the separateness and anonymity of sculptures. Klein's wife kneels before his mutilated body in an anguished *pietà*, and the old peasant woman aids the wounded aviators with the eternal succouring gesture of the women in the crucifixions.

At certain junctures in his novels Malraux calls upon still another art to express his meaning, music. The symbolic image, the plastically rendered processional are employed to express the transformation which art effects on the facts of human existence. The plastic image raises experience to the level of an absolute value in lasting form. But for the rare instants of peace and of happiness, when man rises above the struggles which generally exhaust him, Malraux prefers the art of music. "When it's a question of happiness, literature is a poor means compared with music," writes Malraux.[22] The same aesthetic preference for *sound* which makes Malraux say that he values a writer's tone and the tone of his characters, is evident here. But whereas tone implies a phenomenon of will, the use of music in Malraux's fiction is independent of the mythology of action. Music is decorative and symbolic.

The crowd which follows the funeral cortège of Tcheng-Dai is first noticed as a wave of sound which fills the streets. "A distant rumbling of drums and gongs pierced by the sounds of a monochord violins and flutes, now modulated, now shrill; sounds of bagpipes, fine, linear, in spite of the sharp sounds, in the midst of a muffled crackling of sandals and of words paced by the gongs" (C, p. 127). In *La Voie royale* a beggar chants a folk epic in the midst of the jungle, music played where there is no audience: it exists in and for itself, like the art form lying dormant till an appreciative culture comes to awaken it. Alvéar listens to the "Internationale" sung in the streets of Madrid by a blind man: this music on the eve of defeat becomes the symbol of a hope which surpasses the political setting. It is like Malraux's oracular affirmation that the wretched crew descending the mountain is equal to that mountain—the logic of opposites triumphs. Man affirms himself in action and in art, and in this affirmation reaches beyond his mortality.

Painting and sculpture can transfigure the novelist's vision into an enduring object. Music and its motion can surpass this feat: it can suggest the cycle of man's eternal death and rebirth. Malraux's description of Kassner's auditory hallucination which saves him from total despair is one of his finest passages. The funeral chant becomes a symbol of eternal life.

> Music perpetuated all of the past by delivering it from time, mixing everything in its gathered presence like life and death in the immobility of the starry sky. . . . All memory dissolved in an endless rain which descended on things as if its inexhaustible flight had dragged them to the bottom of the past. Perhaps death was like this music. . . . When he soared in

his dreams, wings spread out, in a long movement like a sail in the wind, little by little he mingled his scattered body with the inexhaustible fatality of the stars, fascinated by the army of the night adrift toward eternity across the silence. (TM, pp. 54-56)

Kassner is able to see beyond death in music. In *La Condition humaine* Gisors moves beyond pain in the imaginary symphony which detaches him from the world of his son's death.

Assimilating many art forms into fiction, André Malraux transmutes his vision of the modern tragedy into "the world of things conceived and dominated." Like the bas-reliefs of the Royal Way which reign over the insects and beasts of the jungle with a majestic secular gesture, the artistic metamorphoses Malraux achieves in his novels rise above the revolutions and wars of men, transforming the substance of defeat and death into a poetry of triumph.

Notes on Some Classic French Folk Ballads Recently Collected in Louisiana

by

Harry Oster

ALTHOUGH ANCIENT FRENCH folk ballads in Louisiana are on the brink of extinction, known only by old people who seldom sing them since their children show no interest in hearing or learning them, nevertheless in this last generation many of the surviving songs are still in a good state of preservation, textually not far removed from their ancestors of hundreds of years ago. There are others with excellent texts in which changes of a positive creative nature have occurred, fresh sprigs blossoming on the tree of tradition. Another group consists of songs in which the text has become corrupt or confused in the course of transmission, and a fourth is made up of fragments. In this paper I will illustrate and discuss ballads of these four classes which I have collected and recorded.[1]

Among the most beautiful and best preserved of the Louisiana French ballads is "Les anneaux de Marianson," an ancient song which probably goes back to the Middle Ages. This variant was sung for me in 1957 by Caesar Vincent, a seventy-four year old native of the farm country adjoining Abbeville, who is a descendant of the Acadian exiles.

1. "Marianson, femme jolie,
   Et oussqu'il est votre mari?"
2. "Et mon mari-z-il est past ici,
   C'est à la guerre il est allé."

239

3. "Oh oui! madam', femme jolie,
   Vous m'donn'riez-ti pas ces trois anneaux d'ces doigts?"

4. Lui dit: "Non, non, non, non, monsieur,
   Mon mari trop fidèle à moi.

5. Mais alle'-y chez lor-lorfèfvr',
   Et fait'-vous-en fair' trois pareils.

6. Et fait'-vous-en fair' trois pareils
   Et ni plus p'tites et ni plus grand'."

7. Le beau galant ne perd pas d'temps,
   Dret à l'orfèv' il est allè les commander.
   C'est trois anneaux, ces trois anneaux
   Jolis d'ces doigts.

8. Ces trois anneaux jolis d'ces doigts,
   Z-et ni plus p'tit et ni plus grandes.

9. Ce beau galant dret qu'il ait yeu ces trois anneaux,
   Ce beau galant ne perd pas d'temps,
   Dret à la guerre il est allé.

10. Le premier homme il rencontre,
    C'était le mari de Marianson.

11. "Ohé, Marie, homme joli,
    Quelles nouvelles apportez-vous de ma famill'?
    Et la nouvell' moi rapporter."
    "C'est moi l'mari de Marianson."

12. Lui dit: "Non, non, non, non, monsieur,
    Ma femme est trop fidèle à moi."

13. "Et croyez-les, croyez-les pas,
    Les voilà ses trois anneaux."

14. Ce beau galant, quand il a vu ça,
    Z'il est tombé, trois jours, trois nuits resta par terre.
    Au bout d'trois jours-z-au bout trois nuits,
    Ce beau galant-z-e-ressussi.

15. "Ohé! ma femm', v'là ton mari qui s'en revient tout enragé,
    Courez-lui presenter son petit
    Pour lui apaiser sa colère."

16. Il a pris son p'tit par les pieds blancs,
    Dret au muraill' il l'a attaché.
    Il a pris sa femm' par les cheveux,
    Drouet au plancher il l'a traînée.

17. Dessu' les butt' et les buttons
    Fesait que vouer passer le sang de Marianson.
18. "Ah, oui, mari, homme jolie,
    Qu'avez-vous vouloir detruir' Marianson?"
19. "Oh, oui, madam', femme jolie,
    Et ioussqu'l' sont mes trois anneaux?"
20. "Prenez la clé du cabaret
    Z-et fait' trois tours, vous les trouverez."
21. Le beau galant ne perd pas d'temps,
    Z-il a bien pris, ah oui! la clé du cabaret.
22. Il avait bien pas fait' trois tours,
    Il entendait ses anneaux sonner.
23. "Oh oui, madam', femme jolie,
    Vouderez-ti m'le pardonner?"
24. "Tant qu'à pour moi je vous pardonne,
    Mais pas pour le sang de mon p'tit enfant."
25. "Oh, oui, madam', femme jolie
    Quel médécin i' vous fauderait?"
26. "E-je vois pas ni médécin, ni pret' ni saint
    Qui pourrait remett' mon corps en sin (sang).
27. Prenez quat' planch', clouez-les ensembl',
    Z-et mettez-moi-z-avec le sang de mon p'tit enfant."

This text is essentially similar to typical French and French Canadian variants, like the following one collected by Dr. Marius Barbeau at Ovide Soucy, Saint-Antoine, Temiskouata, Canada:

1. "Marianson, dame joli'
   Où est allé votre mari?"
2. "Mon mari est allé-z-en guerr'
   Ah! je ne sais s'il reviendra."
3. "Marianson, dame joli',
   Prêtez-moi vos anneaux dorés."
4. "Ils son dans l'coffre au pied du lit.
   Ah! prends les clefs et va les qu'ri.'"
5. "Bel orfèvrier, bel orfèvrier,
   Faites-moi des anneaux dorés,
6. Et qu'ils soient faits aussi parfaits
   Comm' les ceuss de Marianson."

7. Quand il a eu ses trois anneaux,
   Sur son cheval s'est embarqué.

8. Le premier qu'il a rencontré
   C'était l'mari de Marianson.

9. "Ah! bonjour donc, franc cavalier,
   Quell' nouvell m'as-tu-apporté'?"

10. "Ah! des nouvelles je n'en ai pas,
    Que les ceuss de Marianson."

11. "Marianson, dame joli'
    Elle m'a eté fidèle assez."

12. "Oui, je les crois, je le décrois:
    Voila les anneaux de ses doigts."

13. "Tu as menti, franc cavalier!
    Ma femme m'est fidèle assez."

14. Sa femme qu'était sur les remparts
    Et qui le voit venir là-bas:

15. "Il est malade ou bien fâché,
    C'est une chos' bien assuré'.

16. Ah! Maman montre-lui son fils
    Ca lui rejouira l'esprit."

17. "Ah! tiens mon fils, voilà ton fils.
    Quel nom donn'ras-tu à ton fils?"

18. "A l'enfant je donn'rai un nom,
    A la mère un mauvais renom."

19. A pris l'enfant par le maillot,
    Trois fois par terre il l'a jeté.

20. Marianson par les cheveux
    A son cheval l'a attaché'.

21. Il a marché trois jours, trois nuits
    Sans regarder par derrièr' lui.

22. Au bout des trois jours et trois nuits
    A regardé par derrièr' lui.

23. "Marianson, dame joli'
    Où sont les anneaux de tes doigts?

24. Ils sont dans l'coffre, au pied du lit,
    Ah! prends les clefs et va les qu'ri."

25. Il n'eut pas fait trois tours de clef,
    Ses anneaux d'or il a trouvés.

26. "Marianson, dame joli',
    Quel bon chirurgien vous faut-il?"
27. "Le bon chirurgien qu'il me faut
    C'est un bon drap pour m'ensev'lir."
28. "Marianson, dame joli',
    Votre mort m'est-ell' pardonné'?"
29. "Oui, ma mort vous est pardonné',
    Non pas celle du nouveau-né."[2]

According to the typical plot of this ballad, while Marianson's husband is at war, an enemy of his has copies made of the three rings her husband had given her. He then proceeds to the battlefield where he meets her husband. The enemy boasts that he is the real mate of Marianson. As evidence he shows the husband the three rings. The husbands falls into a faint for three days. When he comes to his senses, he returns home. From the ramparts Marianson and her mother (or companion) observe the intense disturbance of the approaching rider, and the mother suggests that Marianson run to him to present him his baby to soothe his anger. When she does so, he seizes the infant by the feet and dashes him against the wall. Then he seizes Marianson by the hair and drags her behind his horse. When she is on the brink of death, he asks for his three rings. When she tells him to look in the cabinet, he takes the key; and then as he opens the drawer he hears the rings jingling. His lady forgives him for her own death but not for the death of her child. Her final request is that he nail together four planks as a coffin for herself and her little child.

The theme of "Les anneaux de Marianson" was among the most popular of the Middle Ages, although most often the innocent survived and the traitor was punished. Shakespeare's *Cymbeline* embodies a similar theme.[3] In works most like the ballad the husband often boasted of the impeccable virtue of his wife, making a bet with an acquaintance that the latter cannot seduce his wife. Although he fails, he brings the husband some sign of having succeeded—a birthmark seen on her body or a favorite jewel obtained by trickery or theft. Again, the nature of the punishment, dragging the victim by the hair, was a traditional feature of many of the ballads of northern Europe, as for example, in the ballad describing the killing of old Queen Brunehaut by the son of Frédégonde.[4]

"Les anneaux des Marianson" has also been imitated by poets. Toward the end of the eighteenth century there appeared in France in the style of the troubadours, "Adélaide et Ferdinand ou les Trois Anneaux," sung to "l'air du prélude de Mina," and later the Suisse-Romande story of "Sire de Vanel."[5]

Let us consider a second well-preserved text. "La danseuse noyée" is a widely known ballad of France and French Canada; the following Louisiana variant, sung by Alma Bartholomew, a fifty-five year old mulatto of Diamond, is not significantly different from typical variants of France and French Canada:

1. Son frère arrive dans un joli bateau.
2. "Bonjour ma mère et où est Hélène, ma soeur?"
3. "Hélène, ta soeur, dans la chambre à pleurer."
4. "Bonjour, Hélène, qu'avez-vous à pleurer?"
5. "A ce beau bal ma mère veut pas je vas."
6. "Hélène, s'habille tout en satin brodé."
7. La première valse était avec son frère.
8. Le pont défoncé, Hélène tomba à l'eau.
9. "Comment, mon frère, tu m'laisseras noyer?"
10. Sonnez les cloches pour Hélène qu'est noyée.
11. J'ai fait un songe qu'Hélène s'avait s'était noyée.
12. Voilà le sort des enfants entêtés.
13. Son père fait fair un' tombe tout en marbre,
    Son père fait faire un cerceuil tout doré,
    Son père fait faire un tombe tout en marbre.

Doncieux's composite text is only slightly more detailed:

1. Au pont de Nantes un bal est assigné.
2. La belle Hélène voudrait bien y aller:
3. "Ma chère mère, m'y lairrez-vous aller?"
4. "Non, non, ma fille, vous n'irez point danser."
5. Elle monte en chambre et se met à plorer.
6. Son frère arrive dans un bateau doré:

7. "Qu'as tu, ma soeure, qu'as tu donc à plorer?"
8. "Hélas! mon frère, je n'irai point danser!"
9. "Oh! si, ma soeure, moi, je t'y conduirai.
10. Met robe blance et ceinture doré."
11. Et fit toris toures, le pont s'est défoncé.
12. La belle Hélène dans la Loire est tombé:
13. "Hélas! mon frère, me lairras-tu noyer?"
14. "Non, non, ma soeure, je vai te retirer!"
15. Dans l'eau se jette, et les voilà noyés.
16. Toutes les cloches se mirent à sonner.
17. La mer' demande: "Qu'a-t-on à tant sonner?"
18. "C'est pour Hélène et votre fils aïé."
19. Voilà le sore des enfants ostinés![6]

Helen longs to go to a dance being held on a bridge, but her mother refuses to let her attend. Her brother arrives and, against their mother's wishes, takes her to the ball. The bridge suddenly collapses, probably under the shaking caused by the dancing, and Helen falls into the stream. Her brother tries to save her but they both drown. (The drowning of the brother does not occur in the Louisiana variant.) The drowning is given as an example of the horrors which can befall a child who disobeys his parents. The moral of the song is of a naïve sort, appropriate to the intelligence of a young child.

This ballad has been found in all the provinces of France, but it is most widely known in western France and in the vicinity of Nantes, where it probably originated. Although many variants begin with "Au pont de Nantes" and mention the Loire, other bridges are also the scene of the tragedy—pont de Londres, pont du Nord, or pont des Morts.

The theme of the mother who refuses her daughter permission to attend a ball has been popular since around the end of the twelfth century, as suggested by this fragment in Old French:

> C'est là-jus c'on dit ès prés,
> Jeu et hal i sont criés;
> Enmelos y veut aler,
> A sa mère en aquiert grés:
> "Par Dieu, fille, vous n'ires!"[7]

The ballad may also be, as Doncieux suggests, a fragmentary and confused survival of the Danish ballad, "Agnes and the Man of the Waters" (a variant of which is the ultimate source of Matthew Arnold's "The Forsaken Merman") ,[8] which was widely distributed in central Europe, as, for example, in the probably related German ballad, "Die schöne Hannele." In the Danish ballad, which is among the most beautiful creations of Scandinavian folk poetry, Agnes asks her foster mother for permission to go to the shore. Her mother refuses, warning her that the man of the sea may come to look for her; nevertheless Agnes makes her way toward the shore. As she is crossing a bridge, suddenly the man of the sea appears. She accepts his love, and he takes her to his underwater palace. Eight years elapse, during which they have seven children. One day, as she is seated at the cradle of her youngest child, she hears the bells of England, the kingdom of her father. Suddenly deeply homesick, she begs the merman to allow her to pray in a church in her native land. Her husband reluctantly grants her permission but insists that her stay be as brief as possible. As precautions he stops her ears and closes her lips. Swimming through the sea, he brings her to the beach, from which she reaches the church of her parents. When she sees her parents, her old ties reassert themselves. The merman pursues her, begging her to return, but she refuses. In some versions, the abandoned one avenges himself by killing her.

The first part of this story may be relevant to the French ballad; it includes the girl's asking permission to go out and her mother's refusal, her appearing on a bridge, the arrival of a swimming man, the disappearance of the couple under the waves, and the ringing of the bells. It may be that the French imitator misunderstood the first part of the story—the girl's rebellion and her falling into the water. The French version includes her brother instead of the supernatural swimmer; the tragedy of the drowning of Helen becomes an accident, which can be explained in terms of a realistic event— the collapse of a bridge during enthusiastic participation in an old custom. The bells which summoned Agnes in the Danish ballad are perhaps represented in the French ballad by those which toll to announce the death of Hélène or Hélène and her brother.[9] Although Doncieux's theory that "La danseuse noyée" is the degenerate daughter of a noble mother is highly ingenious, the parallelism of the French and Danish ballads may well be pure coincidence.

"Trois jolis dragons," as sung by Alma Bartholomew, is another Louisiana ballad which closely resembles French and French Canadian variants, which are usually entitled, "Le jolis tambours":

1. Trois jolis dragons qui reviennent de la guerre
   Romme, plomme, plomme,
   Qui reviennent de la guerre.
2. Le plus jeune de trois avait une jolie rose.
3. La fille du roi était à la fénêt'e.
4. "Joli dragon, donnez-moi votre coeur*e*."
5. "Fille du roi, donnez-moi cettre rose."
6. "Joli dragon, demandez à mon père."
7. "Sire mon roi, donnez-moi votre fille."
8. "Joli dragon, vous n'êtes pas assez riche."
9. "Sire mon roi, j'ai trois navires en mer*e*.
10. Un chargé d'or et l'aut' plein marchandise,
    Et le troisième, c'est pour promener ma mie-se."
11. "Joli dragon, ma fille l'est à vous*e*."
12. "Sire mon roi, je vous en remercie.
13. Dans mon pays, il ya mais des plus belles."

Although in Alma Bartholomew's Louisiana version the young man is described as a dragoon rather than as a drummer, the occupation he holds in most versions of the song, the refrain is an obvious imitation of the sound of a drum. Some variants have an additional interchange between the king and the soldier which is helpful in discovering the approximate date of the first appearance of this song:

> "Joli tambour, dis moi quel est ton père?"
> "Sire le roi, c'est le roi d'Angleterre."
> "Et ma mère est la reine de Hongrie."[10]

The basic plot tells of the passage of three drummers outside the king's palace. The princess, who is seated at the window, notices that the youngest of the three has a pretty rose. When she asks him for it, he replies by asking for her hand. She tells him to request permission from her father. When the soldier presents himself to the king, the king rejects him on the grounds that he is not rich enough. The soldier replies that he has three ships on the sea, one loaded with merchandise, one full of gold, and one just to carry his sweetheart. Impressed, the king offers his daughter, but the soldier answers, "Thank you, but in my country the girls are prettier."

The reference of the young man to his ships to build up his prestige suggests that the song originated among maritime people, probably on the coast of Poitou, Brittany, or Normandy. The hero may well have been a drummer of the royal fleet. The reference to the Queen of Hungary is probably to Maria Theresa of Austria (1717-1780), since over a period of centuries there was no other woman of such a title. Furthermore, the legend of the strangely dramatic circumstances of her coronation at the Diet of Pressburg in 1741 left a deep impression on her contemporaries. Also her name must have been mentioned frequently during a twenty-three year period throughout which her armies met with those of France, either as enemies or as allies.[11]

The ending may be explained in two possible ways. Either the soldier is expressing class-consciousness—the lowly drummer shames the mighty king by rejecting his daughter, or he may be a prince in disguise, as in fairy tales or the comedies of Marivaux, someone who approaches his beloved incognito in order to test her heart to discover whether she will love him for himself alone.[12]

Another ballad of the French-speaking world is "La ville de Mantoue," as sung for me in March, 1958, by Jean Paul Davide, an eighty-six year old native of New Roads, a town about thirty-five miles northwest of Baton Rouge:

1. La ville de Mantoue, eh Dieu! qu'elle est jolie!
   Elle est jolie, oui oui, belle assurément,
   Que Napoléon veut rentrer dedans.
2. Napoléon a envoyé quatre homm' de des gens' d'armes:

Allez voir le président du peupl',
A savoir s'ils veul' se rendre à nous.

3. Le président du peupl' lui a envoyé lui dire:
"De rtoutautoure (du tout au tout)
Nous nous moquons de lui
Aussi bien la nuit comme le jour."

4. Napoléon a fait bloquer son hôtellerie.
Le premier coup d'canon qu'on a tiré.
Tout' la jolie ville n'a tremblé,
Et tout' les dames de Mantoue étaient su' les remparts montées:
"Napoléon, apaisez votre colére,
Nous vous donnons chacun cent mille escus."

5. "De vos cent mille escus, mesdam',
Je ne saurais quoi en faire.
Mes canons bris'ront tou' vos maisons,
Et mes chasseurs vous pilleront, mesdames,
Courage, mes enfants, la ville est au pillage."
Ils ont tant tiré, mais tant de (patronelles),
Que Napoléon éta rentré dedans.

Achille Millien cites a typical variant of France:

1. La ville de Mantoue
Grande Dieu! Qu'elle est jolie!
Elle est joli', parfaite assurément,
O vous, Français, entrez dedans.

2. Bonaparte a t-envoyé
Quatre de ses gendarmes
"C'est Bonaparte qui nous envoie ici,
Si vous voulez vous rendre à lui."

3. "Va dire à Bonaparte,
Ton gouverneur de France
Va donc lui dir' qu'nous f--- de lui,
Autant le jour (e) que la nuit."

4. Bonaparte a fait braquer
Ses canons d'assurance.
Au premier coup que l'canon a tiré,

La jolie ville en a tremblé.
5. Les dames de Mantoue
 Montaient sur les rempar (*es*)
 "O Bonaparte, apaise tes canons;
 Contribution nous te paierons."
6. "Quelle contribution
 Me paierez-vous, mesdames?"
 "Contribution de cinq mille écus,
 Que tes canons ne tirent plus!"
7. "Mesdam', de votre argent
 Je ne saurais qu'en faire
 Oh! mes canons brûleront vos maisons
 Et mes soldats les pilleront.
8. Courage, mes soldats!
 La ville est au pillage.
 Et nous tuerons les petits et les grands,
 Et nous prendrons l'or et l'argent!"[13]

Napoleon approaches the beautiful city of Mantoue. He sends envoys to demand surrender, but the chief of government sends him a scornful reply. When Napoleon bombards the city, all the ladies of Mantoue mount the ramparts to offer him thousands of crowns to stop the bombardment. Napoleon refuses and tells them that he will destroy their houses and his infantry will pillage their city. He instructs his soldiers to begin killing and pillaging.

Although the earliest variants of this ballad grew out of the wars of Louis XIV, the same basic text has been used to describe the taking of Turin in 1690; the insurrections of the Vendée in 1793, in which the city of Montaigu is the object of the attack and the general is de Charrette; and even, in a French-Canadian variant, the fictitious retaking of Toronto by the patriotic Louis-Joseph Papeneau, a Canadian politically quite active in 1837.[14]

An interesting example of a Louisiana ballad which shows a creative local variation is "Le mariage anglais," as sung for me in 1957 by Alma Bartholomew:

1. C'était la fille d'un roi français,

Son pére voulait la marier
Avec un bon Anglais.
    Refrain:
"Car moi, j'estime un bon Français
Que toi, maudit Anglais."

2. Quand c'èst l'heure de souper,
L'Anglais voulait couper son pain.
"Oh coupe ton pain et laisse
Le mien, maudit Anglais."

3. Quand c'est venu l'heure de se coucher
L'Anglais voulait la déchausser.
"Oh déchausse-toi et laisse
Moi, maudit Anglais."

4. Quand c'est venu sur les onze heurs et demie,
L'Anglais pensait à ses amours.
"Oh tourne-toi, embrasse
Moi, maudit Anglais."

5. "O belle, laissez-moi dormir,
Car tout à l'heure je vais être hors du lit;
Vous avez l'argent dans votre pays
Pour vous faire servie, et moi une dame de
Lafourche pour me faire l'amour."

A variant which is typical of those of France and Canada is
printed by Millien:

1. Mon pér' m'a voulu marier,
Un roi z-anglais il m'a voulu donner.
    "Empêch', empêch', mon petit frèr',
      De m'emmener:
     J'aimerais mieux soldat français
      Que roi z-anglais."

2. Ils l'ont prisé, ils l'ont emmené',
Dedans Paris ils l'ont mené' passer.
     Toutes les dames de la vill'
      Font que d'pleurer
     De voir la fill' du roi français
      A un Anglais.

3. Quand ce vint la mer a passer,
   Le roi z-anglais les yeux lui bander.
      "Bande les tiens, laisse les miens,
      Maudit Anglais.
   Puisque j'ai la mer à passer,
      Je la verrai."

4. Quand (*e*) la mer ell' fut passé,
   Tambours, violons de tour les côtés:
      "Apaisez-vous, maudits tambours
   Apaisez-vous!
      Oh! ce n'est pas ça les tambours
         Du roi français."

5. Quand c'est venu pour le coucher,
   Le roi z-anglais voulait la déchausser:
      "Dechaussee-toi, et laisse-moi,
      Maudit Angalis!
   J'ai bien du mond' de mon pays
      Pour me servir."

6. Quand c'est venu sur les minuits,
   La belle pousse un grand soupir:
      "Retourne-toi, embrasse-moi,
      Mon cher Anglais.
   Puisque Dieu nous a mariés,
      Faut nous aimer."[15]

The basic plot of the ballad deals with the marriage of an English king to a French princess who patriotically hates the English. She rebuffs all his efforts to be kind, but finally when they are in bed together, she decides that her patriotism has been carried far enough. The song probably originated as a reaction to the marriage of Henriette of France, daughter of Henry IV, with Charles I of England in June, 1625.[16]

The typical variant quoted by Millien has some dramatic details which the Louisiana one does not: the ladies of the city weeping to see the princess with an Englishman; the princess angrily rejecting his kind offer to blindfold her to spare her some of the terrors of crossing the sea; the princess angrily telling the trumpets and violins of the accursed English to be silent because they are not like those of the king of France. On the other hand, the Louisiana variant has other picturesque incidents—the princess at dinner insisting that she will cut her own bread and at bedtime refusing to let her husband take her shoes off. These details are not unique to Louisiana, but the ending represents a creative addition; the conclusion is even more sophisticated than in the variants from France. The Englishman replies to his French bride's final practical acceptance of the marriage with a rebuff; he needs his rest in order to be fresh for his mistress, who is a native of Lafourche Parish in Louisiana.

As an example of a confused ballad text we may examine this variant of "La marquise empoisonnée," sung for me by Jean Paul Davide in 1958:

1. Le roi-a-a fait faire une lit
   Pour voir toutes les femmes.
   N'en trouverai point-z-a son loisi
   Que le femm' du beau marquis.
2. "Marquis, t'es plus heureux que moi
   D'avoir si jolie femme,
   Mais je te jur', dessur ma foi,
   Nous logerons ensemble."
3. "Si vous avez tout le pouvoir,
   Tout le pouvoir du pays,
   Mais si vous ne seriez point le roi,
   J'en prenderai vengeance."
4. Le roi la prit par la main,
   L'emmena dans sa chambe
   Et la douc' marquise en pleurant,
   Croyait de s'en défende.
5. "Ah! pleurez point tant, la belle,
   Je te ferai princesse.
   Et de mon or et mon argent,
   Tu en seras maîtresse."
6. "J'estim'rais meiux mon doux marquis
   Que le roi avec ses fleurs de li'."
7. Le roi-z-a fait faire un bouquet
   De trois fleurs jolies

Il l'a mis dessus son
En   ?   de la marquise.
8. Le roi i' a fait faire un tombeau
De trois´pierres jolies.
A fait braquer aux quatre coins
Le nom de la marquise.

In this variant the crucial incident of the poisoning has been badly confused, perhaps because of faulty memory or misunderstanding by the singer or others in the chain of oral transmission.

The central plot of the ballad is clear in this variant collected by Dr. Marius Barbeau in Sainte-Anne-des-Monts, Gaspé, Canada:

1. Quand le roi rentrit dans Paris,
   Quand le roi rentrit dans Paris, a salué les dames,
   Le premier' qu'il a salué ell' lui a ravi l'âme.
2. "Marquis t'es plus heureux qu'un roi, plus heureux,
       qu'un roi d'avoir un' joli' femme,
   Si tu voulais m'en fair' l'honneur, j'en aurais l'avantage."
3. "Sire, vous avez tout pouvoir, l'pouvoir et la puissance;
   Car, si vous n'étiez pas le roi, j'en aurais la vengeance."
4. Le roi l'a pris l'a emmené dans la plus haute chambre.
   Nuit et jour ell' ne cess' d'pleurer pour son honneur
       défendre.
5. "La bell', si tu voulais m'aimer, je t'y ferais princesse,
   De tout mon or et mon argent tu serais la maîtresse."
6. "Gardez votre or et votre argent, n'appartient qu'à la reine.
   J'estim'rais mieux mon doux marquis que toutes vos
       richesses."
7. La reine lui fit faire un bouquet de trois roses jolies,
   Et la senteur de ce bouquet fit mourir la marquise.
8. Le roi fit faire un tombeau couvert de pierre grise;
   A fait marquer tout alentour le nom de la marquise.[17]

The king is attracted to the wife of the marquis, who gives her up with great reluctance since he and his wife love each other. In the king's chamber the marquise weepingly resists the king's advances; despite his offers of wealth and the title of princess, she insists that she loves her marquis more than all his wealth. The jealous queen poisons the marquise by placing a bouquet of three poisoned roses near her. Grief-stricken, the king has an imposing tomb built for the marquise.

George Doncieux persuasively attributes the origin of this beautiful ballad to a historical incident involving Henri IV (1553-1610) and his mistress, Gabrielle d'Estrées. Henri IV first saw and desired Mlle d'Estrées when she was a girl living with her father. For the sake of appearances he had her married to a lord of Liancourt, actually a *sieur* rather than a *marquis*. Later the king had the marriage dissolved by Parliament and made Gabrielle, Marquise of Monceaux. In 1599 at Easter time the two lovers separated for eight days as was customary for a monarch with a mistress. Gabrielle, then four months pregnant, full of presentiments, left for the house of a Tuscan financier, Zamet. On her way back from worship at a chapel, she was stricken with convulsions. After forty hours of suffering, she gave birth to a dead child; shortly afterwards she died, frightfully twisted and disfigured. As has happened frequently when a sudden death occurs which stirs up a court and fosters intrigue, there was suspicion that she had been poisoned. Marguerite de Valois, the queen, had for many years been estranged from the court and living in her own chateau. Apparently she had no connection with the death of Gabrielle, but her introduction into the ballad came about as a result of the popular belief that when the mistress of a king dies of poison, the queen must be the poisoner.[18]

Since "La marquise empoisonée" fell under the edict of 1395, forbidding satiric songs against great men of the kingdom on penalty of two months in prison on bread and water, it is relatively rare in France. It spread more freely in the New World, but it is far from common.[19]

Some classic French ballads survive in Louisiana only in fragmentary form. One of the most ancient fragments found is this variant of "Prince Eugène," sung by Alma Bartholomew in 1956:

1. "Oh, Jean, mon petit page,
   Regarde quel bruit c'est ça."
2. "C'est le monsieur de Moncorne,

Vot' grand plus ennemi."
3. "Oh, Jean, si tu en penses,
Je m'en vais t'en fillet."
4. "J'en est tubé quatorze,
Mon épée ne rend plus.
5. "Oh, Jean, mon petit page,
Retourne-toi dans Paris.
6. "Tu diras à Maurice
Qu'il n'a plus de cher' fils.
7. "Tu diras a ma femme
Qu'il l'a plus de mari."
8. "O Vierge, sainte Vierge,
Rendez-moi mon mari."
9. "J'en n'ai tubé quatorze,
Mon épée ne rend plus."

In a more complete variant like the following from Quebec, there are many more verses and complications:

1. Un jour, le prince Eugène, étant dedans Paris,
S'en fut conduir' trois dames,
Vive l'amour!
tout droit a leur logis,
Vive la fleur de lis!
2. S'en fut conduir' trois dames tout droit à leur logis.
Quand il fut a leur porte: "Coucheriez-vous ici?"
3. "Menni, non, non, mesdames! Je vais à mon logis."
4. Quand il fut sur ces côtés, regard derrièr' lui.
5. A vu venir vingt hommes, ses plus grands ennemis.
6. "T'en souviens-tu, Eugène, un jour, dedans Paris,
7. Devant le roi, la reine, mon fils t'as dementi?
8. Arrête ici, Eugène, il faut payer ceci."
9. Tira son épée d'or, bravement se battit.
10. Il en tua quatorze, mais sans qu'il se lassit.
11. Quand ce vint au quinzième, son épée d'or rompit.
12. "Beau page, mon beau page, viens donc m'y secourir."
13. "Nenni, non, non, beau prince, j'ai trop peur d'y mourir!"
14. "Va-t'en dire à ma femme qu'ell' prenn' soin du petit.
15. Quand il sera en age, il vengera ceci!"[20]

While in Paris, Prince Eugène is escorting three ladies to their lodgings. He virtuously declines to spend the night with them. As he approaches his own quarters, twenty men, his worst enemies, attack him. One of them reveals the reason for the ambush—he is avenging Prince Eugène's accusing his son, before the king and queen, of being a liar. Prince Eugène draws his golden sword, and fighting bravely, kills fourteen without growing weary. But in his battle with the fifteenth foe his sword breaks. He pleads with his page to come to his aid, but the page is too afraid to risk death. Prince Eugène's last words are a request that the page tell his wife to take good care of their little son, for when he comes of age, he will avenge his father's death.

Although this song is among the most remarkable of French folksongs, it is not widely known, for like "La marquise empoisonée" it fell under the edict of 1395. The song is a satire directed against Francis I after his defeat by Charles V at Pavia in 1525. Francis was ignominiously taken prisoner and confined in the dungeons of Madrid; the news of his defeat made him unpopular in France. When a false rumor spread that the king had died of sickness in prison, someone composed this ballad, using Prince Eugène as a fictitious name for the king. The song depicts a noble prince who is the exact opposite of the popular image of Francis I; the satire comes from the incongruity of describing him as virtuous, continent, and so heroic that he fights to the death against overwhelming odds. But as everyone recognized at whom the barbs of satire were aimed, the song was suppressed.[21] It is thus of special significance to discover that this rare ballad is still being sung in Louisiana.

Although these recently collected ballads represent the last leaves of the classic French tradition in Louisiana, there is much left worthy of study as poetry and as folklore. "Les anneaux de Marianson" resounds with the dramatic power and poetic fire of such ballads performed centuries ago. "La danseuse noyee" is entertaining in the genre of songs to amuse children, and also of special interest as (in accordance with Doncieux's theory) the degenerate offspring of a great Danish ballad. "Trois jolis dragons" presents in lively style an encounter between a soldier and a princess; its popularity and wide dispersion in folk circles all over the French speaking world are probably in some measure the results of identification with the gallant soldier by humble people—an expression of wish fulfillment. "Le mariage anglais" not only continues to be an amusing commentary on Gallic practicality in marriage, but also represents a creative local variation of a sophistication that a Parisian would respect. "La marquise empoisonnée" and "La ville de Mantoue" demonstrate the process by which texts become confused in oral transmission and the distortion of history which usually occurs in folk tradition. Finally, there is the fragment of "Prince Eugène"; it is of special significance because of its rarity, its antiquity, and (like the other ballads collected from Alma Bartholomew) its appearance in the tradition of French Negroes in Louisiana.

American Literature in Postwar Germany: Impact or Alienation?

by
Horst Oppel

AROUND THE MIDDLE of the nineteenth century Edgar Allan Poe made the well-known statement in his "Letter to Mr. B.": "You are aware of the great barrier in the path of an American writer. He is read, if at all, in preference to the combined and established wit of the world."[1] And now, a hundred years later, it is tempting for me as a German literary critic to change this to read: "You are aware of the great barrier in the path of a German writer. He is read, if at all, in preference to the combined and established wit of America."

This statement brings out the impression which everyone has when studying publishing figures of American novels in Germany or performance statistics on American plays in German theaters. There is not the slightest doubt of the preferences of the general public today. Thus the reception of American literature in postwar Germany is not only the concern of the professional critic, but also of equal interest to journalists, stage managers, publishers, and translators. Of even greater importance is the obvious necessity for German creative writers to realize how this predominance of American literature has come about, and what consequences it will have for our native literature in the future.

In the first few years after the last war there developed a kind of dichotomy in the statements and verdicts of German writers; on the one hand they were glad that German literature was reopened to the valuable influences and stimulation of world literature after a period of artificial isolation and nationalistic

259

narrowness, but on the other hand concern was expressed that German literature would be forced into competition with foreign works, a competition in which, under the circumstances, German literature was doomed to fail. Here an undertone of resentment could be heard quite clearly. In his excellent article on "Postwar German Reactions to American Literature," John R. Frey collected such critical opinions, in which admiration for the variety and vitality of modern American writing was mixed with anxiety about the fate of German literature.[2] On the part of young German authors we find an unreserved receptivity and an explicit desire to imitate. Ernest Hemingway, Thomas Wolfe, and William Faulkner were mentioned again and again as literary models for the guidance which German narrative art was looking for after the war. The irreparable break with the grand tradition of the German *Bildungsroman* as practiced by Goethe's successors became especially evident. German writers were aware that both subject matter and style would have to undergo a decisive change. But in spite of the general willingness to accept American writers as models, doubt was expressed as to whether this fatal attraction of foreign literature might not lead to a stagnation of the creative impulse in new German writing. In this connection Frey mentions a letter of March, 1947, in which the prominent German writer Elisabeth Langgäser (who died in 1950) stated that unless a German author approved of and wrote like Hemingway or Faulkner, he would not be accepted by German readers.[3]

But why has modern American literature been so unusually successful in Germany? There are two points in which it is considered as being definitely superior to German achievements. First, American writers in both fiction and drama are able to construct truly exciting, interesting, and thought-provoking plots. We were already accustomed to adventure and sensationalism as the special province of older American writing (James Fenimore Cooper, Poe, Bret Harte, Jack London), and we found these qualities in undiminished vigor in modern American writing. It is obvious that Thornton Wilder in *The Bridge of San Luis Rey* combines a profound treatment of questions of human fate with a suspenseful plot, that William Faulkner in *Light in August* or *Intruder in the Dust* projects the mysterious complexity of the human soul into a lively external action, and that John Steinbeck in *Cannery Row* gives an unusual picaresque story with both inner and outer tension. But there is still another point. In addition to these adventurous and sensational elements, the German reader is impressed by the courage of American authors in stripping modern life of all illusion. The novels of Sinclair Lewis and Upton Sinclair, with their social criticism, had already made this impression on European readers, and after the Second World War such works as Erskine Caldwell's *Trouble in July* and Steinbeck's *The Grapes of Wrath* showed that the younger generation was continuing to treat life without illusion. In this regard, German receptivity to American writing sometimes went to an extreme; this explains the striking success of such extreme realism as Norman Mailer's *The Naked and the Dead* and James Jones's *From Here to Eternity*. But it must be added that the success here was only ephemeral. The main reason for this is not that the narrative weaknesses of such works were soon perceived, or that doubt was raised as to the documentary value of such fictional reports, but rather that in the past few years a deep change has taken place in aesthetic taste. In any case, it is today mainly other works of American literature than those of 1945-1953 which are considered models, and which can be expected to have a deeper influence on German creative writers.

New research on changes in literary taste indicates that in the recent past more and more attention has been paid in Germany to the so-called classics of American literature.[4] There has been a discovery or rediscovery of the great masters of the nineteenth century: Herman Melville, Nathaniel Hawthorne, Henry James. Formerly, American authors were expected to deal skillfully with elements of sensation and adventure and to present their readers with the hard facts of life, but interest is shifting to the works of those writers who touch upon the timeless essentials of human life: on the problem of good and evil, on the incomprehensibility of divine justice, on the abyss of fatal pride in man, on the mysterious depths of the individual human being. When Melville summons up "the latent horror of life" by means of an almost overwhelming complexity of figures and images, we have the feeling that he is showing us something of the very ambiguity of existence. This rediscovery of the American classics could have quite favorable consequences for German fiction. At least, German writers need not feel obliged to deal over and over with the ugly and brutal sides of reality if they want to be taken seriously, and can advance more confidently towards a deep symbolic setting. As an example, we may take Ernst Jünger (born 1895), who after the First World War attempted to transform the terrors of destruction into an "inner experience" *(In Stahlgewittern,* 1919, and *Krieg als inneres Erlebnis,* 1920), and who after the Second World War has been working on a view of the world in which a "new theology," stressing the eternal nexus of things in the manner of Goethe, is set up as a counterbalance to "nihilistic reduction" *(Strahlungen,* 1949; *Heliopolis,* 1950). Here the heritage of Goethe is mingled in an unusual but fruitful manner with the view of life found in the American classics. In common with Poe and Melville, Jünger is interested in the theme of terror.[5] In Poe, terror is occasionally taken as a test of character, and even more so in Melville, where the conclusion of *Moby Dick* unites fascination with terror and salvation from terror; thus Jünger is trying, in a similar manner, to evoke a sense of man's ultimate conquest of the powers of darkness. Here of course the relation to American literature is a case of affinity rather than dependence.

The growing expectation in Germany that the great American writers can make an important contribution to the orientation of man in the midst of the overwhelming enigma of life has also led to a revision of our judgment of contemporary American writing. This is especially clear in the change of perspective in our view of Hemingway and Faulkner. Today the early works of Hemingway, especially *A Farewell to Arms* and *The Sun Also Rises,* which appealed to a wide reading public, do not seem nearly so attractive as they did a decade ago. German literary criticism still praises Hemingway as a model for German writers, but it is no longer Hemingway as a master in depicting the existing realities truthfully, rationally, precisely, and economically, or as a master of the use of vital everyday language; today, rather, the most impressive thing about Hemingway seems to be his later work with its symbolic realism, through which he creates parables of human existence and, in spite of the force of destiny, maintains the dignity of man. *For Whom the Bell Tolls* is admired for the way in which fear and dread of nothingness are at least occasionally dispelled by the realization that there are situations in which the individual as such is of absolutely no importance, in which everyone is united by a common creed.[6] In this work it is revealed that discipline, duty, and confidence are no longer mere hindrances to the search of pleasure and individual freedom, but rather are common ties uniting and strengthening individual persons.[7] It is striking, from this point of view, that such a controversial novel as *Across the River and into the Trees* was more favorably received by some German critics than by Americans; the German critics were more willing to accept the external events of war (in Hemingway's words, "disheartening as hell") and the love affair between Colonel Cantwell and the young Italian girl as a mere foreground, whereas the actual meaning of the story was found in Cantwell's transformation of "violent death" into a "happy death" through inner "purgation."[8] "Castigation" and "purgation" appear here as true and permanent values giving a final meaning to a life which had apparently lost its meaning. But of all of Hemingway's works, *The Old Man and the Sea* has received especially high praise from German critics. In spite of complete defeat, the old man succeeds in maintaining his inner equilibrium, and his lonely struggle with the elements becomes a symbol of human fate; here we find a surprising return to the same timeless basic questions which give the American classics their permanent value. Not only Hemingway, but also Faulkner seems to have adopted this new point of view. The matter of violence, with which he first impressed us, no longer seems to be the central point in his work. One Swiss critic has even called *A Fable* "the most important achievement in English and American fiction since the Second World War."[9] The critic justifies this high estimate by saying that "the writer has never taken such a clear position in regard to human existence as he does here." Whatever the degree of exaggeration in this statement, such remarks do indicate the truly significant impressions left by the American way of portraying man in his ultimate meaning. And this not only has

determined the point of view of professional criticism, but also
has given the younger generation of German writers a more
clear-cut goal. Thus, we are quite justified in speaking of an
American impact on German literature which promises to be
stimulating and helpful.

But at the same time we find cases in which it is tempting
to speak of "alienation" rather than "impact." This literary
estrangement can only be defined from case to case, by means of
examples; we have no set criteria for gauging the general situation or the degree of alienation. The only thing that is certain
is that in these cases we find an unusually strong literary influence, one, however, which does not stimulate creative impulses
in the recipient literature, but rather thwarts and weakens these
impulses. In extreme cases, these influences have a destructive
effect and can prevent an organic development of the literature
which is exposed to them.

There are two special areas of contemporary German literature
in which there arises this question of alienation through American influence. One is the drama. It is obvious even to the superficial observer that German plays have been largely displaced by
American and French works (Anouilh, Giraudoux, Cocteau,
Sartre, Claudel). We must remember, of course, that this process
has been going on for some time. In the years between the wars
Eugene O'Neill became known in Germany. As Horst Frenz has
shown,[10] O'Neill achieved a *succès d'estime* on the German stage
in the years 1923 and 1924 with *Anna Christie, The Emperor
Jones,* and *The Hairy Ape.* But it was hardly a popular success.
The Berlin production of *Strange Interlude* in 1929 resulted in
a lively discussion of O'Neill's place in modern literature, and
especially of the technical problems in his work, but even this
play did not lead to a widespread influence of O'Neill in Germany. There were definite reasons for this. In the first place, the
framework of ideas in O'Neill was not found to be new or
stimulating, but rather old-fashioned and stale. It reminded one
too much of Ibsen and Strindberg, whose analytical problem
plays had enjoyed a high reputation in Europe around the turn
of the century, but which by the 1920's were considered out-
moded. Thus O'Neill as a dramatist seemed to be pointing backward rather than forward.

There was still another reason why O'Neill had only a moderate success in Germany between the two wars. We must take into consideration that the 1920's constituted a high point in the German drama. There was no lack of native talent. For more discriminating audiences there was a playwright like Paul Ernst, whose plays, with their classical tendencies, marked a break with naturalism. German expressionism was also in full force at this time, with the plays of Ernst Toller, Fritz von Unruh, Franz Werfel, and Sternheim. And especially Georg Kaiser's work was at most confirmed, but certainly not excelled, by that of O'Neill. Kaiser's neoclassical play, *Die Bürger von Calais* (1914), had already placed him in the front rank of modern German dramatists, after his earlier works, *König Hahnrei* (1910) and *Die jüdische Witwe,* had seemed to mark him as a successor to Frank Wedekind. In 1916 Kaiser turned to expressionism, and in plays like *Koralle* (1917) and *Gas* (1918) he introduced a dramatic style which can hardly be exceeded in sharpness and terseness of expression, in which the dialogues and monologues become more and more abstract, further and further removed from daily speech. In spite of the compositional weaknesses in Kaiser's plays, it must be admitted that he succeeded better than any other dramatist of the generation which had just experienced the First World War in producing a genuine feeling of shock at the emptiness of existence. Bert Brecht also dealt with this idea, but in quite a different way; he attracted attention in 1924 with his revision of Marlowe's *Edward II,* and then in 1928 achieved world success with the *Dreigroschenoper.* Furthermore, we must remember that the impressionistic drama and Viennese neo-Romanticism were still flourishing in the works of Hofmannsthal, Bahr, and Schnitzler. But above all, the acknowledged master of modern German drama, Gerhart Hauptmann, was still alive and attracting a wide audience, although he had long since abandoned the naturalistic style of his early works, such as *Die Weber, Vor Sonnenaufgang,* and *Rose Bernd.* In view of this abundance of native talent, there was no danger of an alienation of the German drama.

But after the Second World War the picture changed completely. Today O'Neill is by no means the only American dramatist known in Germany. Also, the modern German audience is attracted by other plays of his than those of twenty years ago. The Frankfort production of *Mourning Becomes Electra* in 1947 made an indelible impression on those who saw it. On the other hand, *Ah, Wilderness!* and *The Iceman Cometh* produced a feeling of strangeness rather than admiration, but the early O'Neill play, *Beyond the Horizon,* was impressive in a German television performance. But today when we think of American plays on the German stage, we see that O'Neill is losing ground, while the younger dramatists are rising to the fore. Among the American authors who contributed to the German repertoire from 1946 to 1954, we may note O'Neill with ten plays, Tennessee Williams with eight, William Saroyan with four, Elmer Rice, John Patrick, and Maxwell Anderson with three each. But in the last four years O'Neill has lost his leading position; today the German public prefers other American playwrights: Tennessee Williams, John Steinbeck, William Saroyan, Arthur Miller, and last but not least, Thornton Wilder. Their undeniable success is all the more striking because of the obvious lack of new German talent in the drama.[11] This is the main difference between the present situation and that thirty years ago. There is hardly a trace left of the Golden Age of modern German drama. Expressionism, impressionism, and neo-romanticism have lost their vigor and have not been succeeded by a new creative generation. Bert Brecht, who was undoubtedly the most gifted of recent German playwrights, became too much involved in the political conflict between East and West to appeal to us for purely aesthetic reasons. Party doctrines have largely blurred his literary view of life. At most, his play, *Herr Puntila und sein Knecht* (1948), which is free of political tendencies and is written in a humorous vein, can be considered a definite contribution to the contemporary repertoire. At present Germany has scarcely any dramatist of equal rank. Carl Zuckmayer, whose name is sometimes mentioned, is actually nothing more than a skilled craftsman, and such plays as *Des Teufels General* and *Das kalte Licht* depend upon their purely topical appeal, without offering any real permanent value. In Albrecht Goes's *Nacht der Entscheidung* there is more of the inner uncertainty, the doubting of all values, connected with the desire to reconsider the basic substance of human life, to reveal something of human dignity in the midst of injustice, and to teach tolerance. The same interest is found in the works of such Swiss playwrights as Dürrenmatt, Fritz Hochwälder, and Max Frisch, who are often used to compensate for the lack of German dramatists. But so far, only American (and French) works have supplied a real substitute.

There is one American dramatist whose acceptance in Germany has been wholehearted to the point of uncritical adulation: Thornton Wilder. *Our Town* especially has been successfully performed again and again, in the big cities, in small-town theaters, on student and experimental stages, and on television. It can be predicted with complete certainty that *Our Town* will prove to have had a permanent effect in Germany. In contrast, *The Skin of Our Teeth,* which was so warmly welcomed at first, has since faded somewhat. We now tend to look at it as a kind of curiosity, however, as a curiosity which is not only funny, but which also makes us stop and think. This past year, Wilder's new play, *The Alcestiad,* with its modern treatment of a classical theme, attracted critical attention, although it was by no means a dramatic sensation or of particular importance as a model for young German authors. But in any case, we in Germany are deeply grateful to Wilder as one of the few writers who in a time of doubt have dared to raise metaphysical questions (about the meaning of human existence, about the predictable course of fate, about the interdependence of life and death in the individual), even if he is not always able to give a convincing answer. There is probably much more skepticism in Wilder's work (cf. *The Ides of March*) than we are willing to admit. But we are also justified in looking at him as a writer who is supported by the ethos of humanity and who is seeking a cure for the wounds inflicted by our age of catastrophes.[12] But here it must be emphasized that among the newer German playwrights there is not a single one who has successfully followed in Wilder's footsteps; neither are there any successful imitators of Tennessee Williams, William Saroyan, or John Steinbeck. Perhaps these three dramatists are too deeply imbedded in their own soil to take root elsewhere. We can hardly expect a real and permanent revitalization of the German drama from this quarter; for one reason, there

has been no serious confrontation between these American models and German efforts. When a writer in the German language
such as the talented Swiss Max Frisch turns to the stage in order
to reveal the hopeless confusion in our concept of human history
in a satirical and ironical manner (*Die chinesische Mauer*) or
to deal with modern problems such as the dangers of the atomic
age (*Biedermann und die Brandstifter*), the structure and char-
acterization techniques which he uses are derived more from
modern French than from American drama. In Heinrich Böll
(*Stunde der Wahrheit*) there seems to be somewhat more of
William Saroyan's fine perceptiveness for the imponderables of
life. But there can be no talk of a "school" of German dramatists
writing under American influence.

If we turn to the short story, in postwar German, we find an
undeniable American influence. The German word for short
story, *Kurzgeschichte*, is obviously a translation of the English
term. It was not until the 1920's that the German term began
to be used in literary discussions; i.e., at the same time that
American short-story writers (especially O. Henry, Theodore
Dreiser, Sherwood Anderson, Faulkner, Hemingway, Steinbeck)
became known in Germany.[13] And it is quite obvious that during
the past three decades German authors have closely studied the
technique of the American short story. In so doing, they have
recognized the peculiar characteristics of the short story and
have also recognized the differences between it and the German
Novelle (novelette) of Romance origin, a form which has been
among the most important in German fiction since the time of
German idealism (Heinrich von Kleist). But it would be a gross
oversimplification of the problem to claim that the older form,
the *Novelle*, has been displaced through the influence of the
American short story. It must be taken into account that the
form of the German short story, the *Kurzgeschichte*, as we find
it in the works of Thomas Mann, Wilhelm Schäfer, Elisabeth
Langgässer, Günter Weisenborn, Wolfgang Borchert, and others,
has native roots. And in this connection we must remember that
the first master of the American short story, Edgar Allan Poe,
was familiar with the work of the German writer E. T. A. Hoffmann.[14] Thus it is possible that the modern American short story

as it has come to Germany is a further development, or even transformation, of a genre which owes its origin at least partially to German literature, or which at least has early connections with German literature.

In drawing parallels between the German *Kurzgeschichte* and the American short story, it is not enough to start with Irving as the first short-story writer or with Poe as the first theorist of the form ("Philosophy of Composition," 1846). Neither is it enough to point out that the *Kurzgeschichte* can be found in German literature throughout the nineteenth century (E. T. A. Hoffman, Friedrich Hebbel, Theodor Storm, Friedrich Halm), and is thus much older than its name, which was coined much later from the American term. The situation is much more complicated, and thus much more attractive for the literary historian. For there is something which we may call the original form of the German *Kurzgeschichte*, a form which goes back much further in time: the so-called "Almanac Story" (*Kalendergeschichte*). These are simple tales written for entertainment and edification during long winter evenings and can be found as early as the seventeenth century in German farmers' almanacs. Thus they are stories written for genuinely simple people in the biblical sense, people whose lives are governed by love and fear of God, upon Whose grace all changes of weather depend. Such almanac stories have a venerable tradition in Germany, and they undoubtedly played a considerable part in the education and mental outlook of the common people. Benjamin Franklin no doubt had something similar in mind with his *Poor Richard's Almanack* (1733-1758), in which he offered rules of conduct for a wide public. For lack of precise knowledge we must leave open the question of whether the popular figure of Poor Richard had an effect on German almanacs.[15] In any case, the German almanac story has gone through various phases of development during the centuries. It reached its high point with the works of one of our most gifted storytellers, Johann Peter Hebel, who published his informative articles and amusing tales in the "Badischer Landeskalender" and, from 1807 onwards, in the "Rheinischer Hausfreund." These deal with everyday happenings in the lives of common people, but in such a manner that each human event loses its individual character and is fitted into the divine plan of salvation. These examples were intended to show the reader that he is constantly in the hands of the Supreme Judge, that all sins will be punished and all good deeds rewarded.

As as example of the more than two hundred stories which Hebel wrote, we may take the one entitled "Kannitverstan." This is the story of a wandering German apprentice who goes to Amsterdam, where he is astonished by the riches of the great Dutch seaport city and envies the possessors of such great wealth. He asks, "Who owns that magnificent house?" and "Who owns that big ship in the harbor?"; but each time the only answer is "Kannitverstan," i.e., "I don't understand you." And in his simplemindedness the German apprentice mistakes this answer, "Kannitverstan," for the name of the owner, and he starts to complain of his own poverty in comparison with the rich Mr. Kannitverstan, who owns so many houses and ships. Then he encounters a funeral procession, and upon asking who has died, he again is told, "Kannitverstan." Hereupon he decides that his poverty is not so intolerable after all, since what use are all of Mr. Kannitverstan's worldly possessions once he is dead? At the end of the story Hebel points out the moral: "And whenever he again started to complain that so many people in the world were so rich and he was so poor, he had only to think of Mr. Kannitverstan, his luxurious house, his great ship, and his narrow grave." Thus the story gives an excellent portrayal of the limitations of human understanding and of the wisdom of the Creator, who can even lead us along the path of misunderstanding to a better comprehension of our own nature.

In the meantime the almanac story has developed into the short story. The transition appears to have been necessary and inevitable, since the short story is the appropriate form of expression for a completely different age—an age of machines and the masses, an age of people who feel themselves cut off from God's grace. This earlier common spirit of the people, the "Volksseele," no longer exists; we now have only individual feelings, impulses, and experiences. We are struck by the senselessness of existence. It is the main task of the short story to comprehend this new and different age in brief, vivid encounters between Man and Fate, born of a feeling of terror.[16]

The two generations of German authors who have gone through two world wars know what it means to succumb without resistance to the horror of senselessness. And thus the moment came in which the American short story was able to exert a deep influence in Germany. German writers learned to make use of a literary form which permits a direct expression of fear, horror, isolation, loneliness, and estrangement. In the works of writers like Wolfgang Borchert ("An diesem Dienstag," 1947) and Gerd Gaiser ("Einmal und oft," 1956) we see how much they owe to the polished technique of American short-story writers: the psychological point of view, the unity of tone and atmosphere, the conclusion which leaves the question open. But at the same time we see that the almanac story is still making its influence felt, and this gives the best of the German short-story writers a security and independence which protects them against domination by foreign models. As an example we may take Borchert's story "Radi." It is a dialogue carried on in a dream with a former schoolmate who was called "Radi" and who was killed during the first winter of the war in Russia. Two expressions of the dead Radi occur again and again, "please don't laugh" and "strange." Everything is strange for the dead man in Russia: the trees, the snow, the stones, the earth. Then he shows his dreaming friend where he is buried: "Please don't laugh, but here I am." It is the same feeling of horror that we find in the old ghost ballads but here it is presented in hard, clear, sober prose. Equally sober is the consolation offered to the dead man: "All earth smells good. This earth smells like real earth. You can be quite satisfied here." The shock of horror is thus caught up in an effective way; it not only is a shock, but also leaves room for the knowledge that in spite of all the destruction brought about by man, the elements of earth, air, fire, and water are still as pure and pristine as they were on the first day of human history. The cosmic order beyond and above human frailty is not spoken of in a preaching or moralistic tone. But in itself, the knowledge that fate and consolation are inter-related in the great pattern of existence dispels the feeling of emptiness. Admittedly, this was only a beginning for Borchert, who died in 1947 at the age of twenty-six. But we must ask ourselves if such a beginning does not point to the form which the

German short story is taking. It is possible to anticipate a fruitful combination of our native *Kurzgeschichte*, with its roots in the tradition of the almanac story, and the American short story, with its sober, precise presentation of psychological reactions. Not only would this mean avoiding the threat of alienation, which is undoubtedly a serious danger for mediocre talent, but the impact of American models could also mean the beginning of a new and fruitful phase in German fiction. And both German fiction and German drama are in desperate need of this.

Notes

FABIAN GUDAS

[1]A bibliography of the "more important" publications of Coomaraswamy was compiled by Helen E. Ladd of the University of Michigan and published in *Ars Islamica,* IX (1942), 125-42. This bibliography of 494 books, articles, and reviews covers the period from 1900-1942. A selected bibliography of Coomaraswamy's writings up to 1945 appeared in *Psychiatry,* VIII (1945), 373-77; this bibliography was reprinted in a Coomaraswamy Festschrift volume edited by K. Bharatha Iyer, *Art and Thought* (London, 1947), 255-59. Ray F. Livingston, *Ananda K. Coomaraswamy's Theory of Literature* (Ph. D. Dissertation, University of Minnesota, 1956), 266, refers to a mimeographed list of Coomaraswamy's writings prepared by S. Durai Raja Singam; Raja Singam has also collected a large number of tributes to Coomaraswamy written by prominent Eastern and Western scholars and men of letters. He has published these tributes in two volumes: *Homage to Ananda K. Coomaraswamy* (Malaya, I, 1948, and II, 1952). Livingston has revised his dissertation and published it as *The Traditional Theory of Literature* (Minneapolis, 1962).

[2]Some of Coomaraswamy's earliest essays on Indian culture are collected in *The Dance of Shiva,* first published in 1918. The edition of *The Dance of Shiva* used for this paper is the Noonday Paperback (New York, 1959).

[3]*The Bugbear of Literacy* (London, 1949), 96. Other editions of this collection of essays on various topics have the title *Am I My Brother's Keeper?*

[4]In spite of his contempt for aesthetics, Coomaraswamy has received some remarkable tributes from contemporary aestheticians. Katherine Gilbert, in a review of two of his books in the *Art Bulletin,* XXX (1948), 157, has told us that "no one else living among us was able so to interweave the languages and cultural perspectives of Sanskrit, Greek, mediaeval Scholastic, American Indian, and modern western European" into such a powerful restatement of traditional views. Thomas Munro, in his *Toward Science in Aesthetics* (New York, 1956), 112, says that "on the whole, his work is among the most valuable of American contributions to the subject he denounced." Munro also reviewed Coomaraswamy's *The Transformation of Nature in Art* very generously in the *Art Bulletin,* XIV (1934), 397-98. These tributes are remarkable in that they come from two of our most knowledgeable aesthe-

273

ticians, both of whom disagree violently with Coomaraswamy's appraisal of modern artistic theory and practice. However, not all aestheticians have been so kind. For example: Helmut Kuhn, in a review of Coomaraswamy's *Why Exhibit Works of Art?* in the *Journal of Philosophy*, XLI (1944), 106-107, expresses the opinion that "Coomaraswamy, outside the field of Indian archaeology, is an amateur," and that his book is a "paradoxical *jeu d'esprit.*" Finally, no list of summary estimates of the work of Coomaraswamy can omit the lyrical praise of Eric Gill, which brightens a page of his *Autobiography* (London, 1940), 174: "Others have written the truth about life and religion and man's work. Others have written good clear English. Others have had the gift of witty exposition. Others have understood the metaphysics of Christianity and others have understood the metaphysics of Hinduism and Buddhism. Others have understood the true significance of erotic drawings and sculptures. Others have seen the relationships of the true and the good and the beautiful. Others have had apparently unlimited learning. Others have loved; others have been kind and generous. But I know of no one else in whom all these gifts and all these powers have been combined. I dare not confess myself his disciple; that would only embarrass him. I can only say that I believe that no other living writer has written the truth in matters of art and life and religion and piety with such wisdom and understanding."

[5]Arthur O. Lovejoy, in *The Great Chain of Being* (Cambridge, Mass., 1936), 26, says that the otherworldly philosophy has been "the dominant official philosophy of the larger part of civilized mankind through most of its history." Coomaraswamy would not like the implications of "official," and he would claim that the otherworldly philosophy has been the philosophy of all "uncivilized" men as well.

[6]Coomaraswamy mentions only one other historical period—that of the Greek decadence—which lived by a this-worldly philosophy. To describe the intellectual commitments of modern Western man, Coomaraswamy uses such terms as "empiricism," "positivism," "secularism," "liberalism," "humanism," "pragmatism," "rationalism," "nominalism," "materialism," and "individualism." To him, all of these are pejorative terms, as are "progress," "novelty," "history," and "civilization." However, some of these terms name points of view which are "relatively" true, and others may still be useful if properly redefined (thus Coomaraswamy speaks of "true" civilization).

[7]*The Bugbear of Literacy*, 1, 20 n. 13, and *passim*. The essays collected in this volume are among the bitterest that Coomaraswamy ever wrote.

[8]*Ibid.*, 17.

[9]The only precedent that Coomaraswamy mentions is naturalistic Greek art in which the gods and goddesses look like athletes and beauty queens.

[10]Coomaraswamy's opinion of post-medieval painting can be gathered from the following quotation from his "Sir Gawain and the Green Knight: Indra and Namuci," *Speculum*, XIX (1944), 124-25: "I have myself remarked that the Amerindian sand-paintings, considered intellectually, are superior in kind to any painting that has been done in Europe or white America

within the last several centuries." The poets fare a little better. Among English and American poets, Coomaraswamy had an almost lifelong admiration for the work of Blake, Whitman, and Morris. Quotations from these poets appear very frequently in his writings. He also occasionally cites Shakespeare, Spenser, Milton, Wordsworth, Donne, Emerson, and T. S. Eliot.

[11]*Figures of Speech or Figures of Thought* (London, 1946), 33. The subtitle of this book, *Collected Essays on the Traditional or "Normal" View of Art,* describes its contents. Only the first of the essays, " 'A Figure of Speech, or a Figure of Thought?' " had not been published previously.

[12]*Ibid.,* 71, 72, 171.

[13]Both Munro and Gilbert have pointed out that the sweeping generalizations by which Coomaraswamy characterizes contemporary aesthetic theory distort seriously the real state of affairs. "Many of the faults for which [Coomaraswamy] berates aesthetics have long been attacked and discarded by modern aestheticians; many of the things he urges have long been done. Holding a narrow definition of aesthetics, and a false conception of modern art as concerned only with sensuous appearances and pleasures, he ignores the tremendous amount of work which has been done in recent aesthetics on the moral, intellectual, and cultural significance of art" (Munro, *Toward Science in Aesthetics,* 111-12). Katherine Gilbert, in her review article cited in n. 4 above, says that Coomaraswamy's intransigence deprives him of the assistance of many "able allies." However, Coomaraswamy will have none of such allies. Almost all contemporary aestheticians ground their views on a this-worldly philosophy. Hence, regardless of how fully and accurately their divergent positions might have been stated, the judgment passed on them as a group would still have been the same. In *Why Exhibit Works of Art?* (London, 1943), 23, Coomaraswamy says that the perennial philosophy of art is "a catholic or universal doctrine, with which the humanistic philosophies of art can neither be compared nor reconciled, but only contrasted." *Why Exhibit Works of Art?* consists of a series of essays, previously published in periodicals, which, like those in *Figures of Speech,* deal with the "normal" or "traditional" view of art. A Dover edition of *Why Exhibit Works of Art?* was published in 1956 with the title changed to *Christian and Oriental Philosophy of Art.*

[14]*Why Exhibit Works of Art?,* 23, 88.

[15]In his "The Vedanta and Western Tradition," *American Scholar,* VIII (1939), 227, Coomaraswamy praises Meister Eckhart as the one "who with the possible exception of Dante can be regarded from an Indian point of view as the greatest of all Europeans." See also the essay on Eckhart in *The Transformation of Nature in Art* (2d ed., Cambridge, Mass., 1935), 61-95. All of the other essays in this volume, the first edition of which came out in 1934, deal with Indian artistic theory and practice. In the preface to *Figures of Speech,* p. 5, Coomaraswamy says that whoever reads *The Transformation of Nature in Art, Why Exhibit Works of Art?* and *Figures of Speech,* together with the sources on which the essays in these

books are based, "will have a fairly complete view of the doctrine about art that the greater part of mankind has accepted from prehistoric times until yesterday."

[16]In his theory of art, Blake is the "nearest and natural descendant" of Eckhart (*The Transformation of Nature in Art*, 202 n. 57). Blake "may well come to be regarded as the supreme prophet of a post-industrial age" (*The Dance of Shiva*, 136).

[17]Coomaraswamy is aware that the modern positivist, if he were to glance at this list of authorities, would impatiently exclaim that Coomaraswamy is blowing on dead coals, trying to revive a fire which had been smothered by British empiricism and completely extinguished by the verifiability principle of meaning. However, it was Coomaraswamy's lifelong hope that the impact of Eastern thought, particularly that of India, would arouse Western empiricism from its dogmatic slumber.

He is also aware that to box these authorities together and say that they are teaching the same metaphysical doctrine is staggering to the (historical) philosophical imagination. Some of his reviewers accused him of "eclecticism" and "distortion," e.g., J. J. Rolbiecki, review of Coomaraswamy's *Hinduism and Buddhism* in *New Scholasticism*, XVII (1943), 298-99; Sidney L. Gulick, "Oriental Conceptions of the Self," *Personalist*, XXVII (1946), 306-13. To defend himself from the charge that he is distorting the meaning of his texts or that he is a mere syncretist or eclectic, Coomaraswamy says that a distinction must be made between the essence of a philosopher's teaching and the localisms in which it is imbedded; the interpreter can frequently show that two (or more) seemingly diverse formulations of a doctrine differ only in "idiom" and actually express the same principle. Furthermore, since "nothing can be known except in the mode of the knower," a distinction between exoteric and esoteric doctrine is indispensable; it is only on the level of the latter that the essential similarity of all metaphysical teaching appears. Again, many of the metaphysical doctrines are necessarily conveyed in symbols; therefore only a reader who is an expert in interpreting symbolic language is qualified as an authoritative commentator on a metaphysical text. And finally, since the truths of metaphysics can be validated only by "living" them, a professed empiricist cannot ever be sure that he really understands what a metaphysician is talking about; hence Coomaraswamy will accept correction of his interpretations only from another "master." As he says in his review of H. Zimmer's *Myths and Symbols in Indian Art*, in *Review of Religion*, XI (1947), 285, "if one does not believe . . . that the content of the recondite subject of our study can contribute to one's own more abundant life, it will remain impenetrable to all mere learning, however extensive."

Coomaraswamy also knows that few Orientalists will agree with him that even Indian philosophy is a single doctrine. It is widely held, for example, that Hindu and Buddhist thought are radically different. Also there are the well-known "six systems" of later Indian philosophy. Coomaraswamy's answer is that these differences are an illusion. His *Hinduism and Buddhism*

(N. Y., [1943]) is intended to prove the essential identity of these two systems of metaphysics; and the six systems, he says, are only " 'points of view' which are no more mutually contradictory than are, let us say, botany and mathematics" *(ibid.,* 4). Such misconceptions arise because the Indian philosophical works are known to the West only in the translations of Western scholars. These men do not have the basic qualification of a reliable translator; they do not believe the doctrines they are translating and therefore unconsciously mistranslate. As a consequence, "it would be hardly an exaggeration to say that a faithful account of Hinduism might well be given in the form of a categorical denial of most of the statements that have been made about it, alike by European scholars and by Indians trained in our modern sceptical and evolutionary modes of thought" *(ibid.,* 3). Coomaraswamy's particular enemy is "that great Orientalist" A. B. Keith, who is "a typical modern nominalist" and holds that " 'such knowledge as is not empirical is meaningless, and ought not to be described as knowledge' " *(Time and Eternity* [Ascona, 1947], 59).

What Coomaraswamy says about translators and commentators on Sanskrit texts applies as well to students of his other authorities. The Authorized Version, for example, does not always render the Bible accurately *(The Bugbear of Literacy,* 56). And Paul Shorey is not properly qualified for a Plato scholar; after quoting an "inane" comment by Shorey, Coomaraswamy continues: "Solecisms such as this must be expected whenever nominalists set out to expound the doctrine of realistic philosophers" ("What Is Civilization?" *The Albert Schweitzer Jubilee Book,* eds. A. A. Roback and Others [Cambridge, Mass., 1945], 274).

[18] Coomaraswamy devotes the opening pages of his article "Two Passages in Dante's *Paradiso,*" *Speculum,* XI (1936), 327-38 to enumerating "remarkable doctrinal and even verbal equivalences" (p. 327) between medieval and Indian texts. Such equivalences, he says, could be cited "almost *ad infinitum*" (p. 330). In *The Transformation of Nature in Art,* 201 n. 56, Coomaraswamy says, "Eckhart presents an astonishingly close parallel to Indian modes of thought; some whole passages and many single sentences read like a direct translation from Sanskrit."

[19]*Hinduism and Buddhism,* 86.

[20]Coomaraswamy discusses these three hypotheses very briefly in several places, e.g., *Speculum,* XI, *passim,* and *Hinduism and Buddhism,* 86.

[21]*The Bugbear of Literacy,* 67.

[22]Coomaraswamy's best brief account of the metaphysics of the perennial philosophy is in his article in the *American Scholar* cited in n. 15 above. A more extended treatment appears in his *Hinduism and Buddhism* and in his early *Buddha and the Gospel of Buddhism* (New York, 1916). *Time and Eternity* is a full discussion of one fundamental metaphysical problem. For further study Coomaraswamy recommends the works of René Guénon ("Eastern Wisdom and Western Knowledge," *The Bugbear of Literacy,* 64-77), some of which have been translated into English. See particularly Guénon's *Introduction to the Study of the Hindu Doctrines,* trans. Marco Pallis (Lon-

don, 1945), and *Man and His Becoming According to the Vedanta*, trans. Richard C. Nicholson (London, 1946); the latter has been reprinted in this country by the Noonday Press, 1958. Alan W. Watts, *The Supreme Identity* (New York, 1950) might also be consulted; in the preface Watts acknowledges his debt to both Guénon and Coomaraswamy.

[23]*American Scholar*, VIII, 231.

[24]This list does not exhaust the number of levels. Also there are levels within levels; for example, the three main levels of reference in man are the spiritual, mental, and physical.

[25]See E. M. W. Tillyard, *The Elizabethan World Picture* (New York, 1944), especially chapters 6 and 7, for the Elizabethan doctrine of correspondences, which was derived from the medieval tradition.

[26]"Symplegades," *Studies and Essays in the History of Science and Learning Offered in Homage to George Sarton*, ed. M. F. Ashley Montagu (New York [1946]), 471.

[27]*Ibid.*, 486.

[28]*Hinduism and Buddhism*, 12-13.

[29]*Time and Eternity*, 30 n. 1.

[30]"This distinction of an immortal spirit from the mortal soul . . . is in fact the fundamental doctrine of the Philosophia Perennis wherever we find it" (*Hinduism and Buddhism*, 57). The fundamental question for every man is, "Who am I?" and the only categorical imperative is the Socratic "Know thyself."

[31]Coomaraswamy does not use "mysticism" as a synonym for "metaphysical realization." He became increasingly suspicious of the term, and in his later works it usually appears within quotation marks. He feels that it is very loosely used and has been degraded by theosophists and occultists who are responsible for widespread misconceptions of the perennial philosophy (see, for example, *Hinduism and Buddhism*, 40 n. 143, and *The Transformation of Nature in Art*, 137). R. C. Zaehner attacks Coomaraswamy, Aldous Huxley, René Guénon, and other perennial philosophers or "super-Popes" in his *Mysticism Sacred and Profane* (Oxford, 1957). Zaehner, a Catholic convert, denies that all mysticisms are alike or that the reports of all mystics describe a single type of experience; thus it is fruitless to call mysticism the Highest Common Factor (Aldous Huxley's term in *The Perennial Philosophy* [New York, 1945], vii) of all religious experience and argue that the diverse religions of the world are therefore essentially the same.

Coomaraswamy also objects to "pantheism," an epithet frequently used to characterize Indian metaphysics. In *Time and Eternity*, 120, he distinguishes the "proper" and "heretical" senses of "pantheism." See also "On the Pertinence of Philosophy" in *Contemporary Indian Philosophy*, eds. S. Radhakrishnan and J. H. Muirhead (New York, 1936), especially p. 116 n. 2. This article is valuable for its clear statement of the relations that should exist between metaphysics, philosophy, religion, and science.

[32]See *Hinduism and Buddhism*, 18, and *Time and Eternity*, 126.

[33]*Why Exhibit Works of Art?*, 91, 89. If, in the second definition quoted,

the clause "that needs to be made or arranged" carries the meaning "that should be made or arranged," it is an irrelevancy in the definition.

[34]*Figures of Speech*, 241.

[35]"An Approach to Indian Art," *Parnassus*, VII (December, 1935), 17.

[36]*Why Exhibit Works of Art?*, 79. The problem of the definition of "art" and "work of art" arises here again. Coomaraswamy frequently seems to be saying that no object should be called a work of art unless its final cause is the satisfaction of both the practical and spiritual needs of man: "From the stone age onwards, everything made by man . . . has been made by art to serve a double purpose, at once utilitarian and ideological" *(ibid.,* 92). Such a definition would exclude from the class of true works of art the products of modern artists and of industry. However, I am assuming in this essay that Coomaraswamy would not regard the nature of the final cause of an object as a condition for determining whether the object should or should not be called a work of art. The effectiveness of the object for the purpose for which it has been made is both the necessary and sufficient condition for its classification as a work of art. Note the following quotations: art is "the general activity of making things for human use, material or spiritual" *(ibid.,* 62); art produces "things required for use, whether an intellectual or a physical use, or under normal conditions both" *(ibid.,* 90); "Christian and Oriental arts had always human uses: mainly *practical* in the case of what we clumsily call the decorative arts . . . and mainly intellectual in the case of what we call the fine arts" ("Understanding the Art of India," *Parnassus*, VI [April, 1934], 21).

[37]*Why Exhibit Works of Art?*, 40; *Figures of Speech*, 224. There is also a metaphysics of checkers *(ibid.,* 190), sexual acts *(ibid.,* 191), and sports, like archery ("The Symbolism of Archery," *Ars Islamica*, X [1943], 105-19).

[38]See p. 24.

[39]*Why Exhibit Works of Art?*, 18; Coomaraswamy's fullest discussion of ornament is in his essay "Ornament," *Figures of Speech*, 85-99.

[40]*Ibid.,* 98 n. 8.

[41]Coomaraswamy practiced what he preached; several of his works were not copyrighted.

[42]*The Transformation of Nature in Art,* 178 n. 7.

[43]I do not have space here for a full discussion of Coomaraswamy's doctrine of form. As synonyms for "form," he uses "type," "idea," "archetype," "pattern," "model," "image," "species," "prototype," "essence," "exemplar," and "paradigm." Form is not the tangible shape of an object (which, however, may be called its "accidental" or "actual" form), for it is not perceptible by the senses. It is like the soul, which is said to be the form of the body, or like the concept "the shortest distance between two points," which is the form for a straight line. An artist may speak of visiting heaven and "seeing" the divine forms which, on his return to earth, he reproduces in the matter of his art; but this is to be taken as a mythological account of artistic inspiration *(Figures of Speech*, 152).

Coomaraswamy says that the doctrine of forms as taught by the perennial philosophy is formulated more correctly in Indian philosophy than in the Platonic tradition (this is one of the few important points on which he admits disagreement among his authorities): Plato's transcendental ideas "are types of being, external to the conditioned universe and thought of as absolutes reflected in phenomena," whereas "Indian types are those of sentient activity or functional utility conceivable only in a contingent world" *(The Transformation of Nature in Art,* 17). The Indian types are "powers" or "operative principles" (necessarily so, because God's manifestations are "acts"), analogous to the "energies" of science ("Energy" is one of the names of God, *Time and Eternity,* 68 n. 11), which, like everything else in this "conditioned" universe, divide themselves into polar opposites (positive and negative electrical charges). (See also *Figures of Speech,* 72-73, 151-53.)

Finally, a single form can be expressed in many different things (both on the same level of reference and on different levels of reference), in the same way that the relations indicated by an algebraic formula are reflected in an indefinite number of phenomena. The knowledge of God must be conceived as consisting of "only one idea": "One does not imagine that the Divine intellect is a sort of dictionary, but much rather a Word or a Form that is the form of many different things, to use the language of exemplarism" *(Time and Eternity,* 133-34).

[44]Coomaraswamy's most extended discussion of this discipline and its relation to yoga is in his essay "The Intellectual Operation in Indian Art," *Figures of Speech,* 145-60.

[45]*Figures of Speech,* 16.

[46]*Parnassus,* VII (Dec., 1935), 17; *Why Exhibit Works of Art?,* 17, 77.

[47]This analysis of true beauty as the attractive power of perfection makes it possible to use beauty as a criterion for distinguishing art from non-art; the class of beautiful objects will coincide with the class of perfect objects. Thus one of the consequences of Coomaraswamy's dialectic is that beauty, truth, and perfection are only "logically" and not "really" distinguishable from one another.

[48]Coomaraswamy discusses rasa at some length in the following articles: "Hindu View of Art: Theory of Beauty," *The Dance of Shiva,* 35-43; "The Theory of Art in Asia," *The Transformation of Nature in Art,* 3-57, especially, 46-54; and "Indian Literary Theory," *Dictionary of World Literature,* ed. Joseph T. Shipley (New York, 1943).

[49]*Figures of Speech,* 83, 203.

[50]It is only on the metaphysical level that man's spirit can find certainties, whether in ethics, politics, or art. Naturally, when such knowledge is not available, opinion, based on accurate empirical observation, is not to be despised. The "circumstantial evidence" for the truth of a scientific hypothesis must be accepted as true for all practical purposes. Furthermore, no purported metaphysical principle can be true if it contradicts experience *(The Transformation of Nature in Art,* 15-16). Similarly, a purely "humanist" society has some chance of providing for the happiness of its mem-

bers if "good will" is present (Radhakrishnan and Muirhead [eds.], *Contemporary Indian Philosophy*, 117).

[51]Coomaraswamy has certainly heard of the Intentional Fallacy. In private correspondence and in print he objected strongly to the tentative formulation of this fallacy which Monroe C. Beardsley and W. K. Wimsatt, Jr., presented in their article "Intention" in the *Dictionary of World Literature;* see Coomaraswamy, "Intention," *Figures of Speech*, 123-33. Beardsley and Wimsatt refer briefly to Coomaraswamy's criticism in their famous article "The Intentional Fallacy," *Sewanee Review*, LIV (1946), 471.

[52]*Figures of Speech*, 132.

[53]*Ibid.*, 22.

[54]Coomaraswamy uses the term "sophistry" as a name for such a work of art; this is a word condemnatory not of the sophist's art but of his influence.

I have not found any explicit discussion in Coomaraswamy's works of the problem of young Socrates who is teased by Parmenides for his hesitancy in deciding whether such vile and paltry things as mud, hair, and dirt have transcendental archetypes *(Parmenides,* 130). If the metaphysical (and only valid) criterion for determining whether or not an object is well made is the measurement of the correspondence of the finished product to its archetype, then the uncomfortable conclusion seems to be that the forms of bombs, pornography, sophistry, and murders must exist in the divine world of ideas along with beauty, love, and cathedrals.

[55]*Why Exhibit Works of Art?*, 85.

[56]*Ibid.*, 145.

[57]Coomaraswamy suggests that "if we propose to use or understand any works of art (with the possible exception of contemporary works, which may be 'unintelligible'), we ought to abandon the term 'aesthetic' in its present application and return to 'rhetoric' " *(Figures of Speech,* 10). "Rhetoric" here carries the meaning given to it by Plato in the *Phaedrus* and accepted by Cicero and Quintilian; that is, no art is entitled to be called "rhetoric" unless its expressive qualities are used to support a true thesis. If expression is used merely for display (to exhibit the talent of the artist) or to pervert the truth (as in propaganda or advertising), the work of art is sophistic or flattery and to be morally condemned.

[58]*Why Exhibit Works of Art?*, 17; *Figures of Speech,* 10. The term "communication" is, strictly speaking, inaccurate for "it is of the essence of a mystery, and above all of the Mysterium Magnum, that it cannot be communicated, but only realized: all that can be communicated are its external supports or symbolic expressions; the Great Work must be done by everyone for himself" *(ibid.,* 170).

[59]*The Transformation of Nature in Art,* 50.

[60]As the spiritual development of a man progresses, what he brings to a work of art increases. Thus he depends less and less on external aids. If he uses them at all, he prefers very simple devices (such as geometrical designs) which, to him, are less distracting.

[61]*Why Exhibit Works of Art?*, 10; *Figures of Speech,* 168.

[62]See *"Samvega,* Aesthetic Shock," *Figures of Speech,* 200-207.

[63]*Ibid.,* 205.

[64]*Figures of Speech,* 115. Coomaraswamy's article "Symbolism," *Dictionary of World Literature* (reprinted, with some additions, as "Literary Symbolism," in his *Figures of Speech,* 114-22) contains numerous examples of adequate symbols. See Wilbur M. Urban, *Language and Reality* (London, 1939) and H. Flanders Dunbar, *Symbolism in Mediaeval Thought* (New Haven, 1929) for a discussion of the "insight symbol" and for the general problem of interpreting religious, poetic, and metaphysical language. Urban, another advocate of the perennial philosophy (though he confines the term to the metaphysical presuppositions of the Greco-Christian "magnanimous philosophers" who belong to the "Great Tradition") is the only contemporary philosopher whose works Coomaraswamy quotes frequently and approvingly.

[65]*Parnassus,* VI (April, 1934), 25.

[66]No doubt Coomaraswamy would have been delighted by this expression of Philip Wheelwright, *The Burning Fountain* (Bloomington, 1954), 155, and by many other things in Wheelwright's book. Wheelwright discusses the participation principle at some length and uses it as part of his analysis of the semantics of poetry. To the positivist who would laugh at the participation principle, Coomaraswamy has the reply, "All that may be nonsense to the rationalist, who lives in a meaningless world; but the end is not yet" *(Figures of Speech,* 144 n. 38); and "no man can safely aspire to higher ideals than are pertinent to his spiritual age" *(The Transformation of Nature in Art,* 161).

[67]For Coomaraswamy's most detailed discussion of Lévy-Bruhl's theories and of the doctrine of participation, see "Imitation, Expression, and Participation" and "Primitive Mentality," *Figures of Speech,* 134-44, 216-38. Coomaraswamy criticizes Lévy-Bruhl severely for his "superiority complex" and cites the testimony of Franz Boas, Paul Radin, and other anthropologists who assert that the "primitives" have a "normal" mental endowment. Lévy-Bruhl's unhappy expression "prelogical," with its implication that logic is to be equated with scientific procedures, not only attributes to the primitives a "lower" mentality but also begs the ontological question as to what is the nature of reality.

[68]*Figures of Speech,* 38 n. 48.

[69]*Ibid.,* 176.

[70]*Why Exhibit Works of Art?,* 113.

[71]*Parnassus,* VII (December, 1935), 18.

[72]*Parnassus,* VI (April, 1934), 23. In "The Virgin Suckling St. Bernard," *Art Bulletin,* XIX (1937), 317-18, Coomaraswamy points out that the Virgin-St. Bernard motif has a parallel in Juno-Hercules, that the metaphysical significance of both is the same, and that these facts prove that "symbols together with a knowledge of their spiritual significance have been continuously transmitted, uninterrupted by religious changes. Iconography and essential meaning represent an artistic constant, where style and application are merely variable accidents."

[73]The common opinion that Blake resorted to a private symbolism is

contradicted by Coomaraswamy. He says that Blake "still respects a traditional iconography" (*Why Exhibit Works of Art?*, 62).

[74]Coomaraswamy would not agree with certain modern views which recognize the power of symbols but say that social change necessarily exhausts the symbols of the past and therefore each age must find new symbols which will reflect its own consciousness. The perennial philosophy is valid for all times, and the symbols which give it adequate expression can come to life in the mind of anyone who returns to the way. On this point see particularly "Walter Andrae: On the Life of Symbols," *Figures of Speech*, 252-56.

Coomaraswamy praised Émile Mâle's pioneer work in medieval symbolism, but I have found no references to the iconographical studies of Panofsky, Gombrich, or other members of the Warburg and Courtauld Institutes. Alan W. Watts' *Myth and Ritual in Christianity* (London, 1954) is an attempt to work out the universal meanings of Christian symbolism in the manner suggested by Coomaraswamy.

Rosemond Tuve's reconstruction of Renaissance literary theory, showing its basis in rhetoric and philosophical realism, her plea for reopening the question of the relation between truth and literary value, her insistence that a poem should be interpreted in accordance with its author's intentions, and her demonstration of the richness of meaning to be found in the poems of Herbert and Milton when their traditional symbolism is understood would no doubt have been strongly commended by Coomaraswamy.

[75]*Parnassus*, VI (April, 1934), 25.

[76]"Whoever, like Jung, insists upon translating the essentials of Indian or Chinese metaphysics into a psychology is merely distorting the meaning of the texts" (*American Scholar*, VIII, 231). "Man in search of spirit has become Jung's 'modern man in search of a soul,' who discovers . . . spiritualism and psychology" (*Figures of Speech*, 198).

[77]*Why Exhibit Works of Art?*, 46.

[78]"On the Loathly Bride," *Speculum*, XX (1945), 403.

[79]Coomaraswamy insists many times that traditional cultures transmit their myths precisely. Since any change in the myth destroys part of its metaphysical meaning, he has no sympathy with reinterpretations of myths by "literary artists." He praises William Morris for his accurate use of mythical materials (*ibid.*, 399) and condemns Tennyson "who does not scruple to modify his narrative for aesthetic or moral reasons" (*Figures of Speech*, 238 n. 50).

[80]*Speculum*, XX (1945), 403-404. Sir J. G. Frazer is neither a theologian nor a metaphysician (nor even, like Jung, a psychologist); hence his *Golden Bough* is "a glorified doctor's thesis" (*Figures of Speech*, 233).

[81]*Speculum*, XX (1945), 392 n. 2.

[82]*Parnassus*, VI (April, 1934), 22.

[83]*Figures of Speech*, 230.

[84]*Hinduism and Buddhism*, 33 n. 21; *Why Exhibit Works of Art?*, 80.

[85]Coomaraswamy denies that he is recommending a return to the "outward forms" of the Middle Ages (*The Bugbear of Literacy*, 11; *Why Exhibit Works of Art?*, 86-88).

[86]*The Transformation of Nature in Art,* 65.

[87]*Time and Eternity,* 68 n. 11.

[88]*An Introduction to the Art of Eastern Asia* ("Academic Reprints: Social Science Papers," No. 2 [Stanford, 1953]) , 12. This essay, first published in *Open Court* (March, 1932) , was considerably revised and lengthened and then published as "The Theory of Art in Asia," *The Transformation of Nature in Art,* 3-57.

[89]*The Transformation of Nature in Art,* 3-4.

[90]The principal parts of my summary come from *Figures of Speech,* 29-32; and *Spiritual Authority and Temporal Power in the Indian Theory of Government* (New Haven, 1942) , 51-60.

[91]"An Indian Crocodile," *Bulletin of the Museum of Fine Arts,* XXXIV (1936) , 28.

ANNETTE M. McCORMICK

[1]J. H. Gardiner, *The Bible as English Literature* (New York, 1906) , 338.

[2]Robert Lowth, *Lectures on the Sacred Poetry of the Hebrews,* trans. G. Gregory (Andover, Mass., 1829) , 157; Lowth's lectures were first printed in 1753 and translated by Gregory in 1787.

[3]L. S. Newman and W. Popper, *Studies in Biblical Parallelism* (Berkeley, Calif., 1918) , 20-56.

[4]E. G. King, *Early Religious Poetry of the Hebrews* (Cambridge, 1911) , viii.

[5]A glance at the desert notebooks, now in the Fitzwilliam Museum at Cambridge, will show that economy was no deterrent to the author's compulsion to find a suitable style; even when a scanty supply of paper made every half-inch valuable, he rearranged clauses and substituted words and phrases.

[6]Charles Montague Doughty, *Travels in Arabia Deserta* (2 vols.; Cambridge, 1888) , I, 169. This, the first edition, is that to which reference is made in the remainder of this study. Cf. Job 3:14.

[7]For clearness I have divided the members as though they were separate poetic lines. The illustrations of various kinds of parallelism in this paragraph are taken either from Lowth or from the summary of S. R. Driver, *An Introduction to the Literature of the Old Testament* (New York, 1942) , 362-65.

[8]*Ibid.,* 363.

[9]*Ibid.,* 365.

[10]I have divided Doughty's lines into members.

[11]See A. S. Cook, *The Bible and English Prose Style* (Boston, 1903) , xv-xxvi, for a succinct account of these differences.

[12]Ernest Renan, *Histoire générale et système comparé des langues sémitiques* (Paris, 1858) , 21.

[13]*The Bible as English Literature,* 69.

ELLIOTT D. HEALY

[1]*Histoire de la littérature occitane* (Paris, 1953), 29. Maurice Valency, in his excellent study of the pre-Renaissance lyric tradition, *In Praise of Love* (New York, 1958), 177, also associates the Comtessa de Dia and Louise Labé as ladies who belong to the same poetic mold.

[2]Notably Jean Larnac in his rather romanticized biography, *Louise Labé* (Paris, 1934), 105 ff.

[3]Jean Boutière and A. H. Schutz, *Biographies des Troubadours* (Toulouse and Paris, 1950), No. XXVII. "The Countess of Dia was the wife of Sir William of Poitiers, a beautiful and worthy lady, and she fell in love with Sir Raimbaut of Orange and composed many good songs about him."

[4]*La Poésie lyrique des Troubadours* (2 vols.; Toulouse, 1934), I, 313; and *The Life and Works of the troubador Raimbaut d'Orange* (Minneapolis, 1952), 12, 25.

[5]Pattison, *Life and Works of Raimbaut d'Orange*, 28. Pattison makes a tentative but reasonable identification of the poetess as the daughter of Isoard of Dia, who was married to Raimon d'Agout, a patron of the troubadours. This lady lived near Orange and was a contemporary of Raimbaut IV, dying only a few years before him; cf., 29.

[6]*Poésie des Troubadours*, I, 316.

[7]The *tenso* in question is attributed only to Raimbaut d'Aurenga in the manuscripts. Because the poet debates with a woman it was once assumed that she must inevitably be the Comtessa de Dia, but this assumption loses validity when we question the identity of her lover. It seems to me, however, that nothing in the lady's role is incompatible with what the Comtessa de Dia might well have said. Pattison, *Life and Works of Raimbaut d'Orange*, 157, takes the opposite view, saying, "The wit of the female role is more in keeping with Raimbaut's other works than those of the countess." As a matter of interest, and in view of lack of genuine proof that the countess could not have had a hand in the composition of this *tenso*, it has been drawn upon briefly in the present discussion.

[8]*Louise Labé, Elégies, sonnets, débat de la folie et de l'amour* (Paris, 1953), 16.

[9]*Ibid.*, 15.

[10]*Histoire sommaire de la littérature méridionale au moyen âge* (Paris, 1921), 80.

[11]*Ibid.*, 29.

[12]*Les Troubadours, leurs vies, leurs oeuvres, leur influence*, (4th ed.; Paris, 1929), 151.

[13]*Louise Labé*, 8.

[14]"Towards him neither mercy nor courtesy avails me, nor my beauty nor my worth nor my intelligence, and thus am I deceived and betrayed, as I ought to be, were I ungracious." All citations from the poetry of the Comtessa de Dia are taken from the critical edition of her works by Gabrielle Kussler-Ratyé in *Archivum Romanicum*, I (1917), 161-82. These passages

will be translated and will be designated by the numbers which the poems cited bear in this edition.

¹⁵This is of course from Petrarch. Quotations from Louise Labé are from the edition of Bernard Jourdan cited in note 8 above. I have followed the spelling, punctuation, accentuation, and numbering of the poems as reproduced by him after other editions based upon the original by Jean de Tournes of Lyons. Since her language is quite modern except for easily recognizable sixteenth-century spellings, it has not been deemed necessary to give a translation.

¹⁶*Louise Labé*, 15.

¹⁷"For I have chosen a worthy and gentle one, because of whom worth improves and is ennobled, generous, and sincere and discerning."

¹⁸"For my love is the gayest one, wherefore I (too) am gracious and joyful" (I, 3-4).

¹⁹"The greatest excellence which dwells within you, and the fine distinction which you possess, disturb me, for I do not know a woman, be she nearby or far away who, if she desires to love, is not drawn toward you."

²⁰"But you, love, are so very discerning that you must indeed recognize (that I am) the most loyal one, and may you remember our covenant."

²¹"I am constrained to sing about that which I would rather not, so bitter am I toward him whose lover I am, for I love him more than anything which exists."

²²"Friend, I am in great distress and in great sorrow because of you, and of the harm which I suffer therefrom I do not believe that you feel anything at all."

²³"Now do I see that I am betrayed because I did not grant him my love, wherefore I have been in great sorrow, both night and day." The last line of this passage has been rendered rather freely, the literal meaning being scarcely in accord with the general sense. Kussler-Ratyé gives a similar translation.

²⁴"In this do I take comfort, that never, love, did I fail toward you in any way. Rather do I love you more than Seguin loved Valensa, and it pleases me greatly that I surpass you in loving, my dear, for you are the most worthy. . . ." We cannot identify Seguin and Valensa, but they must have been noted, at least among the troubadours, for the strength and fidelity of their love, for they are also mentioned with this same implication by both Arnaut de Marueil and Lanfranc Cigala; see Kussler-Ratyé, *Archivum Romanicum*, I, 177.

²⁵"It is not just that another love should take you away from me, for reason of anything that she may say or grant to you, and may you remember what was the beginning of our love; may the Lord God never grant that the separation be fault of mine."

²⁶"And since I am true to him, it is indeed fitting that he be true to me, for never do I turn away from loving him, nor do I have the heart to withdraw from him."

[27]*Louise Labé*, 17.

[28]One of the countess' poems, the last of Kussler-Ratyé's edition, lacks a personal note, dealing in rather general fashion with criticism of flatterers and jealous lovers. This work may belong to a period prior to her amorous involvement, or at the beginning of it.

[29]"My worth and my beauty and my lineage, and most of all my loyal heart should avail me, wherefore I send to you, there where you dwell, this song, that it may be a messenger for me."

[30]"But let the messenger tell you all the more, that from too much arrogance do many people suffer great harm" (II, 36-37).

[31]"I marvel to myself at how arrogant you are toward me, my love, wherefore I have reason to suffer. . . . And I wish to know, my fair and noble friend, why you are so harsh and cruel to me—I know not if it be pride or ill will."

[32]"You are arrogant toward me in both word and deed, and yet you are gracious toward all others" (II, 13-14).

[33]Joseph Aynard in his *Les Poètes lyonnais* (Paris, 1924), 29-30, has made a pertinent comment on this point: "Que Louise Labé ait aimé, cela paraît certain, et le simple fait d'avoir publié des poésies amoureuses a pu suffire pour lui donner une mauvaise réputation. Mais sans prendre parti entre les deux camps qui assez ridiculement attaquent ou défendent sa vertu, on peut supposer qu'au moins il n'y eut pas scandale."

[34]Does not this line at least suggest that her lover is quite real and attainable, perhaps a married man with whom, in the tightly knit Lyonese society of her time, not even she could live openly?

[35]An interesting variation of the troubadour convention which demands that the poet express his complete subservience to the lady's will.

[36]"A lady who turns her thoughts toward excellence should place her affection in a worthy and honorable knight since she recognizes his worthiness and dares to love him openly."

[37]"It pleases me greatly to know that the one whom I desire to possess me is more worthy, and I pray God that great joy may come to him who first brought him (my lover) to me."

[38]"I should like indeed to hold my lover naked in my arms, one evening, and he would hold himself to be happy in this provided that I should serve as a pillow for him."

[39]"Fair friend, handsome and good, when shall I hold you in my power? And when shall I lie with you at eventide and give you a loving kiss? Know that I should have a great desire to have you in place of a husband, provided that you had sworn to me to do all that I might desire."

JOHN J. GUILBEAU

[1]*Le Don Quichotte de Cervantes* (Paris, n. d. [1931]), 112-29, 159-91.
[2]*Some Forms of the Riddle Question and the Exercise of the Wits in*

Popular Fiction and Formal Literature ("University of California Publications in Modern Philology," II [Berkeley, 1911]) , 220.

[3]Besides the two studies already cited, see also J. D. M. Ford, "Plot, Tale, and Episode in *Don Quixote," Mélanges de Linguistique et de Littérature offerts à M. Alfred Jeanroy* (Paris, 1928) , 311-23; A. Krappe, "La Fuente clásica de Miguel de Cervantes," *Romanic Review,* X (1929) , 42-43; S. Barto, "The Subterranean Grail Paradise of Cervantes," *Publications of the Modern Language Association,* XXXVIII (1923) , 401-11; and especially the note and commentaries in the following editions and translations of *Don Quixote:* F. Rodríguez Marín (ed.) , *El Ingenioso Hidalgo Don Quixote de la Mancha* (10 vols.; Madrid, 1947-49) ; R. Schevill and A. Bonilla (eds.) , *Don Quixote de la Mancha* (4 vols.; Madrid, 1928-41) ; J. Ormsby (trans.) , *Don Quixote de la Mancha* (New York, n. d. [1936]) ; S. Putnam (trans.) , *The Ingenious Gentleman Don Quixote de la Mancha* (2 vols.; New York, 1949) .

[4]*The Folktale* (New York, 1946) , 413.

[5]Stith Thompson, *Motif-Index of Folk-Literature* (6 vols.; Bloomington, 1955-58). This is the revised and enlarged edition of the work first published in 1932-36. Hereafter this work will be referred to as the *Motif-Index.* Where the classification number is given in the text, no further reference is necessary since the number is sufficient to locate the item readily; for example, D1318.5.2. The *motif* as here used is defined as "the smallest element in a tale having the power to persist in tradition" (Thompson, *The Folktale,* 415) . And it is made to include any of the elements of narrative structure that have formed part of a tradition, whether oral or literary. (See *Motif-Index,* I, 10-11.)

[6]References to *Don Quixote* are by part and chapter to facilitate finding the passages in any edition.

[7]Other items in this category, with their location in the novel given in parentheses followed by the *Motif-Index* classification numbers where applicable, are: the magic drinking cup as a chastity test (I, 33) H411.4; beaver sacrifices scrotum to save its life (I, 21) J351.1; the cumulative tale: "el gato al rato, el rato a la cuerda, la cuerda al palo . . ." (I, 16) Z20; the parson and the thief (II, 1) X441. The answers of the youth who insisted they could not make him sleep in jail (II, 49) are in the tradition of the clever repartee motifs, J1280 ff. See also Schevill, *Some Forms of the Riddle Question . . .,* 192 n. 10 for the story of Nicolao the Fish (II, 18) , and p. 220 for the folklore aspects of the episode dealing with the enchanted head and the answering of riddle questions (II, 62) . For the otherworld journey in the Cave of Montesinos episode (II, 22, 23) , see Barto, "The Subterranean Grail Paradise," *loc. cit.,* 401-11, and Thompson, *Motif-Index,* F80 ff.

[8]*El Ingenioso Hidalgo Don Quixote,* IV, 291 n. 5.

[9]*Comedias y entremeses de Cervantes* (6 vols.; Madrid, 1915-22) , IV, 199.

[10]"Cervantes as a Dramatist," *Modern Language Notes,* XXIII (1908) , 185 n. 9.

[11]*Don Quixote,* III, 482.

[12]*Ingenious Gentleman,* II, 996 n. 14.

[13]*The Ocean of Story, Being Tawney's Translation of Somadeva's Kathā*

Sarit Sāgara, ed. N. M. Penzer (10 vols.; London, 1924-28), VI, 217-20.

[14]*Ibid.,* 285-88.

[15]R. F. Burton, *Supplemental Nights to the Book of a Thousand and One Nights* (6 vols.; privately printed by the Burton Club, n. d.), IV, 1 ff. See also V. Chauvin, *Bibliographie des ouvrages arabes* (12 vols.; Liège, 1892-1922), VII, 158-61, for an impressive list of analogues and parallels of this tale. He lists Indian, Persian, Arabic, Jewish, Greek, French, Danish, and Russian versions of this tale type.

[16]M. Gaster (ed.), *The Exempla of the Rabbis* (London, 1924), 63-64, No. 51. See pp. 195-96 for many other Jewish references as well as a long list from other parts of the world.

[17]See H. Fischer and J. Bolte (eds.), *Die Reise der Söhne Giaffers aus dem Italienischen des Christoforo Armeno* ("Bibliothek des Litterarischen Vereins in Stuttgart," No. 208 [Tübingen, 1895]), 22-32. See pp. 177-97 for the popularity that this work enjoyed and for the many European versions —German, French, English, Danish, Dutch—that ultimately stem from it. It is interesting to note that Christoforo Armeno's Italian version of the three princes of Serendip, published in 1557, has been suggested as a possible source for the framework of the "El Cautivo" episode in *Don Quixote;* see Ford, "Plot, Tale, and Episode in *Don Quixote,*" loc. cit., 317 n. 1.

[18]Fischer and Bolte (eds.), *Die Reise der Söhne Giaffers,* 200-202, give a long list of analogues from various parts of the world—Persian, Arabic, Hebrew, Indian, and European versions—including a reference to the wine taster episode of *Don Quixote,* and add that an anecdote similar in details to Cervantes' version was reported in a German newspaper in 1879 as a news item.

[19]E. Oliver and F. Powell (trans.), *The First Nine Books of the Danish History of Saxo Grammaticus* (London, 1894), 113-15.

[20]A. Aarne, *The Types of the Folk-Tale,* trans. S. Thompson ("FF Communications," No. 74 [Helsinki, 1928]).

[21]*The Folktale,* 82-83.

[22]For other variations on this motif, see Thompson, *Motif-Index,* F647.1 to F647.12.

[23]*Ibid.,* I, 19; Thompson, *The Folktale,* 414-16; Schevill, *Some Forms of the Riddle Question,* 218 n. 70.

[24]See n. 17 above.

[25]See n. 18 above.

[26]Rodríguez Marín (ed.), *En Ingenioso Hidalgo Don Quixote,* IV, 291 n. 5.

[27]Penzer (ed.), *The Ocean of Story,* VII, 10-12.

[28]*Ibid.,* 204-11. See also J. Bolte and G. Polívka, *Anmerkungen zu den Kinder-und Hausmärchen der Brüder Grimm* (5 vols.; Leipzig, 1913-32), III, 238. It should be noted that this motif is of the same order as the one involving unusual sensitiveness in smelling and drinking. The sub-types listed in Thompson, *Motif-Index* under F647, "Marvelous sensitiveness," include both types.

[29]On this point, see Thompson, *Motif-Index,* I, 19.

[30]It should be noted that the dream experience itself with factual results

occurs, in a more exaggerated and striking form than the one told by the innkeeper's daughter, as a common folk motif: "Realistic dream" (F1068). For instance, a man dreams that he is flogged by two mysterious women and on awakening is so used up that he takes to his bed and lies speechless for a whole year. Another one dreams that he is stabbed and on awakening finds a knife sticking in his side to the haft. For these and many other examples in classical and popular romances, see George L. Kittredge, *Witchcraft in Old and New England* (Cambridge, Mass., 1928), 221-23.

[31]Rodríguez Marín (ed.), *El Ingenioso Hildago Don Quixote*, VII, 25 n. 2.

[32]*Popular Tales and Fiction, Their Migrations and Transformation* (2 vols.; Edinburgh, 1887), I, 29.

[33]A version similar in treatment to that of Cervantes appears in T. F. Crane (ed.), *Exempla of Jacques de Vitry* (London, 1890), 109, *exemplum* CCLV. See pp. xvii ff. for a discussion of the impulse given by this collection to the use of *exempla* in sermons and through them to the diffusion of popular tales in Europe; and pp. 242-43 for a long list of parallels in Latin, French, and German *exemplum* and tale collections of the Middle Ages and the Renaissance, including Johannes Pauli's *Schimpf und Ernst*, ed. H. Osterley (Stuttgart, 1866, No. 15). For a discussion of the possible role played by this latter collection, first published in Strassburg in 1522, and other German jest books in the presence of popular themes in Spanish collections, see Schevill, *Some Forms of the Riddle Question*, 196-201.

[34]T. de Wyzewa (trans.), *Le Légende dorée* (Paris, 1925), 24-25; *Libro de los Ensemplos, ensemplo* CLXV, in P. Gayangos, *Escritores en prosa anteriores al siglo XV* (Madrid, 1922), 487; Gaster, *Exempla of the Rabbis*, 82, No. 121a, and a long list of analogues on pp. 210-11; Reinhold Köhler, *Kleinere Schriften zur Märchenforschung*, ed. J. Bolte (3 vols.; Weimar, 1898-1900), I, 137, and the references given by Bolte; J. Bladé, *Contes populaires de la Gascogne* (3 vols.; Paris, 1886), III, 368.

[35]Rodríguez Marín (ed.), *El Ingenioso Hidalgo Don Quixote*, VII, 19-20 n. 19.

[36]E. Richardson, *Materials for a life of Jacopo da Varagine*, Section II, *Latin Writings* (New York, 1935), 26-30, especially.

[37]It is interesting to note that in the tale-type of "The Three Wise Brothers," the theme of marvelous powers of tasting and smelling merges frequently into another form of the motif in which the process of deduction from observation rather than unusual sensitiveness plays the principal part. See Penzer (ed.), *The Ocean of Story*, VI, 285-86; Thompson, *Motif-Index*, J1661, "Clever deduction" and sub-types.

[38]See Hazard, *Le Don Quichotte*, 171-72; Putnam (trans.), *Ingenious Gentleman*, II, 1019 n. 2 to chap. 51.

[39]For the Solomon legend in folklore, see Thompson, *The Folktale*, 266-67; Schevill, *Some Forms of the Riddle Question*, 204-205.

[40]*Anmerkungen*, II, 209; see also L. Mackensen and Others, *Handwörterbuch des deutschen Märchens* (Berlin, 1931 ff.), II, No. 190a.

[41]*El Ingenioso Hidalgo Don Quixote*, II, 103 n. 6.

[42]It appears in Crane (ed.), *Exempla of Jacques de Vitry*, 10, No. 27.

In his notes to this work Crane, p. 143, cites Pauli's *Schimpf und Ernst* (see n. 33 above) and a number of Latin works.

[43]On this aspect of the diffusion of traditional tales, see Thompson, *The Folktale*, 5.

[44]See R. Schevill, *Cervantes* (*New York*, 1919), 60-77, 153-54, 168, especially. As for his reading, Cervantes himself states in *Don Quixote* (I, 9) that he was extremely fond of reading even though it was but a scrap of paper in the street.

[45]*Ibid.*, 230.

[46]On the character of Sancho, see *ibid.*, 257-58.

JEAN ALEXANDER

[1]The division into two phases is a generally accepted one, but the labels vary. For example, Ernest Martinenche, *La Comedia espagnole en France de Hardy à Racine* (Paris, 1900), divides the era into an heroic epoch and an ironic epoch; Clifford Leech, *Shakespeare's Tragedies* (New York, 1950) and Ludwig Pfandl, *Historia de la literatura española en la edad de oro* (Barcelona, 1933) mention the phases as those of illusion and disillusion.

[2]Theodore Spencer, *Shakespeare and the Nature of Man* (New York, 1945), 21-50.

[3]Willard Farnham, *The Medieval Heritage of Elizabethan Tragedy* (Berkeley, 1936), 341 ff.

[4]Willard Farnham, *Shakespeare's Tragic Frontier* (Berkeley, 1950), 37-38.

[5]Una Ellis-Fermor, *The Jacobean Drama* (London, 1958), 1-5.

[6]Pfandl, *Historia de la literatura . . .*, 407.

[7]Lope de Vega Carpio, *Obras*, ed. Sainz de Robles (Madrid, 1952), 913.

[8]Adolph Friedrich von Schack, *Historia de la literatura y del arte dramático en España* (5 vols.; Madrid, 1887), V, 43-192.

[9]Henry Thomas Buckle, *History of Civilization in England* (3 vols.; London, 1904-1906), II, 388. Buckle quotes and accepts the phrase from Simonde de Sismondi's *Historical View of the Literature of the South of Europe.*

[10]Pfandl, *Historia de la literatura . . .*, 271.

[11]John Owen, *The Five Great Skeptical Dramas of History* (London, 1896), 359.

[12]F. T. Bowers, *Elizabethan Revenge Tragedy, 1587-1642* (Princeton, 1940).

[13]Alfred Harbage, *Shakespeare and the Rival Traditions* (New York, 1952), 3-57.

MARTIN E. ERICKSON

[1]*Foreign Influences in Elizabethan Plays* (New York, 1923), 119.

[2]"On the Influence of Spanish Literature upon English in the Early 17th Century," *Romanische Forschungen*, XX (1907), 604-34.

[3]*Foreign Influences in Elizabethan Plays*, 122.

[4]*The Relations between Spanish and English Literature* (Liverpool, 1910), 23.

[5]"On the Influence of Spanish Literature . . .," *loc. cit.*, 624 n. 2.

[6]"A Probable Source of Beaumont and Fletcher's *Philaster*," *Publications of the Modern Language Association*, XLI (1926), 294.

[7]*Studies in Beaumont, Fletcher, and Massinger* (Chapel Hill, N. C., 1939), 107. Edward M. Wilson in *"Rule a Wife and Have a Wife* and *El Sagaz Estacio*," *Review of English Studies*, XXIV (1948), 189-94, says, "If Fletcher read the novel he read it in Spanish"; see also Edward M. Wilson, "Did John Fletcher Read Spanish?" *Philological Quarterly*, XXVII (1948), 187-90, for the evidence that he read it fairly fluently.

[8]"On the Influence of Spanish Literature . . .," *loc. cit.*, 605-606.

[9]*A History of Spanish Literature* (New York, 1930).

[10]*Historia de la literatura española* (2d ed.; Boston, 1949), 361.

[11]*Historia de la literatura española* (Madrid, 1925).

[12]*An Introduction to Spanish Literature* (2d ed.; Chicago, 1949).

[13]*Historia de la literatura española* (3d ed.; Barcelona, 1950).

[14]*History of Spanish Literature* (2d ed.; New York, 1854).

[15]*Historia de la lengua y literatura castellana* (14 vols.; Madrid, 1915-1922), IV, 187.

[16]*Historia de la literatura nacional española en la Edad de Oro* (Barcelona, 1952).

[17]*Catálogo bibliográfico y biográfico del teatro antiquo español* (Madrid, 1860), 82.

[18]*Catálogo de las piezas de teatro* (2d ed.; Madrid, 1934), I, 220.

[19]*Geschichte der dramatischen Literatur und Kunst in Spanien* (5 vols.; Madrid, 1885-1887),

[20]*Obras completas de Don Guillén de Castro y Bellvis* (3 vols.; Madrid, 1925-1928), I, xxxii.

[21]*Ibid.*, xxix.

[22]*Ibid.*, xxxvi. Courtney Bruerton in "The Chronology of the *Comedias* of Guillén de Castro," *Hispanic Review*, XII (1944), 89-151, bases his conclusions on metrical tests.

[23]Juliá Martínez (ed.), *Obras completas . . .*, I, xxxvii.

[24]*Ibid.*

[25]*Agudeza y arte de ingenio* (Madrid, 1929), 282.

[26]*Obras Completas de Guillén de Castro*, III, xi.

[27]*Scritti vari de erudizione e di critica in onore di Rodolfo Renier* (Torino, 1912), 830.

[28]*L'Art dramatique à Valencia, depuis les origines jusqu'a commencement du XVII₍ siècle* (Toulouse, 1913), 583 n. 1.

[29]Maxwell says, *Studies*, p. 114, "Many have placed the date of *Love's Cure* from sixteen to nineteen years before 1625, and almost every dramatist of the time has been advanced as a collaborating author."

[30]E. K. Chambers, *Elizabethan Stage* (4 vols.; Oxford, 1923), III, 232.

[31]G. C. Macaulay, in *Cambridge History of English Literature* (15 vols.; New York, 1932-1933), VI, 140.

[32]*Ibid.*, VI, 158. D. M. McKeithan in *The Debt to Shakespeare to the Beaumont and Fletcher Plays* (Austin, Texas, 1938), 199, says: "Macaulay

believes (p. 153), however, that there may be a Spanish original not yet discovered. Oliphant (p. 417) quotes Stiefel as saying that De Castro's play was licensed for printing in Spain on February 7, 1624-25, and was published some three months later. While the date of *Love's Cure* is uncertain, practically all scholars agree that it was written before 1624. It does not seem possible, therefore, that its source could be *La fuerza de la costumbre*. I have not read the Spanish play, but if, as Macaulay says, this comedy and *Love's Cure* 'are founded on the same source,' the two plays probably have a common source yet to be discovered."

[33]*Cambridge History of English Literature*, VIII, 146.

[34]Felix Schelling, *Elizabethan Drama* (2 vols.; New York, 1908), II, 214-15.

[35]*Philip Massinger* (New York, 1920), 5, note.

[36]*The Plays of Beaumont and Fletcher* (New Haven, 1927), 414.

[37]*Ibid.*, 418.

[38]*Ibid.*, 431.

[39]R. Warwick Bond, "On Six Plays in *Beaumont and Fletcher, 1679*," *Review of English Studies*, XI (1935), 263-64.

[40]*Ibid.*, 268.

[41]E. H. C. Oliphant, "Three Beaumont and Fletcher Plays," *Review of English Studies*, XII (1936), 199.

[42]R. Warwick Bond, "Three Beaumont and Fletcher Plays," *Review of English Studies*, XII (1936), 444-45; see also McKeithen, *Debt to Shakespeare . . .*, 199-206.

[43]*The Jacobean and Caroline Stage* (5 vols.; Oxford, 1941-1956), III, 363-66.

[44]In R. B. McKerrow (ed.), *The Spanish Curate*, in *Works of Beaumont and Fletcher* (Variorum ed.; 4 vols.; London, 1904-1912), II, 104, 107-20.

[45]"On Six Plays," *loc. cit.*, 266-67.

[46]"Die Nachahmung spanischer Komödien in England unter den ersten Stuarts," *Archiv*, XCIX (1899), 271-310.

[47]*Ibid.*, 282-83.

[48]He refers to his earlier study with the same title published in *Romanische Forschungen*, V (1890), 193-220.

[49]Stiefel, "Die Nachahmung . . .," *loc. cit.*, 271-72.

[50]*Ibid.*, 283.

[51]*Ibid.*, 284-85.

[52]*Mira de Amescua y su teatro* (Madrid, 1931), 72.

[53]*Ibid.*

[54]"On the Influence of Spanish Literature . . .," *loc. cit.*, 609-10 n. 2.

KENNETH R. WILSON-JONES

[1]Theodore Besterman (ed.), *Voltaire's Correspondence* (Geneva, 1953–); volumes I and II contain the texts on which this study is based. Theodore Besterman (ed.) *Voltaire's Notebooks* (2 vols.; Geneva, 1952).

[2]Among the general works on Voltaire's visit to England the following, listed in chronological order, have been the most useful: J. Churton Collins, *Voltaire, Montesquieu and Rousseau in England* (London, 1908), written

in the 1880's; Gustave Lanson, "Voltaire et les *Lettres philosophiques*. Comment Voltaire faisait un livre," *Revue de Philologie* (August 1, 1908), 367-86; Lucien Foulet (ed.), *La Correspondence de Voltaire (1726-1729). La Bastille, L'Angleterre. Le Retour en France* (Paris, 1913); Fernand Baldensperger, "La Chronologie du séjour de Voltaire en Angleterre et les *Lettres philosophiques*," *Archiv*, CXX (1913), 137-53; Archibald Ballantyne, *Voltaire's Visit to England (1726-1729)* (London, 1919); Fernand Baldensperger, "Voltaire anglophile avant son séjour en Angleterre," *Revue de Littérature Comparée*, IX (1929), 25-61; Voltaire, *Lettres philosophiques*, ed. Gustave Lanson (5th ed.; 2 vols.; Paris, 1937); and René Pomeau, *La Religion de Voltaire* (Paris, 1956). C. P. Gooch, "Voltaire in England," *Contemporary Review*, CXCV (1959), 349-53, and CXCVI (1959), 31-36, 90-93, has added nothing new to the subject.

[3]Besterman (ed.), *Voltaire's Correspondence*, I, 329. In 1718 Voltaire had sent a copy of *Oedipe* together with a flattering little poem to George I through the English ambassador to France, Lord Stair. In acknowledgment the king presented Voltaire a gold medal and a gold watch. See Baldensperger, "Voltaire anglophile," *loc. cit.*, 29-30.

[4]Besterman (ed.), *Voltaire's Correspondence*, I, 91.

[5]Baldensperger, "Voltaire anglophile," *loc. cit.*, 34-43.

[6]Pomeau, *La Religion de Voltaire*, 91-92, insists on the importance of Bolingbroke in the formation of Voltaire's thought. In this he is opposed to the view of Norman L. Torrey in "Bolingbroke and Voltaire—a Fictitious Influence," *Publications of the Modern Language Association*, XLII (1927), 788-97. Pomeau's opinion is strengthened by a letter of Bolingbroke to Voltaire of June 27, 1724, first published by Besterman (ed.), *Voltaire's Correspondence*, I, 245-49.

[7]George Sherburn (ed.), *The Correspondence of Alexander Pope* (5 vols.; Oxford, 1956), II, 221-22 (February 18, 1724).

[8]Pope to Bolingbroke, April 9, 1724, in Sherburn (ed.), *Correspondence of Pope*, II, 228-29.

[9]Pope to Caryl, December 25, 1724, in Sherburn (ed.), *Correspondence of Pope*, II, 354. "I had read Mariamne before our friend sent it, having formerly had some correspondence (about the poem on the League) with its author." Sherburn's note seems to indicate that he interprets Pope's statement as a reference to some exchange of letters with Voltaire. E. Audra, in *L'Influence française dans l'oeuvre de Pope* (Paris, 1931), 69, denies the existence of any lost letters between Pope and Voltaire. The whole chapter on Voltaire and Pope seeks to demonstrate a lack of interest on the part of Pope.

[10]Foulet (ed.), *Correspondence de Voltaire*, Appendice I, "Voltaire et Rohan-Chabot," 211-32.

[11]*Ibid.*, 28-29, notes; and Besterman (ed.), *Voltaire's Correspondence*, II, 23, 33, the commentary.

[12]Ballantyne and Collins relate many anecdotes of this sort. Their sources, however, are usually sworn enemies of Voltaire writing many years after his English visit.

[13]Besterman (ed.), *Voltaire's Correspondence*, II, 34-40 (Letters 291-295).

[14]Voltaire had done this several times already—after his first imprisonment in the Bastille, and again in 1723 when he had almost died of smallpox.

[15]There are many references to the difficulties of mastering English pronunciation in Voltaire's letters to Thiriot and to Madame du Châtelet, 1726-1734.

[16]The letter has been reproduced several times since its first publication in fairly complete form in 1892. The notes in Foulet's edition are more complete than those of Besterman. Foulet (ed.), *Correspondence de Voltaire*, 53-64; Besterman (ed.), *Voltaire's Correspondence*, II, 36-39.

[17]The comment is Foulet's, repeated by Besterman.

[18]For a description of the two notebooks and a history of the publication, see Besterman (ed.), *Voltaire's Notebooks*, Introduction, I, 1-3. The text is found in I, 31-88.

[19]Lanson, in his fifth edition of the *Lettres philosophiques* (1937), used the fragmentary and incomplete edition of Fernand Caussy *(English Review,* 1914) rather than the excellent critical edition of Norman L. Torrey in *Modern Philology*, XXVI (1929), 308-25. Torrey traces some of the ideas in this notebook into later works of Voltaire. Besterman indicates in his notes some of the entries which Voltaire later developed. A thorough study of the transformation of the material in the notebooks into Voltaire's finished works remains to be done.

[20]Lanson (ed.), *Lettres philosophiques*, I, xlvi-xlvii, mentions his unsuccessful attempts to examine the Cambridge notebook.

[21]Besterman (ed.), *Voltaire's Notebooks*, I, 34.

[22]*Ibid.*

[23]*Ibid.*, 35. See Torrey's edition, 314-15.

[24]Lanson, using the incomplete edition of Caussy, is rather vague when giving his doubts about the early composition of this notebook. "Je ne crois guère, malgré certaines indications du texte, que ces notes rédigés en anglais par Voltaire aient pu l'être dès 1726. Les passages embarrassants (ceux qui contiennent la date 1726, ou les mots 'the present year') pourraient être des extraits pris dans les livres ou des journaux. . . ." *Lettres philosophiques*, I, 77; see also II, 303. Almost all of Voltaire's literary sources are newspapers or anthologies published some years before his visit; the dates are not references to these sources.

[25]Besterman (ed.), *Voltaire's Notebooks*, I, 72.

[26]*Ibid.*, II, index. The index is not complete; several interesting comments by Voltaire on English authors are not mentioned. The translations into French are found in I, 70-71, 76-77, 79, 80.

[27]*Ibid.*, I, 82.

[28]"Discours sur la tragédie. A milord Bolingbroke" (preface to *Brutus)* in Voltaire's *Oeuvres complètes*, ed. Louis Moland (52 vols.; Paris, 1877-1885), II, 311-12.

[29]Besterman (ed.), *Voltaire's Notebooks*, I, 82-85.

JOHN ROLAND DOVE

[1]*Existentialism and the Modern Predicament* (New York, 1958), 9.

[2]*Le Diable et le bon Dieu* (Paris, 1951), 64.

[3]*Gesammelte Werke* (6 vols.; Leipzig, 1930), III, 290.

[4]*Stendhal* (Cambridge, 1939), 235.

[5]All page references in parentheses in the text are to the edition by Henri Martineau (Paris, 1948).

[6]*Stendhal*, 237.

[7]All page references in parentheses in the text are to the Chiltern Library edition (London, 1950).

[8]For a fuller discussion of James's attitude to love, see John Roland Dove, "Tragic Consciousness in Isabel Archer," *Studies in American Literature*, ed. Waldo McNeir and Leo B. Levy ("Louisiana State University Studies, Humanities Series," No. 8 [Baton Rouge, 1960]), 78-94.

CARL HAMMER, JR.

[1]Henry Wadsworth Longfellow, "Journal" of January 7, 1848, quoted by Samuel Longfellow, *Life of Henry Wadsworth Longfellow, with Extracts from His Journals and Correspondence*, vols. XII-XIV in *The Works of Henry Wadsworth Longfellow* (14 vols.; Boston, 1886-91), XIII, 280. Hereinafter cited as *Works*.

[2]*The Poets and Poetry of Europe, with Introduction and Biographical Notices* (Philadelphia, 1845).

[3]James Taft Hatfield, "The Longfellow-Freiligrath Correspondence," *Publications of the Modern Language Association*, LXVIII (1933), 1227.

[4]"Longfellows Beziehungen zur deutschen Literatur," *Zeitschrift für den deutschen Unterricht*, VI (1892), 272-74. Thiergen refers to the translations of Luther's *Ein' feste Burg* and Goethe's *Wanderers Nachtlied I* and *Wer nie sein Brot mit Tränen ass*. For a discussion of correspondences of trochaic and iambic lyric verse in English and German, with particular reference to Longfellow, see A. L. Kroeber, "Parts of Speech in Periods of Poetry," *Publications of the Modern Language Association*, LXXIII (1958), 309-14.

[5]"Longfellow and German Romance," *Poet Lore*, XVII (1906), 69.

[6]"German Poetry," in *An Anthology of World Poetry* (New York, 1928), 816-941.

[7]*New Light on Longfellow, with Special Reference to His Relations to Germany* (Boston, 1933), 143. Appendix B, 164-78, contains an indispensable summary of Longfellow's German studies and reading.

[8]*Amerikanische Dichter und die deutsche Literatur* (Goslar, 1950), 92, 94.

[9]*Longfellow: A Full-Length Portrait* (New York, 1955), 31.

[10]See Iris Lilian Whitman, *Longfellow and Spain* (New York, 1927), 143; and Andrew Hilen, *Longfellow and Scandinavia* (New Haven, 1947), 53, 76.

[11]*Works*, VIII, 369.

[12]Out of 766 double-column pages, 191 (pp. 180-370) are devoted to German poetry and introductory essays on the poets.

[13]*Longfellow:A Full-Length Portrait,* 7.

[14]*Works,* VI, 181 f.

[15]*Ibid.,* 183. With few exceptions, Longfellow's published translations of German poems are found in this volume, pp. 260-89, 417-21 (Appendix). The following were included in *Voices of the Night* (1839) : "The Happiest Land," "The Wave," "The Dead," "The Bird and the Ship," "Whither," "Beware!," "Song of the Bell," "Song of the Silent Land," "The Castle by the Sea," and "The Black Knight"; in *The Belfry of Bruges and Other Poems* (1845) : "The Hemlock Tree," "Annie of Tharaw," "The Statue over the Cathedral Door," "The Legend of the Crossbill," "The Sea Hath Its Pearls," and "Poetic Aphorisms." Most of these, together with "The Luck of Edenhall," were reprinted in *The Poets and Poetry of Europe.*

[16]*Works,* VII, 112 (ll. 205-12, from two consecutive stanzas) .

[17]Edward Wagenknecht (ed.) , *Mrs. Longfellow: Selected Letters and Journals of Fanny Appleton Longfellow* (New York, 1956) , 146.

[18]"Hoffman and Longfellow," *Nation,* LXXXVI (1908) , 32.

[19]Lawrance Thompson, *Young Longfellow* (New York, 1938) , 240-63; Hatfield, *New Light on Longfellow,* 167; Orie W. Long, "Goethe and Longfellow," *Germanic Review,* VII (1932) , 166, 174; and Carl L. Johnson, *Professor Longfellow of Harvard* (Eugene, Oregon, 1944) , 86 f.

[20]Thompson, *Young Longfellow,* 231, 396 n.

[21]"Longfellow's Attitude Toward Goethe," *Modern Philology,* XVI (1918) , 65.

[22]Thompson, *Young Longfellow,* 265 f.; see also Henry A. Pochmann and Others, *German Culture in America: Philosophical and Literary Influences, 1600-1900* (Madison, Wis., 1957) , 410-26: "Henry Wadsworth Longfellow." The is the best concise general account of Longfellow's relations to Germany and her literature.

[23]See Andrew Hilen (ed.) , *The Diary of Clara Crowninshield: A European Tour with Longfellow, 1835-36* (Seattle, 1956) , 211-13, 218.

[24]"Longfellow and German Romance," *loc. cit.,* 69.

[25]Why Novalis was not included in *The Poets and Poetry of Europe,* despite intentions to the contrary, is set forth by Percy Matenko, "Fragments from Longfellow's Workshop: Novalis," *Germanic Review,* XXII (1947) , 32-41.

[26]Longfellow endeavored to translate the *Hildebrandslied* for an undated lecture. For his version of the first eight lines of the Low German *Reinke de Vos,* see Hatfield, *New Light on Longfellow,* 35.

[27]Found in the "Interlude: Martin Luther," in *Christus: A Mystery* (1871) , *Works,* V, 293-97. The individual stanzas are interspersed through Luther's soliloquy, which is largely a commentary on them.

[28]*Bibliothek deutscher Dichter des XVII. Jahrhunderts* (14 vols.; Leipzig, 1822-27) .

[29]Long attributed to Dach, this Low German poem is believed by some

to be the work of Heinrich Albert (1604-51), of Königsberg. Cf. August Closs and T. Pugh Williams (eds.), *The Heath Anthology of German Poetry* (Boston, 1957), 142 n.

[30]Hatfield, *New Light on Longfellow*, 113.

[31]*Works*, VIII, 189.

[32]*Ibid.*, VI, 418-21 (Appendix). Longfellow devoted a lecture to Matthisson, with illustrative passages in translation from several poems, including *Die Kinderjahre*, which apparently influenced "My Lost Youth"; see Hatfield, *New Light on Longfellow*, 53. Matthisson (born near Magdeburg in 1761) was, of course, not a "Swiss poet," as Hatfield calls him, *ibid.*, 54.

[33]*Ibid.*, 135.

[34]"Longfellow's Translation of Goethe's 'Ueber allen Gipfeln,'" *Modern Language Notes*, LXXI (1956), 344 f.

[35]*Goethe, The Lyrist: 100 Poems in New Translations Facing the Originals, with a Biographical Introduction* ("University of North Carolina Studies in the Germanic Languages and Literatures," No. 16 [Chapel Hill, N. C., 1955]), xv, 79. Even so, this final version represents an improvement upon the form in which it originally appeared in *Hyperion; Works*, VIII, 195.

[36]Like "Wanderer's Night-Song II," it was revised for inclusion in the second edition of *The Poets and Poetry of Europe;* the first effort is found in a letter to Samuel Ward, dated September 17, 1841.

[37]All three have been printed by Hatfield, *New Light on Longfellow*, 59 f. Besides the titles already mentioned, there are fragments of numerous poems, including the following: Goethe, *Der Fischer*, as well as a number of short passages from *Faust;* Hahn-Hahn, *Lass, O Herr;* Heermann, *Herzliebster Jesu;* Hölty, *Mailied;* Matthisson, *Die Sterbende* and *Adelaïde;* Müller, *Abendreihn;* and Schiller, three lines from *Wallenstein*.

[38]*Works*, VIII, 291.

[39]See Longfellow's article, "Heinrich Heine" (with selections from *Reisebilder*), *Graham's Magazine*, XX (1842), 134-37.

[40]*Works*, VIII, 87-90.

[41]First published in full in *Keramos and Other Poems* (1878). The beginning stanza had served as the motto for the second book of *Hyperion* forty years earlier.

[42]*Longfellows Wechselbeziehungen zur deutschen Literatur* (Leipzig, 1907), 72.

[43]For example, F. E. Pierce and Carl F. Schreiber, *Fiction and Fantasy of German Romance* (New York, 1927), 351.

[44]"Longfellow and German Romance," *loc. cit.*, 70.

[45]When Miss Ashburton objects to the "grim and ghostly" character of "this striking ballad," Flemming replies: "It begins joyously enough with the feast of Pentecost, and the crimson banners at the old castle. Then the contest is well managed. The knight in black mail, and the waving in of the mighty shadow in the dance, and the dropping of the faded flowers, are all strikingly presented to the imagination. However, it tells its own story and needs no explanation." *Works*, VIII, 184.

[46]*Ibid.*, VIII, 114.

[47]Hatfield, *New Light on Longfellow*, 75.

RICHARD M. PAYNE

[1]*Cubism,* trans. Stuart Gilbert (Geneva, 1959), 120-21.

[2]*La Conquête des étoiles, poème épique* (Paris, 1902); *Destruction, poèmes lyriques* (Paris, 1904).

[3]*Roi Bombance, tragédie satirique en 4 actes, en prose* (Paris, 1905); *Re Baldoria,* trans. Decio Cinti (Milan, 1906).

[4]*The European Caravan,* ed. Samuel Putnam (New York, 1931), ix.

[5]*Apollinaire, le mal-aimé* (Paris, 1952), 6-7.

[6]*Ibid.,* 163.

[7]*Les Peintres cubistes,* 27.

[8]"Lettera di F. T. Marinetti a G. Severini," in *Gli Archivi del futurismo,* eds. Maria Drudi Gambillo and Teresa Fiori (Rome, 1958), I, 294.

[9]"L'Esprit nouveau et les poètes," *Mercure de France* (December 1, 1918), 386.

[10]All quotations from *Le Futurisme* as appearing in *Le Figaro,* September 20, 1909, p. 1.

[11]See Mario M. Rossi, "Il futurismo ed il movimento della Voce'," *Italica,* XXXVI (1959), 155-80.

[12]*Vita e tumulti di Marinetti* (Milan, 1959), 203-11.

[13]*Les Peintres cubistes,* 7.

[14]*Ibid.,* 12.

[15]*Ibid.,* 91.

[16]*Ibid.,* 8.

[17]*Ibid.,* 13.

[18]*Ibid.,* 15.

[19]*Ibid.,* 21.

[20]Robert Goldwater and Marco Treves (eds.), *Artists on Art* (New York, 1947), 420-21.

[21]Francesco Flora, *Dal romanticismo al futurismo* (Milan, 1925), 198.

[22]André Billy, *Apollinaire vivant* (Paris, 1923), 104.

[23]*Cubism, A History and an Analysis, 1907-1914* (New York, 1959), 185.

T. R. REES

[1]F. W. Bateson, "Contributions to a Dictionary of Critical Terms II: Dissociation of Sensibility," *Essays in Criticism,* I (1951), 302-12.

[2]T. S. Eliot, "The Metaphysical Poets," in *Critiques and Essays in Criticism, 1920-1948* (New York, 1949), 51-53.

[3]He cites this definition from *The Prompter* of 17 June 1735. A similar definition is listed in the *New English Dictionary.*

[4]Sir James A. H. Murray (ed.), *A New English Dictionary on Historical Principles* (Oxford, 1914), VIII, a.v. "sensibility."

[5]Alexander Spiers and Gabriel Surrenne, *English and French Pronouncing Dictionary* (New York, 1918), 570.

[6]Rémy de Gourmont's *Decadence and Other Essays on the Culture of Ideas* (New York, 1921), "Introduction," x.

[7]"Literary Criticism in France II," in *Critiques and Essays in Criticism, 1920-1948*, 441.

[8]*Ibid.*, 443.

[9]*Ibid.*, 441.

[10]Eric Thompson, "The Critical Forum: 'Dissociation of Sensibility I,'" *Essays in Criticism*, II (1952), 208.

[11]*Ibid.*, 209.

[12]*Ibid.*, 210.

[13]Samuel Taylor Coleridge, *Biographia Literaria*, Chap. XIV, in *The Great Critics*, eds. James Harry Smith and Edd Winfield Parks (New York, 1951), 529.

[14]"Subconscious Creation," in *Decadence and Other Essays*, 191.

[15]*Ibid.*, 195.

[16]*Ibid.*, 189.

[17]*Ibid.*, 191.

[18]Sir Joshua Reynolds, "The Thirteenth Discourse," *Discourses on Art* (London, 1887), 212. Note the reference to sensibility as a faculty of the mind; here it could mean only susceptibility of impression, or mental perception.

[19]*Ibid.*, 213.

[20]*Ibid.*

[21]*Ibid.*

[22]*Ibid.*, 214.

[23]*Ibid.*, 229.

[24]William Wordsworth, "Observations Prefixed to 'Lyrical Ballads,'" in Smith and Parks (eds.), *The Great Critics*, 501.

[25]Percy Bysshe Shelley, "A Defence of Poetry," in Smith and Parks (eds.), *The Great Critics*, 578.

[26]*Ibid.*, 579.

[27]*Milton and Wordsworth: Poets and Prophets: A Study of Their Reactions to Political Events* (New York, 1937), 11-12.

[28]*Ibid.*, 6.

[29]Rémy de Gourmont quoting Alexander von Humboldt, in "Subconscious Creation," *Decadence and Other Essays*, 205.

[30]"Tradition and the Individual Talent," in *The Sacred Wood* (London, 1920), 15.

[31]Smith and Parks (eds.), *The Great Critics*, 528.

[32]*Ibid.*, 535.

[33]"Introduction," *The Alien Vision of Victorian Poetry: Sources of the Poetic Imagination in Tennyson, Browning, and Arnold* (Princeton, 1952), x.

[34]*Ibid.*, 118.

[35]*English Poetic Theory, 1825-1865* (Princeton, 1950), 154.

[36]"The Fall of the House of Usher," in *Great Tales and Poems of Edgar Allan Poe* (New York, 1951), 81.

[37]*Ibid.*, 86.

[38]Frank Kermode, "Dissociation of Sensibility," *The Kenyon Review,* XIX (1957), 181.

JOHN T. KRUMPELMANN

[1]*The Divine Comedy of Dante Alighieri* (New York, 1950), xii.

[2]See the reviews of *The Green Pastures: The Literary Digest,* CV (June 21, 1930), 22, quotes J. H. Barton, editor of the *London Mail:* "How any creature can dare to personate and caricature our ineffably Holy God . . . passes all understanding." *Ibid.,* CVII (December 20, 1930), 19 f.: "House of Commons Debates 'The Green Pastures.' " Here the play is called a "terrible profanity" (p. 20), and we are told "law and custom have prohibited the appearance of a person representing the Deity on the stage." *Theater Magazine,* LIII (March, 1931), 14, reports: "The play has been banned by England's censor because of its representation of God upon the stage." See also William Frederic Hauhart, *The Reception of Goethe's "Faust" in England in the First Half of the Nineteenth Century* (New York, 1909), 37.

[3]Bayard Taylor (trans.), *Faust. A Tragedy by Johann Wolfgang von Goethe* (2 vols. in 1; Boston, 1870), 11. 1112-17. This translation is the one most likely to have been known to Taylor's fellow-Pennsylvanian, Marc Connelly.

[4]Marc Connelly, *The Green Pastures,* in *Pulitzer Prize Plays 1918-1934,* eds. Kathrun Coe and William H. Cordell (New York, 1935), Part II, scene vii, p. 646, and scene viii, p. 648. Lines are not numbered in this edition. (ll. 11,605-85)

[5]Neither of these works actually presents a physical hell on the stage, although there are references to devils and hell in both. In *The Green Pastures* (Part II, scene i) God orders Gabriel, if he is "goin' anywhere near de Big Pit to lean over de brink" and deliver a message to Satan. In *Faust* not only is Mephistopheles omnipresent but in the "Burial Scene" (Part II) Act V, ll. 11,605-85) there are on the stage "The Fearful Jaws of Hell, open on the left," accompanied by a dumb show of devils.

[6]In each drama Gabriel is the second archangel to be presented.

[7]Italics are mine. Cf. the words of "de Lawd" in Roark Bradford's *Ol' Man Adam an' His Chillun* (New York, 1928), 203: " 'Hey-ho, Satan!' say de Lawd. 'I ain't seed you in a month of Sundays. How's Miz Satan and de gals?' "

" 'Finest kind, Lawd,' say Satan. 'How's all yo' folks?' "

[8]Taylor (trans.), *Faust,* II, 455 n. 181.

[9]To Goethe, 3 April 1801. *Schillers Briefe,* ed. Fritz Jonas (Stuttgart, n. d.), VI, 266.

[10]Lines 12,069 ff. Italics are mine.

[11]Lines 12,102 f. Italics are mine.

[12]Cf. *Faust,* 11. 11,936 ff. Italics are mine.

Whoe'er aspires *unweariedly*
Is not beyond redeeming.
And if he feels the *grace of Love*
That from On High is given,
The Blessed Hosts, that wait above,
Shall welcome him to Heaven!

[13]The original begins:

Schlage, heil'gen Stabs Gewalt,
Dass der Boden bebt und schallt!

Taylor's rendering is somewhat free.

[14]*The Green Pastures,* scene ii, p. 608. Italics are mine.

[15]*Ibid.,* p. 630. Note also: to Gabriel's suggestion that God annihilate the race of "man," God replies, "An' admit I'm licked?"

[16]Lines 280 ff. It is interesting to compare Noah's opinion of "man" (I, vii, pp. 620 f.,) with that of the Imperial Kanzler (II, 4,780 ff.) :

"Everybody is mighty busy, gamblin', good-timin' an' goin' on. . . . Dey just all lazy, and mean an' full of sin. . . . Doggone, I come in de church Sunday 'fo las' 'bout an hour befo' de meetin' was to start, and dere was a woman stealin' de altar cloth. . . . Dey ain't got no moral sense. . . . Dere is a boy seventeen years old. Doggone, if he didn't *elope* with his aunt."

Wenn's fieberhaft durchaus im Staate wütet
Und Übel sich in Übeln überbrütet?
Wer schaut hinab von diesem hohen Raum
Ins weite Reich, ihm scheint's ein schwerer Traum,
Wo Missgestalt in Missgestalten schaltet,
Das Ungesetz gesetzlich überwaltet,
Und eine Welt des Irrtums sich entfaltet.
Der *raubt* sich Herden, *der ein Weib,*
Kelch, Kreuz und Leuchter vom Altare,
Berühmt sich dessen manche Jahre
Mit heiler Haut, mit unverletztem Leib.

Italics are mine.

[17]Satan is mentioned immediately after the passage quoted in n. 16: "Why, doggone it, de good man is de man dat keeps busy."

[18]The last two verses, spoken to the angels, recall "de Lawd's" realization quoted in n. 16 that *"quod licet angelis non licet hominibus."*

[19]Lines 4,738 f. Taylor translates:

Adorned and prinked with wondrous art,
Yet so grotesque that all men start.

[20]Cf. the "Candidate Magician" in the corresponding scene of Connelly's play.

[21]See, for example, "Murmurs," 11. 4,951 ff.:

Two rogues they are, in league they've grown,
Dreamer and Fool—so near the throne!
. . . .
Der Tor bläst ein—Der Weise spricht.

Note that Moses prompts and Aaron performs. Also in *The Green Pastures* the Hebrew pair are accused of having resorted to "a new trick." "It's got 'lectricity in it" (p. 636). The pair of German tricksters are accused (1. 4,974) of using "stuff stale and flat. 'Tis quackery! [Kalenderei]—'tis Chemistry! [Chymisterei]."

²²See Goethe's *Sämtliche Werke,* ed. Eduard von der Hellen (41 vols.; Stuttgart, 1902-12), XIV, 389, note "Vor 11,143," concerning Faust's age. In Bradford's *Ol' Man Adam an' His Chillun,* 141, we read of the expiring Moses: "He ain't hardly a hund-ed and twenty, yit."

²³Auf freiem Grund mit freiem Volke stehn (1. 11,580).

²⁴*The Green Pastures,* p. 641; and Bradford, *Ol' Man Adam an' His Chillun,* 147. "About dat time somethin' caught him up and before he could bat his eye he was settin' in de middle of de air. . . ."

²⁵Lines 9,599 ff. Taylor's translation amended by me.

²⁶Taylor (trans.), *Faust,* II, 425 n. 120.

²⁷*Goethes Werke,* XIV, 370.

²⁸Note Helena's words to her "imp" shortly after his birth: "Beware of flying! for prohibited is flight to thee": Aber hüte dich zu fliegen, freier Flug ist dir versagt (1. 9,608).

²⁹Connelly took over the family name "Rucker" as well as these characters from Bradford, *Ol' Man Adam an' His Chillun,* 19.

³⁰"Jake," German "Jakob" (James), is not a popular name among Negroes. "Jim" or "Jimmy" is quite common.

³¹Coe and Cordell (eds.), *The Pulitzer Prize Plays,* 601.

³²Grandgent, *The Divine Comedy,* vii.

³³Coe and Cordell (eds.), *The Pulitzer Prize Plays,* 600.

³⁴*Goethes Werke,* XXXVII, 184 ff., 321.

RIMA DRELL RECK

¹André Malraux, "Préface à *Sanctuaire* de W. Faulkner," *Nouvelle revue française,* XLI (1933), 746-47; all translations from the French are mine.

²André Malraux, "Journal de voyage d'un philosophe, par Hermann Keyserling," *Nouvelle revue française,* XXXII (1929), 886.

³Armand Hoog, "Malraux, Möllberg and Frobenius," *Yale French Studies,* XVIII (Winter, 1957), 87.

⁴André Malraux, "Préface," *Qu'une larme dans l'océan,* by Manès Sperber (Paris, 1952), x.

⁵R. M. Albérès, "André Malraux and the 'Abridged Abyss,'" *Yale French Studies,* XVIII (Winter, 1957), 47-48.

⁶E. W. Knight, *Literature Considered as Philosophy, The French Example* (London, 1957), 131.

⁷André Malraux, "Les traquées, par Michel Matvéev," *Nouvelle revue française,* XLII (1934), 1015.

⁸André Malraux, "Préface," *Indochine S.O.S.,* by Andrée Viollis (Paris, 1935), vii.

⁹André Malraux, *Les Conquérants* (Paris, 1952), 11. Included in this

edition are also *La Condition humaine* and *L'Espoir;* subsequent page references are given in the text, preceded by, respectively, C, CH, E.

¹⁰André Rousseaux, "André Malraux," *Revue de Paris,* No. 10 (October, 1946), 123.

¹¹André Malraux, "Laclos," *Tableau de la littérature française* (Paris, 1939), 420.

¹²André Malraux, *La Voie royale* (Paris, 1930), 21; subsequent page references are given in the text, preceded by VR.

¹³Jean de Pontcharra, "André Malraux, révolutionnaire et romancier," *Études,* CCXXXV (May 20, 1938), 463.

¹⁴Marcel Savane, *André Malraux* (Paris, 1946), 16.

¹⁵Albert Ollivier, "La Mythologie d'André Malraux," *Critique 6,* I (1946), 485.

¹⁶Rachel Bespaloff, *Cheminements et carrefours* (Paris, 1938), 46.

¹⁷Victor Brombert, "Malraux, Passion and Intellect," *Yale French Studies;* XVIII (Winter, 1957), 72-73.

¹⁸André Malraux, *Esquisse d'une psychologie du cinéma* (Paris, 1946), Part V.

¹⁹W. M. Frohock, *André Malraux and the Tragic Imagination* (Palo Alto, Calif., 1952), x.

²⁰André Malraux, "Lignes de force," *Preuves,* XLIX (March, 1955), 12.

²¹André Malraux, *Le Temps du mépris* (Paris, 1935), 153; subsequent page references are given in the text, preceded by TM.

²²*Malraux par lui-même* (Paris, 1956), 56.

HARRY OSTER

¹I wish to thank the Graduate Research Council of Louisiana State University for a grant which enabled me to carry out this work.

²Marguerite and Raoul d'Harcourt, *Chansons Folkloriques Françaises au Canada* (Quebec, 1956), 65-66.

³W. W. Lawrence, *Shakespeare's Problem Comedies* (New York, 1931), 174-233.

⁴George Doncieux, *Le Romancero Populaire de la France* (Paris, 1904), 227-29.

⁵Henri Davenson, *Le Livre des Chansons* (Paris, 1946), 169.

⁶Doncieux, *Le Romancero Populaire,* 399-401.

⁷Davenson, *Le Livre des Chansons,* 241.

⁸C. B. Tinker and H. F. Lowry, *The Poetry of Matthew Arnold* (New York, 1940), 129.

⁹Doncieux, *Le Romancero Populaire,* 401-404.

¹⁰Davenson, *Le Livre des Chansons,* 334-35.

¹¹Doncieux, *Le Romancero Populaire,* 433-34.

¹²*Ibid.,* 434-35.

¹³Achille Millien, *Chants et Chansons Populaires Recueillés et Classés* (3 vols.; Paris, 1906-1910), I, 304-305.

[14]d'Harcourt, *Chansons Folkloriques*, 431-32.

[15]Millien, *Chants et Chansons*, I, 218-19.

[16]Doncieux, *Le Romancero Populaire*, 309-310.

[17]d'Harcourt, *Chansons Folkloriques*, 81-82.

[18]Doncieux, *Le Romancero Populaire*, 298-301.

[19]Marius Barbeau, *Romancero du Canada* (Montreal, 1937), 108.

[20]Marius Barbeau, *Folk-Songs of Old Quebec* (Ottawa, n. d.), 34.

[21]Barbeau, *Romancero du Canada*, 21-23.

HORST OPPEL

[1]Edgar Allan Poe, "Letter to Mr. B," *The Works of Edgar Allan Poe*, Tamerlane Edition, I, 54.

[2]*Journal of English and Germanic Philology*, LIV (1955), 173-94.

[3]*Ibid.*, 182.

[4]See, for example, Heinrich Straumann, "Amerikanische Literatur in Europe," *Anglia*, LXXVI (1958), 208-16.

[5]H. F. Peters, "Ernst Jünger's Concern with E. A. Poe," *Comparative Literature*, X (1958), 144-49.

[6]Consider the words of Robert Jordan in *For Whom the Bell Tolls* (New York, 1945), 466: "You can do nothing for yourself but perhaps you can do something for another."

[7]Helmut Papajewski, "Die Frage nach der Sinnhaftigkeit bei Hemingway," *Anglia*, LXX (1951), 186-209.

[8]See Horst Oppel, "Hemingway's *Across the River and into the Trees*," *Die Neueren Sprachen*, N. S., I (1951), 473-86.

[9]Heinrich Straumann, "Eine amerikanische Seinsdeutung: Faulkners Roman *A Fable*," *Anglia*, LXXIII (1956), 484-515.

[10]"Eugene O'Neill in Deutschland," *Euphorion*, L (1956), 307-27.

[11]Lawrence M. Price, " 'Überfremdung' and 'Nachwuchs' in the German Theater Today," *Modern Language Forum*, XLII (1957), 146-51.

[12]The true reasons for Germans' fondness for Wilder can hardly be explained by the superficial arguments advanced by Paul Fussell, Jr. in "Thornton Wilder and the German Psyche," *Nation*, CLXXXVI (May 3, 1958), 18. He goes so far as to say: "This 'canonization' of Wilder indicates something pathetic in the German psyche."

[13]Klaus Doderer, "Die angelsächsische short story und die deutsche Kurzgeschichte," *Die Neueren Sprachen*, N. S., II (1953), 417-24.

[14]Gustav Gruener, "Notes on the Influence of E. T. A. Hoffmann upon E. A. Poe," *Publications of the Modern Language Association*, XIX (1904), 1-25; and P. Cobb, *The Influence of E. T. A. Hoffmann on the Tales of E. A. Poe* (Chapel Hill, N. C., 1908).

[15]See Horst Oppel, "Amerikanische Literatur," *Reallexikon der deutschen Literaturgeschichte* (2d ed.; Berlin, 1955), I, 49.

[16]Hermann Pongs, "Die Anekdote als Kunstform zwischen Kalendergeschichte und Kurzgeschichte," *Der Deutschunterricht*, IX (1957), 5-20.

Contributors

ALEXANDER, JEAN, b. Forest Grove, Oregon, 1926; B. A., University of Oregon, 1947; M. A., University of Washington, 1955; Ph. D., 1961; Phi Beta Kappa, University of Oregon; Fulbright Scholar, University of Paris, 1957-58; Assistant in English, University of Washington, 1953-57; Instructor in English, Louisiana State University, 1958-61; Assistant Professor of English, University of Alberta, 1961-; paper read at Pacific Northwest Renaissance Conference, 1957.

DOVE, JOHN ROLAND, b. London, England, 1924; B. A., Oxford, 1949; M. A., 1953; Ph. D., University of Texas, 1956; Instructor in Humanities, Hobart College, 1949-51; Teaching Fellow and Instructor in English, University of Texas, 1953-56; Instructor in English, Louisiana State University, 1956-58, Assistant Professor of English, 1958-; author of articles in University of Texas *Studies in English* and *Studies in Humanities;* contributor to *Studies in American Literature* (Baton Rouge, 1960).

ERICKSON, MARTIN E., b. Duluth, Minnesota, 1900; B. A., University of Oregon, 1928; M. A., 1930; Ph. D., University of Washington, 1940; grants from American Council of Learned Societies, 1943 and 1948; grants from Graduate Research Council of Louisiana State University, 1951, 1952, and 1956; Teaching Fellow in Spanish and English, University of Oregon, 1930-36; Teaching Fellow in Spanish, University of Washington, 1938-40; Assistant Professor of Spanish, University of Texas, 1940-42; Assistant Professor of Spanish, Northwestern University, 1942-44; Assistant Professor of Spanish, Louisiana State University, 1944-47; Associate Professor, 1947-50, Professor, 1950-; author of articles and reviews in *Revista Iberoamericana, Hispania, Modern Language Quarterly, Italica, Latin American Studies.*

GUDAS, FABIAN, b. Boston, Massachusetts, 1917; A. B., University of Chicago, 1938; Ph. D., 1952; Phi Beta Kappa, University of Chicago; Graduate Scholar, University of Chicago, 1938-40; Instructor in English, University of Minnesota, 1945-53; Instructor in English, Louisiana State University, 1953-56, Assistant Professor, 1956-61; Associate Professor, 1961-; author of articles in *American Business Writing Association Bulletin;* contributor to *From Jane Austen to Joseph Conrad* (Minneapolis, 1958); Editor, *Extrasensory Perception* (New York, 1961).

307

GUILBEAU, JOHN J., b. Golden Meadow, Louisiana, 1913; B. A., Louisiana State University, 1935; M. A., 1936; Ph. D., University of North Carolina, 1950; Bonne Volonté Franco-Américaine scholar, 1935; Institute of International Education scholar in France, 1936-37; Chairman of Program Committee, South-Central Modern Language Association, 1960-; Assistant d'anglais, Lycée M. Montaigne, Bordeaux, 1936-37; Instructor in French and Spanish, University of North Carolina, 1939-41; Instructor in French, Louisiana State University, 1945-47, Assistant Professor, 1947-54, Associate Professor, 1954-60, Professor, 1960-; contributor to *Comptes Rendus de l'Athénée Louisianais.*

HAMMER, CARL, JR., b. near Salisbury, North Carolina, 1910; A. B., Catawba College, 1934; M. A., Vanderbilt University, 1936; Ph. D., University of Illinois, 1939; Fellow, University of North Carolina, 1934-35; Fellow, Vanderbilt University, 1935-36; Phi Beta Kappa, University of Illinois; Faculty Fellow, Fund for the Advancement of Education, 1953-54; Schiller Bicentenary Medallion from Federal Republic of Germany, 1955; Assistant in German, University of Illinois, 1936-39; Instructor in German, Vanderbilt University, 1939-45; Assistant Professor, 1945-47; Associate Professor of German, Louisiana State University, 1947-55, Professor, 1955-; Associate Editor (German), *South-Central Bulletin,* 1959-61; Vice-President, South-Central Renaissance Conference, 1960-61; President, Louisiana chapter, American Association of Teachers of German, 1959-61; National Counselor, Delta Phi Alpha, 1950-53; Editor (with John G. Grank), *Deutsch für Mediziner* (New York, 1941); Editor, *Goethe After Two Centuries* (Baton Rouge, 1952); author of *Rhinelanders on the Yadkin* (Salisbury, N. C., 1943); (with John G. Frank and C. M. Lancaster), *Two Moods of Minnesong* (Nashville, 1944); *Goethe's "Dichtung und Wahrheit," 7 Buch—Literaturgeschichte oder Bildungserlebnis?* (Urbana, 1945); *Longfellow's "Golden Legend" and Goethe's "Faust"* (Baton Rouge, 1952); articles and reviews in *Journal of English and Germanic Philology, German Quarterly, American-German Review, Monatshefte, Germanic Review, Modern Language Quarterly, Modern Language Journal, Romance Notes, Books Abroad, South-Central Bulletin;* contributor of three papers to *Southern Illinois Goethe Celebration: A Collection of Nine Papers* (Carbondale, 1950).

HEALY, ELLIOTT D., b. Revis, Virginia, 1909; A. B., College of William and Mary, 1931; M. A., University of North Carolina, 1937; Ph. D., 1941; John Archer Coke scholar and Graves scholar, College of William and Mary, 1931; Phi Beta Kappa, College of William and Mary; Institute of International Education scholar in France, 1931-32; guest of French Government at 2000th anniversary of founding of Paris, 1951; Croix de Chevalier dans l'ordre des Palmes Académiques, 1959; Instructor in French, University of North Carolina, 1937-41; Professor of French and Spanish, Meredith College, 1941-42; Assistant Professor of Romance Languages, University of Texas, 1946-49; Associate Professor of French, Louisiana State University, 1949-60,

Professor, 1960-; Editor, *South-Central Bulletin*, 1950-53; Editor, *Foreign Language News Letter*, 1953-54; author (with S. T. Stocker), *A Vocabulary of Naval Terms, English-French and French-English* (2 vols.; Washington, D. C., 1943); author of section on "The Old Provençal Lyric" in *A Critical Bibliography of French Literature*, I, The Medieval Period (Syracuse, 1947); articles in *Script, Studies in Philology, French Review, Romance Studies, Louisiana Schools.*

KRUMPELMANN, JOHN T., b. New Orleans, Louisiana, 1892; B. A., Tulane University, 1915; M. A., 1916; A. M., Harvard University, 1917; Ph. D., 1924; Traveling Fellow, Harvard University, 1924-25; Attaché, U. S. Department of State, in charge of exploitation of archives of German Foreign Office, 1945-47; guest of Federal Republic of Germany at Goethe Bicentennial, 1949; Fulbright Lecturer, University of Frankfurt, 1955; Schiller Sesquicentennial medal from Federal Republic of Germany, 1956; Associate Editor (German), *South-Central Bulletin*, 1944-59, Business Manager, 1952-53; President, South-Central Modern Language Association, 1959-60; Instructor in German, Lehigh University, 1917-18; Instructor in German, University of North Carolina, 1919-21; Instructor in German, Harvard University, 1921-24; Assistant Professor of German, University of North Carolina, 1925-27; Associate Professor of German, Columbia University, 1927-33; Lecturer in German, Institut für Ausländer, University of Berlin, 1933; Professor of German, Marshall College, 1934-38; Assistant Professor of German, Louisiana State University, 1938-42, Associate Professor, 1942-48, Professor, 1948-; author of articles and reviews in *Modern Language Notes, Journal of English and Germanic Philology, Modern Language Journal, American Speech, Harvard Graduates' Magazine, Germanic Review, Monatshefte, American Notes and Queries, Die Neueren Sprachen, Archiv für den Studium der neueren Sprachen, Louisiana Historical Quarterly, American-German Review, Louisiana State University Alumni News, South-Central Bulletin, The Bridge, Jahrbuch für Amerika-studien; Bayard Taylor and German Letters* (Hamburg, 1959); contributor to *Goethe After Two Centuries* (Baton Rouge, 1955); *Festschrift für Walther Fischer* (Heidelberg, 1959); translator, Sachs' *Brooding Calves*, in *Poet Lore*, 1927; Gryphius' *The Beloved Hedgerose*, in *Poet Lore*, 1928; Kleist's *The Broken Jug*, in *Poet Lore*, 1939; Schiller's *The Maiden of Orleans* (Chapel Hill, 1959).

McCORMICK, ANNETTE M., b. Cambridge, Massachusetts, 1919; A. B., Smith College, 1940; A. M., University of Chicago, 1941; Ph. D., University of London, 1951; Scholar, Smith College, 1938-40; Scholar, Bedford College, University of London, 1947-48; Instructor in English, Western College, 1945-47; Assistant, Bedford College, University of London, 1948; Instructor in English, University of Colorado, 1949-50; Instructor in English, Bryn Mawr College, 1950-52; Instructor in English, University of Kansas, 1952-54, Assistant Professor, 1954-56; Visiting Assistant Professor of English, University of Iowa, 1956-57; Visiting Assistant Professor of English, Wheaton College (Norton, Mass.), 1957-58; Assistant Professor of English, Louisiana State

University, 1959-; papers read for South-Central Modern Language Association; English Department Lecture Series, Louisiana State University, 1960.

OPPEL, HORST, b. Halle, Germany, 1913; Universities of Bonn, Leipzig, and Oxford; Ph. D., University of Bonn, 1935; ausserordentlicher and ordentlicher Professor of English, University of Mainz, 1946-56; Professor of English and Director of Englisches Seminar, University of Marburg, 1956-; author of articles and reviews in *Anglia, Deutsche Vierteljahrsschrift für Literaturwissenschaft und Geistesgeschichte, Die Neueren Sprachen, Shakespeare-Jahrbuch, Comparative Literature,* and other journals; contributor of "Methodenlehre der Literaturwissenschaft" and "Der Einfluss der englischen Literatur auf die deutsche" in *Deutsche Philologie im Aufriss,* and of "Die Einwirkung der amerikanischen Literatur auf die deutsche" in *Reallexikon der deutschen Literaturgeschichte;* author of *Komik und Humor im Schaffensgefüge Friedrich Hebbels* (Bonn, 1935), *Die Literaturwissenschaft in der Gegenwart: Methodologie und Wissenschaftslehre* (Stuttgart, 1939), *Morphologische Literaturwissenschaft* (Mainz, 1947), *Peregrina: Vom Wesen des Dichterischen* (Mainz, 1947), *Das Shakespeare-Bild Goethes* (Mainz, 1949), *Die Kunst des Erzählens im englischen Roman des 19. Jahrhunderts* (Bielefeld, 1950), *Die tragische Dichtung Georg Büchners* (Stuttgart, 1951), *Shakespeares Tragödien und Romanzen: Kontinuität oder Umbruch?* (Wiesbaden, 1954), *The Sacred River: Studien und Interpretationen zur Dichtung der englischen Romantik* (Frankfurt, 1959), *Stand und Aufgaben der deutschen Shakespeare-Forschung* (Stuttgart, 1960) *Titus Andronicus: Studien zur dramengeschichtlichen Stellung von Shakespeares früher Tragödie* (Heidelberg, 1961); Editor, *Die Neueren Sprachen,* 1952-; *Festschrift für Walther Fischer* (Heidelberg, 1959).

OSTER, HARRY, b. Cambridge, Massachusetts, 1923; A. B., Harvard University, 1946; M. B. A., Columbia University, 1948; M. A., Cornell University, 1950; Ph. D., 1953; Buckley Scholar, Harvard University, 1946; Fellow, Cornell University, 1950-53; Friends of Music Scholar, Cornell University, 1952; Fellow, Ford Education Forum, 1956; four grants from Graduate Research Council of Louisiana State University; Instructor in Accounting and Industrial Management, Syracuse University, 1948-49; Instructor in English, University of Toledo, 1953-55; Instructor in English, Louisiana State University, 1955-57, Assistant Professor, 1957-; papers read for Folklore Institute of Indiana University, Ohio Folklore Society, American Folklore Society, Louisiana Folklore Society, and South-Central Modern Language Association; lecture-concerts on folk music given at various colleges and on radio and television; author of articles in *New York Folklore Quarterly, McNeese Review, Notre Damean;* contributor to *Louisiana Folklore Miscellany* (1958, 1959), *Studies in American Literature* (Baton Rouge, 1960); thirteen long-playing records of folk music published by Louisiana Folklore Society, Folkways, Selection Limited, Folk-Lyric Recording Co., Heritage Records.

PAYNE, RICHARD M., b. Oakland, California, 1925; B. A., University of California (Berkeley), 1947; Ph. D., Stanford University, 1960; Fellow, Southern Fellowship Fund, 1957; grant from Graduate Research Council of Louisiana State University, 1958; Instructor in Italian, Stanford University, 1949-54; Instructor in Foreign Languages, Louisiana State University, 1954-61; Fulbright Scholar in Italy, 1961-62.

RECK, RIMA DRELL, b. New York, 1933; B. A., *summa cum laude*, Brandeis University, 1954; Ph. D., Yale University, 1960; Fulbright Scholar, Universities of Caen and Paris, 1954-55; University Fellow, Junior Sterling Fellow, Boies Scholar—Yale University, 1955-58; Instructor in French, Tulane University, 1958-61; Assistant Professor of English and Comparative Literature, Louisiana State University in New Orleans, 1961-; papers read for Louisiana College Conference, South-Central Modern Language Association, Modern Language Association of America; author of articles, reviews, and translations in *The Turret, Yale French Studies, Modern Drama, French Review, University of Kansas City Review, Books Abroad,* and *Tulane Drama Review.*

REES, THOMAS R., b. Washington, D. C., 1925; A. B., American University, 1949; M. A., University of Washington, 1958; Instructor in English, Louisiana State University, 1959-; Editor, *The Listening Post,* 1955-56; author of articles in *Musicland* and Baton Rouge *State-Times;* paper read for Philological Club of Louisiana State University, 1959.

WILSON-JONES, KENNETH R., b. Monroe, North Carolina, 1929; B. A., Davidson College, 1951; M. A., University of North Carolina, 1955; Ph. D., 1957; Phi Beta Kappa, Davidson College; Fulbright Scholar, University of Dijon, 1951-52; Instructor in French, Louisiana State University, 1957-59, Assistant Professor, 1959-.